New Television, Globalisation, and the East Asian Cultural Imagination

Hong Kong University Press thanks Xu Bing for writing the Press's name in his Square Word Calligraphy for the covers of its books. For further information, see p. iv.

NEW TELEVISION, GLOBALISATION, AND THE EAST ASIAN CULTURAL IMAGINATION

Michael Keane, Anthony Fung, and Albert Moran

香港大學出版社

HONG KONG UNIVERSITY PRESS

Hong Kong University Press
14/F Hing Wai Centre
7 Tin Wan Praya Road
Aberdeen
Hong Kong

© Hong Kong University Press 2007

Hardback   ISBN 978-962-209-820-6
Paperback ISBN 978-962-209-821-3

British Library Cataloguing-in-Publication Data
A catalogue record for this book is available from the British Library.

Secure On-line Ordering
http://www.hkupress.org

Printed and bound by Kings Time Printing Press Ltd., Hong Kong, China.

Hong Kong University Press is honoured that Xu Bing, whose
art explores the complex themes of language across cultures, has
written the Press's name in his Square Word Calligraphy. This
signals our commitment to cross-cultural thinking and the distinctive
nature of our English-language books published in China.

"At first glance, Square Word Calligraphy appears to be nothing
more unusual than Chinese characters, but in fact it is a new way
of rendering English words in the format of a square so they
resemble Chinese characters. Chinese viewers expect to be able to
read Square Word Calligraphy but cannot. Western viewers, however
are surprised to find they can read it. Delight erupts when meaning
is unexpectedly revealed."

— Britta Erickson, *The Art of Xu Bing*

Contents

Acknowledgements

This book is the culmination of a long journey that has taken us to many destinations. The project was first conceived in 1999 when Professor Tom O'Regan, then Director of the Key Centre for Cultural and Media Policy at Griffith University, Queensland, Australia, brought Michael Keane and Albert Moran together. The first stage of the project was made possible by an Australian Research Council (ARC) Small Grant awarded by Griffith University in 2000. Results in this timeframe alerted us to the potential of the Asia Pacific and we were able to extend the scope and deepen the significance of this research thanks to the award of an ARC Discovery Grant in 2002–2004 for the project entitled 'Economic, Legal and Cultural Dynamics of Format Flows in the Asia/Pacific Region'.

There are many people to thank. Meaghan Morris recognised the importance of our research at a very early stage, even to the extent of noting how academics were in fact formats. Koichi Iwabuchi contributed a great number of valuable ideas to the project. Ran Ruxue (Beijing) was instrumental in setting up several of the interviews and providing materials. The following persons contributed greatly to the intellectual process: Liu Yu-Li and Chen Yi-Hsiang (Taiwan), Lee Dong-Hoo (Korea), Tania Lim (Singapore), Keval Kumar and Amos Owen Thomas (India), Philip Kitley (Indonesia), and Josephina Santos (the Philippines). Others who have provided suggestions, encouragement and criticism along the way are Stuart Cunningham, Terry Flew, Michael Curtin, Justin Malbon, Wang Xuechun, Stephanie Hemelryk Donald, Li Hui, Jiannü Bao, Christina Spurgeon and Zhang Wuyi.

In China we would like to thank Chen Qiang (Beijing Weihan Company), Gao Yusong (CCTV), Zhang Wei (CCTV), Feng Qi (Hunan TV and Huayu TV), Ning Xiaoxhou (Guangzhou TV), Long Mei (Hunan TV), Hong Tao (Hunan TV) and Long Danni (Hunan Economic TV). In Australia we would like to thank Mark Overett and in the United Kingdom, Eugene Ferguson (Granada). Some producers and actors interviewed in China expressed a wish to remain anonymous. We appreciate their comments and thank them for participating.

Susan Jarvis provided cheerful and dedicated editorial assistance by smoothing out the chapters and helping bring the collection together. We would also like to thank our commissioning editor, Colin Day, who had faith in the project, and our copyeditor at Hong Kong University Press, Phoebe Chan, who helped see the book through the publication stage.

Finally, we would like to thank our partners, Noela Moran, Leigh Zhang-Keane and Cindy Cheung, for their support and help.

We would also like to point out that every effort has been made to realise correct translations of program titles. In the People's Republic of China, we used the *hanyu pinyin* system of romanisation, while in the Republic of Taiwan we used the *zhuyin* system.

1

Out of Nowhere

> For decades, we worked under the assumption that mass culture follows
> a steadily declining path towards lowest-common-denominator
> standards, presumably because the 'masses' want dumb, simple pleasures
> and big media companies want to give the masses what they want. But
> in fact, the exact opposite is happening: the culture is getting more and
> more intellectually demanding, not less.
>
> — Johnson (2005: 9)

For more than five decades since television was introduced into East Asia,
widespread debate has ensued concerning the pervasive influence of American
and Western popular culture. The key arguments can perhaps be summarised
as follows: Hollywood is the dominant centre of production; it produces
movies and television that have global recognition; this content promotes
individualist values; these values are damaging to Asian social traditions.

Since 1998, viewers in Japan, China, Taiwan and South Korea have been
introduced to a new kind of entertainment television. Celebrity chefs compete
in highly stylised culinary combat; winners 'take all' in survival reality shows;
quiz contestants walk away with extraordinary prizes; and instant celebrities
are created in documentary-style talent quests. Of course, one can speculate
that economic recession in East Asia during the late 1990s led people to choose
escapist diversionary activities. But when *Time Asia* announced its annual
survey of 'Asia's heroes' in October 2005, the person featured on the cover
was not someone who had performed heroic deeds in the wake of the Asian
tsunami or who had fought against endemic corruption, but rather an
androgynous tomboy called Li Yuchun, the winner of *Super Girl* (*chaoji
nüsheng:* literally 'Super Female Voice'), a Chinese version of the popular *Idol*

format. With the headline 'Li Yuchun: loved for being herself', *Time Asia's* correspondent pointed out that the show had drawn the largest audiences in the history of Chinese television, producing a media frenzy comparable with coverage of a war or the O. J. Simpson trial (Jakes 2005). In China, critics moved quickly to either praise or condemn this media event which was staged by Hunan Satellite Television in south China. Not for the first time, this upstart broadcaster had challenged the purity of China Central Television (CCTV) whose own soporific talent quest *Special 6+1 Dream China* suddenly encountered a ratings freefall.

Reactions to the spread of global television ideas are not isolated. As integration of the world economy increases, and as products and services rapidly replicate around the globe, cultural globalisation fears persist. And as we travel from country to country, we may be reassured or discomforted — depending on our political position — in being surrounding by familiar products, images and brands. Franchise capitalism has reproduced Starbucks, Disney product stores and McDonald's in the United Kingdom, in Europe and in East Asian cities. In television industries, the franchising model is also on the ascendant. This model of production is recognisable in reality TV, game shows, and a range of lifestyle and infotainment programs. While many critics berate the banality, viewers of such shows have highly individualised reactions. Many consume with discrimination, ambivalent to a show's origins, while accepting these global developments as indicators of what constitutes new television.

In this book we examine the contribution these shows make to social and economic relations in East Asia. If what was once deemed bad is now good — to take Johnson's opening provocation on board — is Western-style popular culture now good in East Asia? Is the injection of individualistic values into Asian reality TV now 'good' for cultures that have traditionally espoused co-operation and hierarchical relationships? Or are there more nuanced processes of accommodation occurring between individualised models of material progress and the social interdependency that frames Confucian family values?

United States success in global media and advertising markets forms a common theme within cultural studies and political economy. Recent studies have asserted that Hollywood continues to relentlessly impose its presence on 'weaker' cultures. Miller et al.'s *Global Hollywood* thesis sees dominance reproduced through a combination of distribution, marketing, exhibition, and production efficiencies. This so-called New International Division of Cultural Labour (NICL) is consolidated by influence over global copyright regimes (Miller et al. 2001). In another account, aptly entitled *Hollywood Planet* (Olsen

1999), American cinema and television programming achieves dominance across cultures through 'narrative transparency'. Many American popular cultural texts make sense in international markets due to the formulaic presentation of themes such as good and evil. In the end, whether it is *Global Hollywood* or *Planet Hollywood*, we contend that such approaches undervalue the importance of local content by denying a sense of agency to viewers in non-English-speaking regions.

This book traces a different narrative of the globalisation of television. It looks at distribution channels and production strategies that manifest outside the purview of mainstream English-language scholarship. And it works on a different premise than the *Global Hollywood* and *Hollywood Planet* models. Our assertion is that Hollywood is a dominant centre of production; it produces blockbuster movies with a global cachet; it exploits competitive advantage in distribution and marketing; its content is associated with individualist values; but its television products have a diminishing influence in East Asian schedules.

The reassertion of regionalism in television production is a result of several factors: the integration of East Asian economies within global markets has produced more opportunities in television production and distribution; increased levels of trade and exchange of creative personnel across the East Asian region have resulted in new niche markets; transfer of technologies through joint ventures and co-productions has created efficiencies; rising cosmopolitanism in cities has led to demand for content reflecting everyday life; and new flexible models of production have emerged as a response to multi-channel platforms and digitisation. It is apparent from these environmental changes that we are not concerned with the United States, except to point out that constant focus on the success and dominance of Hollywood perpetuates a scholarly imbalance and contributes to misunderstandings of how East Asian media engage within the global cultural economy.

Globalisation is a topic that has been widely addressed by scholars with varying degrees of definitiveness, and where Asian media studies is concerned there has been a tendency within much English-language literature to emphasise the political economy of global media penetration and the (often assumed) 'effects' of Western programming. Our intention in this study of new television in East Asia is to shift the focus of debate towards processes of cultural exchange, and in doing so, further challenge the West-East imperialism model that is framed on culturally destabilising effects imposed on recipient nation value systems. Of course, this presupposes that we are not focusing our intention on finished programs — that is, the sale of programs across national borders. Our key propositions are: first, that trade in format licenses is significantly different from trade in 'finished program' rights; second, that adaptation is increasingly widespread as media producers search for compelling content; third, that a shift to conceptual and interchangeable 'media artefacts' is accounting for a greater percentage of the market (Aris and Bughin 2005); and fourth, that East Asia is generating more tradable media content. These propositions underpin a different model of trans-border program flows, and they challenge totalising theories such as the NICL and 'narrative transparency'.

Our approach will test sociological notions of cultural value, cultural studies' celebrations of hybridity and political economy evaluations of Western influence. Our research methods combine interviews with producers and distributors, industry data, academic critique and policy research. While we visited eleven countries in Asia in conducting our fieldwork (Moran and Keane 2004), in this book we are concerned with the internationalisation of television trade within the People's Republic of China (PRC), Hong Kong, Japan, Taiwan, and South Korea.

The examples we present straddle cultural theory and industry practice: they are fundamentally about how new programming ideas are created, shaped and sold to television stations — and how these ideas are creatively redeveloped in different global locations. In terms of distribution and marketing, this book is also about how new program concepts are repackaged and targeted at different cultural demographics. While the focus is on the role of formats within this region, the stimulus for this study comes from examining change in programming strategies within global television networks and media production companies. Growth in independent production during the past decade — a response to multi-channelling and diminishing advertising revenue for in-house production — has stimulated new models of television production in the countries of East Asia.

While many of the television programs in this study have Western origins (particularly Europe and the United States), it is their take-up and creative adaptation within East Asia that illustrates what we term the *East Asian cultural imagination*. In other words, the scope of the research is not just the licensing of programs into East Asia, but the refashioning of ideas into new versions, spin-offs and ancillary products. In fact, the key concern of this project is to understand processes of adaptation. More importantly, we are considering not just the West-East trade flow, which has been the dominant theme of political economy, but the equally important East-East and East-West dynamics of television program trade.

Globalisation and Localisation

Globalisation is one of the key themes of this book. In embracing the concept of global media, we acknowledge that sale of television programs constitutes the core business for transnational media companies. Alternatively, we note that imitation, localisation, co-productions and niche programming are a strategic means for new or under-capitalised production companies to compete against high-budget international programs. Do we therefore make a distinction between the globalisation strategies of transnational media corporations and the internationalisation aspirations of smaller domestic companies? If domestic companies are endeavouring to tap into new markets, are they globalising, internationalising, or regionalising their business, or are they just being savvy about the opportunities that exist in the marketplace? We find evidence of economic exchange and cultural translation across cultures. In many instances this activity is hard to categorise as either globalisation or localisation. As we shall see in the study of television formats, globalisation discourses need to be grounded in economic and social contexts.

Other themes that recur are cultural transfer, translation, discount, proximity, and compatibility. The cultural transfer model that we develop in this study draws on a new international division of cultural production (*in addition to* cultural labour). Technology is transferred in several ways, not least being the exchange of expertise. Translation occurs as ideas are localised. Cultural discount, where non-familiarity with international cultural nuance undercuts the tradability of many audio-visual exports — except for American drama and sit-coms in English-language markets — is avoided (Hoskins and Rolf 1988). Adaptation avoids the problem of cultural discount by substituting local accents and cultural references such that many viewers fail to distinguish the program's true origins. Cultural proximity refers to the capacity for film and television content to be read symptomatically in countries where cultural traditions, values and structures of feeling are aligned (see Straubhaar 1991). For instance, television dramas made in Japan achieve great success in Taiwan (Iwabuchi 2002). By the same measure, programs made in Japan have less success in mainland China, where compatibility is a function of enduring national sensitivity to Japanese imperialism.

The Universality of Adaptation

In the present stage of audio-visual industry development, the most significant dynamic seems to be one of adaptation, transfer, and recycling of narrative and other kinds of content. This tendency is not limited to television, but is characteristic across many media and related areas of cultural production. Nor is it unique to the present epoch. However, in the present age of international media conglomerates, the recycling and adaptation of content across different media platforms is rapidly multiplying to the point of marginalising other economic and cultural practices. Many kinds of adaptations are familiar. For example, films become television series just as television series trigger feature films. Remakes are equally common, although these are sometimes known under other names such as the sequel, the spin-off or even the prequel. This general phenomenon of a content-genealogy does not end there. Narratives can span several media: theatrical film, television, video, DVD re-release, video games, CD soundtrack, radio, comics, novels, stage shows, musicals, public concerts, posters, merchandising, theme parks and so on. Fanzines and internet websites further spin out these contents. Individually and collectively, this universe of narrative and content constitutes a loosening of the notion of closure and the self-contained work of art (Thompson 1999, 2003).

Behind this proliferation of transfers — this ever-expanding recycling of content — is a set of new economic arrangements designed to secure a degree of financial and cultural insurance not easily available in the present multi-channel environment. Adapting already successful materials and content provides an opportunity to duplicate past and existing successes. In other words, media producers are attempting to take out financial and cultural insurance by using material that is in some way familiar to the audience (Fiddy 1997; Moran 1998). Having invested in the brand, it makes good business sense to derive further value from it in these different ways. This tendency of recycling is further facilitated by the fact of owning the copyright on the property in the first place.

Although we identify a great deal of adaptation activity based on Japanese programs, many of the programs identified in this study originate in Europe. Important questions considered here include: whether the practice of emulating, copying, and adapting is cultural diversity in action, an attempt to localise and claim the *de facto* intellectual property, or just recycling what sells? It is our contention that increasing demand for content dictates that adaptations are economic solutions to increased pressures in the multi-channel marketplace, rather than 'nationalistic' desires to propagate local content using international models. Of course, the strategies inherent in producing local versions constitute a significant part of our analysis. But the bottom line is that the successful localisation of a television program is about using cultural identity to deliver ratings.

Adaptation is an exemplar of post-Fordist practices intersecting with the new logic of creative production. The logic of post-Fordism evokes recent work on creative industries where media industries are understood as dependent on a range of mainstream services: finance, legal, management, advertising and marketing. Writing about the new symbiosis between Japan and Hong Kong's audio-visual industries, Yeh and Davis (2002:2) have written of flexible accumulation as a means of corporative survival in which there are ready-made models and sources of material to 'allude to' or 'copy outright'. This in turn echoes Jeremy Rifkin's thesis of a shift from ownership to access which refers to the 'new Hollywood model' of outsourcing that has largely displaced the old studio system in which every facet of production was managed by the vertically integrated company (Rifkin 2000; Storper 1989). Rifkin also speaks of leasing and franchising as new economy management strategies. Rifkin's tag-line — 'the age of access' — denotes a global shift towards more flexible models of service provision.

In the same way, the international franchising of TV represents a stage in the evolution of TV production. The formatted adaptation is a franchise in which the core intellectual property is licensed to producers or television networks. The idea of business franchising is predicated on an arrangement between the owner of a concept (the franchisor) who enters into a contract with an independent actor (the franchisee) to use a specific model to sell goods or services under the former's trademark. As Karin Fladmoe-Lindquist notes, 'This approach to franchising involves a set of procedures, designs, management approaches, and services that are to be delivered exactly as specified by the franchisor' (Fladmoe-Lindquist 2000: 198). In cases where the franchise is taken up in new markets, the challenge is to retain the original image and service of the franchise.

Cultural Imperialism Versus Cultural Geography

In the space of the past several years, shows such as *Who Wants to Be a Millionaire?, The Weakest Link, Survivor,* and *Idol* have formed a new currency of program exchange. As they trade across cultures and networks, such formats demonstrate the importance of cultural geography while countering some of excesses of Marxist political economy, which remains resolutely wedded to the media imperialism thesis. Various accounts of media and cultural imperialism have surfaced since the 1960s, reaching a high point in the McBride Commission New World Information and Cultural Order, instigated by UNESCO in 1980. The influential study of television flows by

Nordenstreng and Varis (1974) provided empirical support for the 'one-way flow' thesis. It was not until the 1980s that scholars began to challenge this model. In 1988, Michael Tracey presented an image of increasing complexity. He spoke of 'a patch-work quilt' rather than a one-way street. In 1991, Joseph Straubhaar nominated 'cultural proximity' and 'asymmetrical interdependence' as key determiners of markets, while Oliver Boyd-Barrett and Daya Thussu (1992) looked at outbreaks of local 'resistance' in the global media and 'contra-flows' of information. In 1996, John Sinclair, Liz Jacka and Stuart Cunningham (Sinclair et al. 1996) examined how 'peripheral centres' had created a presence and reputation in world content markets — albeit mostly through analogue and narrative formats (movies, telenovella, television drama) targeted at diasporic communities and geo-linguistic regions.

During the late 1990s, the media and communications field witnessed a reassertion of the media imperialism thesis, coinciding with an upsurge in mergers and acquisitions activity among global media companies (Schiller 1999). The pendulum has swung from the one-way street (1970s) to main thoroughfares with a series of smaller roads (1980s–1990s), and finally back to globally networked capitalist superhighways and new international divisions of cultural labour (Miller et al. 2001). However, accounts emanating from political economy and the cultural geography tradition have been premised on the licensing and syndication of finished programs in multiple markets. Little information has been produced about the TV format business, which developed in scale during the late 1990s, and which now constitutes an alternative model of media globalisation, providing new evidence as well as new models of integration within global media markets (Moran and Keane 2004).

There is ample evidence from our fieldwork to suggest that program flows and cultural influences are more regional than global. This may seem self-evident, but in much global media literature, the local is often glossed over. In other words, while the Western global program may be the vehicle of transfer, the important dynamic occurs within East Asian regional cultures where modification is based on cultural compatibility factors. To fill in the history of the model of program adaptation that we call 'formatting', however, it is important to acknowledge another regional origin. The role of European production in the new movement of ideas is central. Witness the various adaptations of the *Survivor* format. Originally devised in the United Kingdom and piloted in Sweden by the reality television production company Strix Television as *Expedition Robinson*, it has morphed into a growing number of spin-offs in various cultural landscapes including the United States, Japan and Australia, to name but a few of the more than 30 variants (Mathijs and Jones

(2004). This is the mother of the 'survival of the smartest and fittest' reality shows in which contestants and viewers 'vote off' those they consider are threats or unworthy to progress. The attraction here comes in seeing how different personalities cope under the stress of a supposedly dangerous environment and a struggle for an ultimate prize.

These northern European reality shows — and much of the associated cross-media promotion — have found their way into East Asian mediascapes. An example of adaptation into a most unlikely market is the Chinese show *Into Shangrila (zouru xianggelila)* which manages to blend elements of the Chinese Communist Party's Long March from south China to its revolutionary base in Shaanxi, north-west China in the 1930s and the Liberation of Tibet in the 1950s into an escapist game show (see Chapter 8). Central to the analysis, therefore, is a theorisation of cultural exchange. What happens when new ideas are introduced through adaptation and formatting? How are these programs refashioned, resignified, modified — and how are they subsequently read and evaluated? In the past, academic responses to phenomena of cultural flow have ranged from charges of cultural imperialism against the sending culture to celebrations of local resistance on the part of the receiving host culture. Many accounts of resistance seek to describe the manner in which texts (or television programs) are creatively appropriated and refashioned for local distribution and consumption (Erni and Chua 2005). The concept of hybridity is construed as a kind of 'clearing house' in the process of localisation. Some proponents of globalisation contend that hybridity implies a pure origin and that humanity lives in cultural formations that are already hybrid (Cowan 2002; see Kraidy 2005). Pure origin has resonance when we talk about traditional knowledge invested in cultural artefacts; however, anthropology confirms that most ancient myths and symbols were a result of interaction across communities and cultures. Pure origin, like the concept of copyright (see Chapter 11), becomes more problematic in discussions of contemporary popular media texts which are constantly mutating and absorbing different cultural inputs. Moreover, the application of hybridity within media studies often tends towards uncritical celebration of adaptation. Nor are producers reluctant to evoke the idea of the hybrid: they enthusiastically celebrate hybridity when referring to their own output, but are often scornful of others' hybridity, seeing it as opportunistic use of their ideas to make short-term gains.

The polarisation of critique into global domination scenarios and local resistance and hybridity is ultimately unsatisfactory and somewhat misleading. Television programming is a commodity form. However, television is unlike cultural technologies such as the internet and mobile phones that relentlessly innovate in content and applications (for example, producing a churn effect).

Television production tends towards the mundane, the conservative and the formulaic. Much of its audience is aged over forty. Ironically, the high degree of standardisation within television industries drives the circulation of low-risk ideas. From this perspective, adaptation of television programs and the shift toward the media artefact (or franchise) model may be seen as television's response to increasing competition from new media technologies. The globalisation of successful formats is the industry conducting research and development internationally rather than nationally. In the words of Steven Johnson:

> The forces at work in these systems operate on multiple levels: underlying changes in technology that enable new kinds of entertainment; new forms of online communications that cultivate audience commentary about works of pop culture; changes in the economics of the culture industry that encourage repeat viewing; and deep-seated appetites in the human brain that seek out reward and intellectual challenge. (2005: 11)

The inquiry into television program adaptation and trade in the following chapters leads us to the following two propositions:

Significant remodelling of local production occurs where adaptation is genuinely responsive to local values.

Globalisation creates tensions as societies encounter ideas that are incompatible with their own cultural values and political ideologies. Much finished programming (movies, TV drama) encounters intractable obstacles in East Asian markets. In other words, programs are subject to censorship or are forced into black market distribution networks. However, globalisation proceeds on another level through adaptation as inappropriate elements of foreign programs are stripped away and substituted with local flavour and values. For many writing within cultural studies, there is a temptation to celebrate hybridity and overlook the economic logic of the imported idea. The foreign program provides the DNA, the recipe, and the technology for invigorating local television industries that are struggling to commit funds to program development. In many cases, the knowledge provided from outside is taken without any form of payment. Claims and counter-claims of copyright infringement circulate.

Transnational media companies that localise a foreign program as a strategy for gaining entry into the national market usually accrue short-term benefits.

Transnational media companies encounter resistance when breaking into culturally and linguistically distinctive markets. Localisation is the mantra of the market. The successful international brand is invested with local characteristics: strategies are developed to make it speak to local cultures, and to reduce the emphasis on individualistic values. In many examples we find that the international program, professionally localised and marketed, out-rates local imitators. However, the project-based formulaic nature of such television programs means that there is a use-by date.

Chapters

The chapters in this book may be read in any order, as each focuses on different aspects of the TV program trade and adaptation. Part I is entitled 'Adaptation and local production in East Asia', and attempts to introduce fresh theoretical approaches to the globalisation literature and to the field of Asian media studies. Part II, 'Formats, clones, and generic variations', examines program adaptations familiar to audiences, as well as addressing sociological issues of adaptation and localisation. The examples are the licensed brand format, the information challenge, the mass participation talent quest, the reality game show, and the advertising magazine program. The final section, 'New television', returns to the theme of globalisation through the lens of industry volatility, re-examining the value of trans-border format licences, and the implications for the future of television.

Any claim to offer a complete inventory of new television programs is beyond the scope of this book. The focus is on the increasing occurrence of adaptation as a modality of cultural exchange and translation; the impact of formats (and formatting) upon television scheduling; the hybridisation of genres; the role of audiences in informing the direction of program development; and ultimately the economic and cultural value of these new programs. In examining cultural dynamics of localisation in the second section of the book, we offer interpretations of success factors. We have selected several noteworthy case studies that have drawn both audience and critical response.

Chapter 2 argues that there are cultural dynamics which predispose the production, distribution, and reception of particular forms of content in China,

Hong Kong, Japan, Taiwan and South Korea. We discuss the role of television in each country, including background to development and historical influences. The evolving television production environment sees new television (reality television, quiz shows, and family formats) reincarnating and stimulating ideas that are both familiar and foreign. In short, we observe logics of production that have been based upon a rapid turnover of ideas within institutions that have limited financial capacity. These changes are situated within existing indigenous genres (e.g. tele-dramas, 'restaurant' shows, *wanhui*, news genres, etc.) and newer genres (idol dramas) that have claimed large audience followings. We ask whether traditionally popular forms are giving way to new formats and ideas. What are the impacts of new technologies and distribution platforms upon the way that television addresses its audiences in these countries?

Chapter 3 looks closely at cultural exchange, examining globalisation, localisation and cultural translation, and their relation to cross-border flows of television formats. The discussion interrogates the idea of cultural exchange through the work of the Russian writer Yuri Lotman, who proposed that countries progress through stages of sending and receiving texts (Lotman 1990). The initial discussion centres on how texts are exchanged and adapted as they cross cultural borders. On a more material level, however, we look at the economics of global media. How does creative content from East Asia find its way into world markets? Is there a television strategy that will take Asian ideas out of their domestic containers and into international living rooms? The missing dimension in many accounts, particularly those emanating from political economy, is the idea of 'conditions of possibility' — that is, the factors that have led, are leading, and could lead to success. The chapter provides a bottom-up model of cultural production which is a necessary corrective to the domination-resistance models that currently abound in cultural studies.

Chapter 4 provides definitions and conceptual frameworks that will allow us to investigate the fertile ground of adaptation: from formatting as a mode of cultural production and exchange to specific examples that we identify as reality television, docu-soap, talk shows, and quiz shows. While the practice of adaptation is not new, imitation is accelerated by a proliferation of media channels. The chapter reveals the format behind the genre, and argues that that much critical analysis currently operates on the basis of conventions that have evolved from screen and literary theory. In order to make distinctions clearer, we provide historical background to the format industry and introduce the role of intellectual property, which — although regularly abused — nevertheless functions to caution against direct duplication of programming.

In the final part of the chapter, we introduce the concept of program 'engines' to describe some of the innovations that have become widely recognisable within new television. These include million-dollar prizes, lifelines, exotic locations, and contestant elimination by audience voting.

In Chapter 5 we look at the idea of technology transfer through adaptations — both licensed and unlicensed. We adopt an industrial perspective to the logic of cultural production, and in particular to cultural borrowing. We utilise the idea of cultural technology transfer to explain how the transfer of formats embodies change in the creative stage of production (Ryan 1992). This concept supports the argument that the format adaptation is a vehicle for extending the product life cycle and for organising production in order to minimise costs. When formats are introduced across television systems through licensing arrangements they inevitably involve a degree of co-production, the extent of which depends on how closely the new program resembles the original.

Chapter 6 examines the internationalisation of perhaps the best known television format — *Who Wants to Be a Millionaire?* The program's success illustrates the value of cascading rights, in particular how to monetise branded content. Despite many attempts to copy the format, the original — with its distinctive catchphrase 'lock it in' — has beaten off competitors and brought profits to its licensees. Chapter 7 continues a discussion of how information challenges formats. The popularity of 'winner-take-all' quiz shows within the East Asian landscape demonstrates how wealth is linked to knowledge and technology as the knowledge-based economy looms as a blueprint for twenty-first century supremacy. While the values of contemporary quiz formats might clash with local cultural values, nevertheless, the presentation of wealth as an outcome of knowledge acquisition echoes local political and economic discourses, and perpetuates aspirations for material success. The information challenge show, best exemplified by *The Weakest Link*, incorporates elements developed in reality television, such as the tendency towards forming coalitions among contestants in order to maximise the chances of survival.

Reality formats are the subject of Chapter 8. Reality formats in East Asia provide examples of legitimate licence sales through international networks, as well as a multitude of generic variants and clones. While there are many reasons for the abundance of reality television programs in East Asia, their success is an indication that viewers are increasingly predisposed towards interactive forms of popular culture that allow connectivity across platforms, particularly exploiting the pervasiveness of SMS (short message services via mobile phones). The chapter proceeds from an investigation of the reality genre and its sub-genres (docu-soap, reality game shows) to specific instances that echo global formats. We look at the 'survival of the fittest' format in East Asia — how resourceful participants use relationships with fellow contestants and community dynamics to progress. We investigate the concepts of reality, performativity, and authenticity in adventure formats in which contestants compete for an elusive prize, often by 'voting off' fellow contestants.

Chapter 9 concerns mass participation through talent quests — the by now familiar *Idol* format. *Super Girl (chaoji nüsheng)* from China, a generic variant (some would say clone) of the global *Pop Idol* formats was produced by the Hunan Satellite Channel and has taken the Middle Kingdom by storm, in the process raising debates about embedded democracy and the quality and moral comportment *(suzhi)* of its participants. Ironically, the previous occasion in China's history when amateurs took centre stage was the Great Proletarian Cultural Revolution. This current revolution, however, is less about overthrowing 'stinking intellectuals' than establishing a voice for popular expression. The chapter also looks at the uptake of the *Idol* format in Hong Kong, Taiwan, and Japan. While international debate on the mass popularity of *Super Girl* in China has taken up the theme of democratisation, we find that issues of authenticity and the secularisation of celebrity are equally important.

Chapter 10 addresses cultural compatibility, illustrating the convergence of politics and economics through examples drawn from Hong Kong. The intersection of familial governance, cultural value systems, and discourses concerning cosmopolitanism explains why television stations are predisposed to programs that can incorporate merchandising and integration of products. This is a region of paradoxes where conspicuous consumption and accumulation of wealth are held as mutually reinforcing principles. We discuss how cultural compatibility admits certain forms of representation. Then we illustrate how economic progress opens the door for new models of funding. We look at episode insertion formats, advertising magazine shows, and weight loss reality formats that might be paradoxically entitled 'survival of the fattest'. The final section looks at how new formats may indeed undermine cultural compatibility norms by allowing new ideas to enter into formerly restricted public viewing spheres.

We turn to the vexed question of ownership of ideas. The propensity to imitate raises a number of important questions. Is this behaviour exploitative or expedient, excessive or necessary? Alternatively, is the idea of copyright — defined as the legal right to make copies — a means of assuring market growth or just a Western notion with little relevance to East Asian television? In the age of multi-channel television where the value of license and syndication rights is diminished, there is a clearly identified need to derive as much financial mileage out of an ownership as possible. However, the adaptation of television shows proceeds largely under the radar of formal intellectual rights regimes, despite threats of litigation over copyright and trademark. In this chapter, we look at the *Castaway Television Production Ltd v Endemol Entertainment International* dispute, as well as infringement incidents that have occurred in East Asia.

The final chapter returns to our title theme and advances the idea that formats represent a progression to a new mode of television production, one in which producers and consumers meet as co-creators of hybrid programming. While the imminent death of reality television has become a constant refrain from television critics nostalgic for a glorious past of quality programming, the reality pulse is still strong. Meanwhile, the logic of formatting and franchising extends globally. Evidence from our research points to the fact that formats have impacted significantly upon the logic of production, and have spawned new business alliances and models, bringing together independent producers, broadcasting networks, advertisers, and telecommunications companies. In this coalition of the willing, where does creativity reside?

Other Contexts: What's New?

If our research findings are correct, adaptation has significantly reshaped not only the television landscape in East Asia, but also the way we understand the globalisation of information and cultural commodities. The tendency to proclaim newness is symptomatic of business literature. However, what is radically, disruptively or pervasively new for some might be construed as a standard evolutionary process by other observers. In drawing a more macro-perspective on our case studies of television formats, we can reflect on Nigel Thrift's notion of 'soft capitalism' (Thrift 2005) which signifies the adaptive capacity of capitalism — and, more specifically for media industries, the acceptance of a greater role for end-users in determining the shape and direction of innovation. Greater recycling of products and knowledge, however, is not simply illustrative of an excess of commodification. Utility and expediency, as well as cultural development, are embedded in these processes — particularly for users (adopters) of knowledge.

What this tells us is that there is something important occurring in the process we are outlining in this book. TV formats have not come on to the radar of critical academic research in any major form, until recently (Moran 1998; Moran and Keane 2004). While the term 'new television' might be a premature assessment of what is always going to be an evolving phenomenon, at least we can confidently state that change is driven by bottom lines as television industries confront rapid flows of ideas across national television systems, as interactivity challenges business assumptions, and as adaptation services a need for novel content.

PART I

Adaptation and Local Production in East Asia

2

Performing the Local in the Global

What does it mean to conduct research into Asian television? More particularly, do established research agendas hold back new knowledge of Asian television? If we accept that the purpose of research is 'the systematic pursuit of the not-yet-known' (Appadurai 2001: 10), it is evident that legitimate new knowledge is something that is theoretically or empirically novel, while being of intrinsic interest to the field.

The field of television studies — from the histories of television production to the development of new television technologies — is circumscribed by prior knowledge and inherited frameworks. These frameworks devolve from ideological and institutional perspectives that underpin television studies. In many examples of television research over the past decades, public service broadcasting models have been influential (Collins 1998). Indeed, this approach has relevance to the East Asian field. Writing from the liberal democratic world, many scholars typify television producers in China as lacking in freedom, and television content as being subject to excessive governmental intervention. Similar criticisms had applied previously to television in Taiwan, Korea and Japan — countries where direct government control in the name of the public has given way to commercial imperatives. Over time, the field of East Asian television has been sown and cultivated by scholars who have viewed television as a tool of state-building. Alternatively, on another level of analysis, East Asian television systems and Asian audiences have been construed as victims of cultural imperialism. The key point to note here is that such research is predominantly focused on finished programming that is traded in and across regional markets.

Brunsdon (2004: 2300) writes that television studies emerged in the 1970s and 1980s from three major streams: journalism, literary/dramatic criticism and the social sciences. The first two of these sources focused directly on the text, while the social sciences cultivated non-textual elements of television as legitimate new knowledge. Social science approaches thus produced new ways of understanding the medium of television. These included television's role in the maintenance of social order (by privileging certain forms of representation and modes of address); relationships of power (between the state and owners of broadcasting media); international cross-media ownership; national and international regulation of media production and consumption; professional ideologies; public opinion; and audiences.

We note echoes of these themes in much of the work that characterises East Asian television research. Prior to the 1990s, there was little research published on television in Asia — at least in the English language. As television studies gained momentum globally, researchers within Asia turned to 'media effects', 'uses and gratifications' analysis, and discussions of the vagaries of state regulation. Aside from studies that attempted to measure the effects of 'bad programming' on good citizens, work published during the 1990s concentrated heavily on governmental regulation of content. Writers have frequently detailed how television reproduces systems of ideological hegemony (see Curran and Park 2000). Political economy accounts have addressed the persistence of cultural and media imperialism in varying guises (Goonasekera and Holaday 1998; Goonasekera and Lee 1998; Chadha and Kavoori 2000; see Chapter 3 for an extended discussion of this field). A few book-length accounts have described the struggle for control of satellite broadcasting (Thomas 2005; Page and Crawley 2001) and the penetration into Asia of Western communications networks (Schiller 1999).

Alternatively, Brunsdon notes a tributary of 'innovatory work' in television studies focusing on 'the definition of the television text' (2004: 2301) — from William's early work (1974) on television flows through to Caldwell's concept (1995) of 'televisuality', the latter addressing the changing forms of television as aesthetic and industrial practice, and as socially symbolic acts. These newer approaches — or at least revisions of the pioneering work of thinkers such as Williams — have much to offer the field of television studies in East Asia. Indeed, scholars from Asia have begun to move on from inherited political economy of the media frameworks, integrating cultural studies and media economics. Moreover, in the transition from old to new media, researchers have drawn attention to the forms that television adopts through the critical lenses of media literacy, cultural technologies, and cultural geography. In short, literacy relates to citizens' ability to understand the many varieties of media messages that emanate from proliferating media channels. In relation to television, it concerns how to access, evaluate, and make sense of texts. The cultural technologies approach examines how media are diversifying and, in many instances, becoming more responsive to the individual user or consumer — from the use of media blogs to SMS interactivity and, in the case of television, niche consumption and pay-per-view. Cultural geography also alerts us to the importance of rethinking the 'local in the global'.

It is precisely the local aspect of global production that concerns us. As Waisbord (2004) notes, with the media becoming even more global, international and domestic producers have sought new ways to exploit the resilience of national cultures. Meanwhile, national cultures in East Asia have responded to increasingly integrated networks of production and distribution. During the past several years, new creative content breakthroughs have occurred within East Asia. The manifestations are not entirely new: Japanese consumer electronics, music, animation and video games software industries (Iwabuchi 2002), Hong Kong music, film and television industries (Curtin 2003; Lo 2005), and Taiwanese music (Lee and Huang 2002) and TV drama industries (Iwabuchi 2002; Liu and Chen 2004) have shared the spoils of the East Asian popular culture marketplace for the best part of two decades.

More recently, the so-called Korean Wave — expressed most dramatically in music, TV drama, cinema, and video games (Jeon and Yoon 2005; KNTO 2003) — has recaptured East Asian cultural imaginations and extended the scope and directionality of East Asian media production. Rapid transformations in production networks, and the capacity to trade goods and services across proximate cultures, have in turn facilitated media internationalisation and globalisation. The processes wrought by global investment in communication services and by the expansion of media industries across national borders are unprecedented in scope, even if the return on investment of some these border-crossings is minor. In other words, global elements are woven into a rich regional tapestry. Meanwhile, cultural exchange — mostly in the form of co-productions and formats — has increased as regulatory barriers have fallen and as the internet has made more information available.

Regional Identities and Cultural Imaginations

These developments demonstrate how the landscape of production is reshaping, and how the creative industries are being drawn into closer correspondence with theories and models of social transformation. While internationalisation, globalisation, and modernity are analogous concepts in some respects, there are distinctions that need to be clarified. Throughout the following chapters, we draw attention to these distinctions, as well as to issues of cultural proximity. Cultural specificity is important, though it does not always win hearts and minds. 'Trait geographies' — a term used by Appadurai (2001) — implies that consumption of programs is characteristic of national communities within culturally coherent 'areas'. The consumption of TV programming, even more so than cinema, testifies to the importance of pre-existing cultures — the intangible assets of countries and their peoples. However, it is important to bear in mind that regional production is always in flux. In short, as Appadurai writes, 'Regions are best viewed as initial contexts for themes that generate variable geographies, rather than fixed geographies marked by pre-given themes' (Appadurai 2001: 8).

One such theme is an emerging East Asian cultural imagination. This embodies audience receptiveness to 'proximate' cultural artefacts while maintaining connectedness to the global cultural economy through aspirations for international brand products. This compound cultural imagination, in turn, foregrounds material processes. Along with global shifts in the economic alignment of transnational media industries, new cultural technologies have allowed the generation and distribution of creative content in the region. A technology introduced via Japan in 1979, the Sony Walkman, brought about a synthesis of walking and listening. Cultural technologies in East Asia have since evolved from karaoke devices to Music TV to Karaoke TV — now accessed in home entertainment systems (Otake and Shuhei 2005). More recently, SMS and mobile content downloads of TV *Idol* show merchandising and news (see Chapters 9 and 10) have linked the performativity formerly associated with karaoke to the mass participation of media events. In the area of narrative audio-visual content, Japan's Sky Perfect Communications launched a 51-episode drama to mobile phones in 2005 (Keshishoglou 2005), while in China episodic content is a nascent business model for short messaging services (SMS).

In the meantime, business is looking to cash in. This focus on economics underpins the internationalisation of television programs and formats across national boundaries. In short, internationalisation is a rational activity rather than a transformative 'end of history'. And it is not a new phenomenon. Internationalisation describes the expansion of individual firm economic activities across national boundaries in an effort to attain economies of scale and scope. To achieve internationalisation, producers need to understand the local context, including the socio-political and economic processes of acquiring and exploiting local knowledge. In television industries financial returns on program development and production are extended across and within new territories. Dicken (1998) argues that internationalisation is essentially a quantitative process.

In contrast, globalisation is more qualitative. It concerns the functional integration of internationally dispersed activities into broader social, cultural, political and economic realities. Giddens (1990) and Robertson (1992) represent a number of contemporary writers who have associated globalisation with late modernity — although such assertions have provoked claims of *just whose* late modernity; namely, that the concept of modernity is very much European, predominately capitalist, and applies less to developing countries where people have uneven access to global communications, travel and real lifestyle choices (see Anthios 1999). Others have opted for more flexible concepts, such as 'ubiquitous modernity' (Iwabuchi 2004) and 'alternative modernities' (Liu 2005). In the former, Iwabuchi argues that the Western gaze, which has determined discursive constructs of non-Western modernity, has melted into a 'global gaze' in which the forces of media globalisation and consumer culture play important roles. People attest to feeling the same and feeling dissimilar within globally franchised consumer culture — from eating at Subway, an American food franchise, to watching franchised reality TV.

Shops in Chinese cities now display the same products found in downtown New York. More often than not these are cheap copies, often embodying so-called 'Chinese characteristics' — that is, subtle variations that allow local producers or fabricators to claim some degree of originality and to avoid charges of intellectual property violation. Echoing this variety, Liu Kang argues for a multiplicity of modernities because, as he says, 'the uniqueness and specificities of each nation-state's encounter with modernity constitute irrefutable differences and alternatives to Eurocentric capitalist modernity' (Liu 2005: 27). In this view, modernity does not develop teleologically, despite capitalism's global reach and quantifiable indicators of 'progress' such as the spread of transnational firms and increased flows of trans-border information, money, population and symbolic goods.

Calls for the convergence of modernity on the one hand, and its fragmentation into alternative or plural modernities on the other, illustrate a world in which the nation-state no longer over-determines cultural representations. Regions and localities generate 'variable geographies' and alert us to the illusion of permanent associations between space, territory and cultural organisation (Appadurai 2001: 8). The key issue is that modernity implies a coming into being, whereas globalisation suggests that 'we live in an almost/not yet world' (Thrift 1996: 257, cited in Shami 2001: 220). Whereas modernity (along with modernization theory) is concerned with rupture, process and innovation — and in doing so, recalls a series of bracketed pasts identified by big ideas such as tradition, history, evolution, antiquity and civilisation — globalisation captures 'the in-betweenness of a world always on the brink of newness' (Shami 2001: 220). Impermanency is captured by the concept of 'interim globalisation'. Fung (2004) writes of the limited lifespan of TV formats in Hong Kong. Likewise, franchised products in Tokyo, Taipei, Seoul and Shanghai show that difference is often incremental as international formulas are adjusted, appropriated and licensed. Globalisation by franchising thus provides a very different model of development — one that is flexible, post-Fordist and highly subject to user-led innovation.

Theories of globalisation are often associated with cultural and media imperialism — as is regularly noted in critiques of power by the political economy of the media scholars Herman and McChesney (1997), Herb Schiller (1989), and Dan Schiller (1999). A central premise of media globalisation theses is that transnational media conglomerates, by drawing on economies of scale and financial muscle — assisted by powerful distribution networks — produce homogenisation effects within and across national cultures. The result, according to some, is the imposition of Western value systems or even standardised forms of global culture. Indeed, there are numerous instances where cultural globalisation effects have been detrimental to native traditions. The cultural economist Cowan notes that, 'destruction of ethos can cause non-Western cultures to lose their uniqueness, thereby faltering in their artistic creativity' (Cowan 2002: 47). Indeed, the *déja vu* of globalisation often reveals itself to travellers who see franchised versions of global goods and services while walking the streets or viewing programs on hotel televisions.

In acknowledging the reality of cultural globalisation, moreover, we note that, while the cultures of the world are becoming strikingly similar in many aspects, local cultural specificity is not discarded. Global cultural forms and formats may demonstrate greater uniformity, but content is increasingly adaptable and multi-purpose. Economic globalisation implies that countries and regions are becoming more integrated within a global economy (Ohmae 2005). Regional variations propel the dispersion of ideas. Ironically, while the global media are consolidating through mergers and alliances, content is being exchanged or cloned so rapidly that there is an increasing sense of connectedness. Success in one market is very quickly transferred to another market. This does not just apply to the sale of 'finished' programming, but also to the transfer of templates and techniques. Is this the new model of globalisation — and, for now, of new television? The question of how effective globalisation is as a descriptor of what is occurring in Asian communication landscapes remains, given new patterns of media flow within Asia. If media globalisation retains relevance in a period in which local content is reasserting, it is perhaps most evident in the transfer of television genres and formats across regions and national cultures.

The Regional Mediascape

This following sections look in closer detail at the development of television systems and national content in mainland China, Hong Kong, Japan, South Korea and Taiwan — and in doing so, provide background for the extended discussion of new television that follows. In these countries, television viewing has established an important connection to people's lives. Local production has responded accordingly with the consolidation in recent years of local industries and the implementation of regulatory policies to protect and nurture local content. Despite such new growth areas in Asia, the television production environment remains in a state of flux, echoing global developments in media convergence and multi-channelling. Industry analysts tell us that audience fragmentation — notably, the same audience numbers spread over many channels — has led to fewer viewers per channel with pressure to reduce the cost of producing an hour of television (Looms 2005; Griffith 2002; Aris and Bughin 2005). This is occurring in East Asia in a manner analogous to developments elsewhere. Reality television, quiz shows, and family formats provide solutions to this bottom-line crisis. Not only are they economically expedient forms of production, but they function to reincarnate and stimulate ideas that are both familiar and foreign. In this sense, we are witnessing an economic logic of production based on a rapid turnover of ideas, the extension of program life cycles, and the generation of hybrid forms and genres.

The countries that we describe in this collection are collectively referred to as East Asia, and sometimes even as the Far East. The latter description harks back to a time when colonial empires prevailed and the world was subdivided according to its geographical positioning relative to the centres of civilisation as they existed in the European imagination. Somewhat ironically in the contemporary era of disintegrating nation-states, the naming of the Far East is in contradistinction to China's own self-identification as the middle of the known world ('China', written in characters, literally means Middle Kingdom). In contrast, Japan's self-identity is ambiguous in that it is geographically situated in East Asia, while its economy 'is closer to and more competitive with the West than East Asia' (Otake and Shuhei 2005: 54).

Despite historical legacies and the political emergence of the region-state (Ohmae 2005), we address the countries in this study as distinct entities, acknowledging cultural proximity and difference, while cognisant of the role of national regulatory bodies. In doing this, we explore discourses of modernity and globalisation as they impact upon the kinds of content that is deemed fit to broadcast in China, Japan, Korea and Taiwan — whether for political purposes, or in more recent times, for commercial considerations. Television program development in Asia therefore needs be located in an historical and governmental context, and to be understood from the perspectives of both hardware and software. In other words, the effectiveness of this unique cultural technology across time is due to the development of the infrastructure (the technology) and the exploitation of the medium's capacity to instantaneously broadcast words and pictures (content) as a means of informing and influencing mass populations.

Nuances of television content, and the phenomenon in which programming is *both similar and different* in these locations, can be seen as an effect of global flows of culture on one hand, and a response to popular taste on the other. Lest this might appear to be over-simplifying the global–local dynamic by collapsing it into consumer sovereignty, we are mindful that the medium of television is itself embedded within cultural contexts. Of course, culture pre-dates the electronic media. Rather than take the position that television is inimical to culture, we suggest that television is a powerful medium for the transmission, exchange and fusion of culture; in this sense, it provides viewers not only with an unparalleled window on the world, but with a composite of the indigenous and the imported. The television receiver remains the prime means of communication in today's society despite the pervasiveness of the internet and mobile messaging.

Television as a Global Communications Medium

The modern technology of television — or at least the analogue transmission of signals — was developed in tandem with mass broadcasting and was free to users. The principal reason for television being free to air was that it was terrestrial — that is, it was virtually impossible to prevent anyone from watching it except by removing the television receiver. Television content in most Asian nations was until the 1990s largely mandated by governmental concerns to deliver programs that reflected cultural and nation-building objectives. Spectrum was scarce and channels were often monopolised by government interests or shareholders. The issue of globalisation and the impact of the internet would emerge much later.

In a broad sweep of television systems across the globe, we can make a number of claims that pertain to the nature of content. First, governments of all countries have recognised the significant role that television plays in the maintenance of national cultural identity. As well as regulating foreign ownership of television media, national communication policies frame the nature of content that is allowed to be broadcast. Moreover, in many countries there are support mechanisms for local industries, such as content quota requirements that mandate the carriage of particular kinds of programming (public interest) and encourage the development of other forms (low-budget game shows, local drama).

Second, television operates across several markets. Geographic markets help to determine the specific nuances of content. Many programs succeed only in local markets, while others are able to be sold in national and international markets. In addition, there are 'upstream' and 'downstream' product markets. The former concerns the sale of programs to channels by producers, while the downstream market is about the sale of programs to advertisers based on audience loyalty.

Third, the free-to-air analogue system of delivery that has prevailed globally has supported a business model whereby production was almost entirely supported by advertising (with the exception of public broadcasting). With the migration to pay-per-view (cable TV, satellite) and digital multi-channelling, this advertising support is eroding while viewing is becoming more discretionary. To compensate for this transformation, television formats that allow product placement and product synergy have found increasing support within program development meetings, despite misgivings about the banality of many of these offerings (see Adair and Moran 2004).

Fourth, television is being influenced by the fast-evolving computer industry where business models are founded on the vision that television will effectively become a conduit for branded electronic content. Digital television transmission via terrestrial transmitters, satellite or cable, television over broadband internet (IPTV), program reception via third-generation mobile phone, and digital multimedia broadcasting (DMB) all mean that new business models are required if television is to maintain its audience. The consumer uptake of digital TV and IPTV (the simultaneous provision of television and the internet through broadband) is occurring more rapidly in East Asia than elsewhere in the world. The importance of branding and identifying genres and formats grows as more channels appear on our screens. Reality, news, lifestyle and special interest channels are now familiar while game shows replicate themes of 'fastest, smartest and the fittest'.

TV Culture: Oxymoron or Sense-making Repertoire?

Before embarking on a discussion of each country's specific cultural context and television programming, it is worth investigating in more detail the idea of 'television culture' from the standpoint of what the medium of television presents in relation to other media. The broader context of televisual sense-making includes industrial, technological and policy issues, as well as the processes of consumption that adjudicate on the value of television programming. Television culture, therefore, is not something that is imposed by networks. It is different in every country, and more distinctive in countries that have strong domestic industries and national cultures.

Despite the claims of some pundits, the term 'television culture' is not oxymoronic. For Raymond Williams, the medium of television was a crucial cultural form, as relevant to education as the printed word. Due to a greater technical capacity to represent social reality, television offered greater social horizons to its viewers than art forms such as theatre (Williams 1979: 223–242). Whereas the humble receiver was once considered merely a neutral technology, a box in the corner of the living room, in today's multi-channel environment it is the set-top box that has allowed television to present and repackage varieties of cultural experiences. Television brings to our living rooms, and now to our computer monitors, images of the ordinary and the extraordinary, soaps and coups, movies and documentaries, and chat and confessionals.

The popular science writer Stephen Johnson (2005) makes a compelling claim for the complexity of television culture, arguing that while television viewing may still be widely regarded as essentially passive, the evolution of content is destabilising that view. Part of the cognitive work associated with understanding television is its complexity. Multiple threads and interwoven plots in television drama now require viewers to 'fill in'. There is a difference between intelligent shows and shows that force the viewer to be intelligent. Moreover, the advent of new television formats — reality TV and information challenges — requires viewers to think *as if* participating, *as if* performing. This challenges the dominant view. The 'effects' tradition of media studies has long been premised on how meanings encoded into television messages impact on the value systems of viewers. Ethnographic research has confounded simplistic media effect claims. Audiences make multiple meanings, and audiences are engaging with more interactive cultural technologies in their daily lives. The advent of reality TV, for instance, 'provides the ultimate testimony to the cultural dominance of games in this moment of pop culture history' (Johnson 2005: 92). Now there is a different and yet untested dynamic. The psychological activity of 'watching as if participating in television' may well intensify the normative functions of the texts.

As Anthony Smith (1998) writes in the introduction to *Television: An International History,* 'what the inventors never quite realized was that television would become *normative,* that so much of what we see on the screen would contrive to suggest how things ought or ought not to be' (1998: 1, italics in original). In addition, the development of television culture into interactive participatory formats further inscribes the notion of how to conduct oneself in the most unforgiving public arena, but in doing so, promotes acceptable variations of normative social roles.

By the time television reached Asia in the 1950s, its normative role was firmly established. Nevertheless, television in East Asia appears like global television. Or, to put it another way, it is apparent that many formerly distinct 'national' television programs and modes of address have converged into an international style, which is itself a product of the commercial logic of broadcasting. For instance, prime-time news anchors are usually paired (male and female), talk shows address live audiences, and game shows embody interactivity via audience participation and voting. Such evidence appears to support an erasure of cultural specificity. In order to test such a proposition, however, we will briefly look at each national television system, phases of development and the evolution of programming.

The People's Republic of China

The People's Republic of China is a good place to begin this journey, due to the simple fact that it challenges many global assumptions about industry structure. Is Chinese television following an international style, absorbing foreign investment, responding to regional templates, or it is resolutely Chinese? Indeed, government regulation has played an important role in how Chinese television has internationalised, and how it continues to do so. In adopting a Structure–Conduct–Performance paradigm (S-C-P) (Young 2000), we note that television production in China since the 1950s has been subject to overtly interventionist and non-competitive market structures. The resultant 'conduct' of television professionals, moreover, has followed the dictates of bureaucrats, while the output (performance) has been low relative to that of its East Asian neighbours.

The arrival of the medium of television in the late 1950s heralded a new frontier of propaganda .work. Despite an inauspicious development period, hampered by a lack of infrastructure and the temporary cessation of development during the Cultural Revolution, television soon became the primary cultural technology through which the Chinese leadership consolidated its hegemony. The technological revolution of satellite delivery and fibre-optic cable allowed television to extend its reach to an unprecedented degree, far displacing radio and the print media as the preferred medium by which people received information about the world.

The development of television following the Cultural Revolution became a major platform of socialist modernisation. The impetus for the expansion of television, however, came from the opening of the television market to private investment. Decentralisation of administration during the mid-1980s allowed local stations the opportunity to chart their own course in financial management and program development. By the end of 1995, there were some 2740 stations made up of terrestrial broadcasters, cable stations and university television channels (Tu 1997: 4). By way of contrast with the development of terrestrial stations, cable networks had their origin in the 1970s. In 1982, the government decided that all new residential blocks would be equipped with ducts for cable television, although no decisions were made about standardising networks. By 1998, China's rollout of cable exceeded 1.34 million kilometres, and by 1999 there were 80 million subscribers to cable television (Tu 1997).

Television stations, mindful of diminishing state funding and competition, readily embraced advertising as a means to maintain viability. Under new policies of market competition during the 1990s, investors had to be sought out and their whims catered to, even if this meant having sponsors' products inserted into program scripts, or allowing investors a say in production. One of the facts of the early expansion of the television industry was a shortage of programs. The limited capacity of Chinese stations to originate programs created a demand for foreign programs. Whereas, prior to 1980, most foreign programs originated from other socialist countries, during the 1980s programs came mostly from East Asian countries (Taiwan, Hong Kong and Japan), as well as from the United States and Western Europe (Chan 1994: 75). The difficulty for Chinese television stations wishing to procure foreign programs was a lack of capital — a situation that led to the widespread industry practice of exchanging advertising space for programs.

The most widely viewed form of programming is television drama, although game and reality shows are increasingly found in the peak viewing period from 7.00 p.m. to 9.30 p.m. Programs are generically classified into three broad categories: news (news broadcasts, current affairs); arts and entertainment (variety shows, dramas, game shows and music); and education (talk shows, children's shows, university programs). Indigenous forms include the Chinese evening variety show *(wanhui)*, in which performers such as comedians, singers and dancers perform live and often lip-synch. Dramas have consistently performed well and underline audience fascination with the melodrama of daily life (Zhu et al. 2007). While the national news remains the highest rating program, other traditional forms of factual television are not faring so well, leading to innovations in new documentary and docu-soap formats (see Part II). The demand for new content, and the competition from Taiwanese and Hong Kong broadcasters, has in turn put more pressure on stations to experiment, not by buying licences or scripts, but simply by copying the production values and ideas of more successful stations. In this context, the issue of intellectual property remains a complex one, as we will see later in the discussion of reality television and game shows.

An example of the practice of mimicking was the program called *Larry Lang Live*, which was broadcast on Shanghai cable television until deemed problematic in 2006 by China's media censors. In what was ostensibly a copy of *Larry King Live* (CNN), the host Lang Xianping, engaged in soft interviews with celebrities (Dyer and McGregor 2005). The popularity of talk show genres is reflected in the term now used to describe these shows — they are literally 'rattling shows' *(tuokou xiu)*. It should also be noted that the direction that such 'rattling' talk shows adopt in mainland China is also influenced by the Hong Kong-based Phoenix TV *(fenghuang weishi)*, a satellite broadcaster that is co-owned by Liu Changle and Rupert Murdoch. Phoenix, like Murdoch's Starry Skies channel *(xingkong weishi)*, is partly accessible in China and features a buffet of hard-hitting late night news formats, such as *Newsline* and *Behind the Headlines with Wentao*. In the latter, the host Dou Wentao interrogates a range of personalities and newsmakers, also drawing heavily on the interlocutory style of Larry King.

Hong Kong

The first point to note is that Hong Kong has only two commercial free-to-air (terrestrial) stations — TVB and ATV, founded in 1967 and 1969 respectively. TVB maintains about a 70 percent audience share. The dominant practice in the past was for stations to challenge each other by producing television dramas. This category of programming was, and remains, highly popular. Television drama became the most important source of entertainment for Hong Kong as it developed into a global city. The narratives and prime-time intrigues of locally produced soaps were invariably hot topics for private discussion and the focus of public agendas. For example, a soap opera called *The Good, the Bad, and the Ugly (wangzhong ren)*, produced by TVB in 1979, attracted such attention that it galvanised negative sentiment towards mainland

Chinese immigrants (see Ma 1999: 62–96). During the 1970s, TVB's prime-time ratings often reached 40 points (1 point is equivalent to about 65 000 people), capturing more than half of the territory's population. The publicly funded government station Radio Television Hong Kong (RTHK) also produced its own documentaries, but relied on broadcasting time on TVB and ATV.

From the mid-1980s, television serial drama ratings registered a loss of one quarter, signalling the decline of television as a source of entertainment (Chan 1990). Fung and Lau (1993) have argued that television's popularity diminished in Hong Kong as alternative sources of entertainment became available. In the 1970s, mass transit and highway systems were not well developed. The first tunnels linking the New Territories (the northern and major part of Hong Kong) and the Cross-harbour Tunnel were built in 1967 and 1972 respectively, and only short non-cross-harbour subways connecting central and western Kowloon in Hong Kong operated in 1979. With less mobility in terms of transport infrastructure, locals preferred returning home after work to pursue sedentary leisure activities such as watching television. But as Hong Kong developed networks of transport connecting the entire region, people became more inclined to choose new leisure activities (Fung and Lau 1993). In terms of social and cultural development, this represents a positive indication as it reflects greater social mobility. At the same time, it was less beneficial to the local television industry. Nevertheless, despite the overall reduction in television's popularity over the past two decades, TVB still manages to enjoy an average rating of about thirty for most prime-time programs. Furthermore, TVB's continued ascendancy helps to explain why new television formats were piloted by TVB's major competitor, ATV, which traditionally enjoys a smaller audience share.

Prior to the 1990s, when the government implemented the 'open sky' competition schedule, there were few real competitors in the marketplace. Even in the early 1990s, only a relatively small percentage of the population could view the new pan-Asia STAR Television as this required installation of a satellite dish. Wharf Cable, the local cable television system, was launched in October 1993 and delivered fifty-seven channels; however due to charges and access issues, its penetration had reached only 600 000 household audiences out of a population of 6.9 million. As for competing services, border-crossing signals from Mandarin-language programs from the nearby provinces of China are not strong enough to penetrate to the former colony. Moreover, with the popularity of the programming of the two major terrestrial networks anticipated to continue long term, there is limited incentive to introduce new elements, aside from internal competition.

A second characteristic of Hong Kong has been the high proportion of in-house program production. In-station teams are largely responsible for the bulk of programming. Years of experience in the operation of prime-time production teams have established a very efficient and smooth operational schedule, drawing on a skilled personnel pool, a strong organisational culture, and a high degree of autonomy (TVB producer, interview by Fung, 18 June 2002). In effect, this allows a television station to produce their own programs for their own needs within a manageable budget.

This represents a different way of managing the production chain than in most Western television systems where stations and production companies are operationally independent. When the franchise format mode of production was introduced to Hong Kong, the same producers and personnel were involved, but were compelled to change their operational patterns to fit the production requirements of the franchise format. This, in turn, upset the routine and autonomy of the teams.

Taiwan

One of the anomalies of Taiwan's television industry is an abundance of privately funded channels servicing a population of just under twenty-three million. Taiwan has a dual television system, with both commercial and public television. Viewers enjoy a smorgasbord of channel options, although there is a heavy emphasis on infotainment genres and formats. Broadcasting began with commercial free-to-air television while public television is a recent addition. The public television service (PTS) now supplements four terrestrial commercial stations, 68 cable operators, and more than 128 satellite channels (Liu and Chen 2004).

The current mix of cable and satellite television stations has evolved from a competitive and at times chaotic environment. To some extent, this background explains the low value program model that typifies the production environment. Before the Cable Television Law was passed in 1993 (revised in 1999), there were about 300 illegal cable system operators (Liu 1994). In 1994, these operators were made to apply for licences, and a period of mergers and acquisitions subsequently reduced the number to the current level. The pay TV penetration rate exceeds 80 percent of households, although most of the channels are delivered via satellites. Since the early 1990s, the Taiwanese government has been instrumental in bringing about major technological transitions in the television industry. The government has used several strategies to entice market actors into cooperating in the upgrading of infrastructure, including funding for research and development initiatives in digital video, high-definition displays, and other components of digital TV systems.

The liberalisation of Taiwan's mediascape is perhaps best understood from the perspective of political economy. Since the government regulated the cable television industry in 1993, Taiwan's media have embraced pluralism. As Liu and Chen (2004) write, the high number of private channels looking for a slice of the market has contributed to conservatism which includes stations copying formats. An example of this practice is the program *2100 All the People Talk (2100 quanmin kaijiang)*, a live call-in program instigated in 1994. Host Lee Tao invites representatives from all the major political parties to debate a major issue of the day. Lee even tries to dress and act like CNN's Larry King. Following the success of this show, many cable television channels adopted similar call-in formats. This does not, however, imply diversity: most of the time topics are the same, and sometimes the same guests appear on different channels on the same day (Liu and Chen 2004).

Tried-and-tested schedules with recognised formats and genres are guarantors of success. In this kind of production environment, formats can play an important role. For instance, from 7.00 pm to 8.00 pm most stations and full-service channels broadcast news, and in doing so, follow an American exemplar. Mimicking American news formats, Taiwanese stations persist with a solitary anchor which creates a tendency towards isomorphism in the scheduling of television programs. Prime-time schedules in all the commercial terrestrial television stations and some full-service cable channels are almost identical. Indeed, when there is a change in programming it brings about a kind of herd mentality. As Liu and Chen (2004) point out, news and weather reports are almost identical, and they follow each other's leads: if one anchor broadcasts on-the-scene news, others will follow suit.

From 8.00 pm to 9.00 pm, most channels (except the niche cable television channels) broadcast dramas. Taiwan television drama series have liberally borrowed ideas from Japanese television dramas. This cultural borrowing has given Taiwan's entertainment program formats a more Japanese look rather than simply imitating American models.

Japan

One of the most remarkable features of the Japanese audio-visual market is its near self-sufficiency in television programming. Iwabuchi (2004) writes that Japan is the only country, apart from the United States, where more than 95 percent of television programs are produced domestically. In recent years, however, the success of Korean dramas has disrupted Japanese insularity. As in Taiwan, Japanese popular culture has been deeply influenced by American media. In his discussion of Japanese television formats, Iwabuchi (2004) points out that no regulatory policies were implemented to counter the influx of American media culture. Japan, however, successfully imitated the foreign programming. In other words, Japanese television producers were appropriating rather than being dominated and colonised by American products. At the time of the inception of Japanese television in 1953, Japanese television programming relied heavily upon imports from the United States. However, by the mid-1960s the imbalance had drastically and quickly diminished. As early as 1980, Japan was importing only 5 percent of all programs (Kawatake and Hara 1994).

Japan's economic miracle — together with a large domestic market — made rapid development possible in audio-visual industries. With a population of more than 120 million and an economy sustained by strong growth, the Japanese television market was able to prosper. Domestic production is characterised by a constant supply of original dramas, variety shows, quiz shows, reality television, and infotainment programs. While American products undoubtedly have worldwide distribution, they fail to dominate in markets where there is a strong tradition of local content or where there is significant linguistic difference. Since the 1980s, programs directly imported from the United States have not fared well in Japan, with a few occasional exceptions such as *The X-Files* (Iwabuchi 2004).

This is not to say, however, that foreign popular culture is no longer consumed in Japan. In fact, American popular culture continues to exert a strong influence. People in Japan have been saturated with American popular culture and information about the American way of life frequently appears in the mass media. Japan remains one of the most important and profitable markets for Hollywood movies and American pop music. Furthermore, Japanese television has been able to develop a variety of original programming for its nearly self-sufficient market through the indigenisation of many program formats and concepts influenced by, and borrowed from, American programs.

South Korea

Television was first introduced in Korea in 1956. However, it was not until the early 1960s — a period of national modernisation — that the Korean television industry was regulated. As Lee (2004) notes, in 1961 the military regime founded KBS-TV, the national broadcasting system, to 'cure the citizens' sick minds' and to display an image of 'the renewing nation' (Jung 1991: 135). The 1960s was characterised by dependency on foreign — mostly

American — programs, especially during prime-time (Choe and Kang 2000: 183–84). The national broadcaster, the Korean Broadcasting System (KBS), and the commercial Tongyang Broadcasting Company (TBC) competed to schedule foreign programs. The broadcast of foreign programs in prime time continued until 1969 and in the early 1970s another commercial broadcaster joined the ratings competition. As competition intensified between the one national and two commercial stations, Korean broadcasters developed local genres — especially daily soap operas — which accommodated local audience's 'structures of feeling' (Williams 1961), rather than merely relaying foreign programs. Korean soap operas made the most of limited production resources and eventually substituted foreign programs.

Several factors impacted upon the gradual decrease of the Korean television industry's dependence on foreign programs during the 1970s. During this time, production facilities and technologies stabilised. The augmentation of local relay stations and the domestic production of television sets encouraged larger local audiences to watch television. The rapid growth of audience availability enlarged the pie for television advertisement, facilitating the development of the Korean television industry. However, the development of local genres did not mean that broadcasters' preference for foreign programs suddenly disappeared. During the following decade, KBS2 and the Munhwa Broadcasting Corporation continued to schedule foreign programs at weekends in prime-time rating slots. By the 1990s, the preference for foreign programs had declined. With the local productions garnering greater popularity, foreign programs were moved to marginal timeslots, such as 10.30 pm on weeknights or the early hours of weekend evenings (Lee 2004). In the early 2000s, cable and satellite television have become the major channels for foreign programs to flow into Korea. While multi-channelling has accelerated the inflow of foreign programs, especially American programs, ratings of cable and satellite stations still lag far behind those of network television.

Concluding Remarks: Inter-Asian Flows

Beginning with television content targeted primarily at local audiences for purposes of ensuring citizenship and entertaining local constituencies, Hong Kong, Japanese, Taiwanese, Korean and, more recently, Chinese television productions have moved outwards into East and South-east Asia. The cross-border traffic in programs and formats during the past few years is a result of a growing acknowledgement of the pan-Asian cultural marketplace which has received further impetus from co-production agreements and television trade shows such as MIP Asia. The cross-border trade in finished programs observes a fundamental economic logic of television industries — namely, that when initial production costs have been met, further profits can be attained in secondary markets. Marginal costs of duplication are quite low, even taking into account the translation costs of subtitling (see Bates 1998). Despite this, there are obvious 'cultural discounts' attached to the cross-cultural sale of programming in environments where local programming is perceived to be most relevant (Hoskins et al. 1991).

In the past, most international sales into Asia have operated on the basis of selling finished programs. Indeed, Hong Kong's cross-border influence dates from the days when Run Run Shaw established TVB and built markets for Hong Kong drama in Malaysia, Taiwan, Singapore, and Indonesia. Much of Hong Kong's television production comes with subtitles added so that it is marketable across various Chinese dialects in China, Singapore, Taiwan, and Indonesia (Lo 2005).

Japan's influence in the region is particularly evident in TV formats. However, Japan's other cultural strengths include the direct sales of television teen idol dramas and *anime* (animation). Japan has had most success in selling finished programs into Taiwan which lifted restrictions on Japanese popular culture in the early 1990s at a time when Taiwan's cable stations were expanding and seeking content (Liu and Chen 2004). A cultural proximity argument would suggest that South Korea and Singapore ought to be potentially strong markets for Japanese television. However, the Korean government had legislated to stop the import of Japanese culture. In the period during the 1990s when Japanese television was banned, Korean producers openly imitated Japanese programs. As Waisbord (2004) has noted, protectionist policies on importing foreign programs lead local producers to pursue other models, either purchasing scripts (see Liu and Chen 2004) or simply copying ideas (Keane 2004). With full opening to Japanese culture pending at the end of the 1990s, Korean producers moved to co-produce TV serial dramas — *Friends* in 2001 and *Sonagi, an Afternoon after Showers* in 2002 (Lee 2005). When Korea eventually lifted final restrictions on Japanese culture in 2004 — including Japanese songs and movies — there was no subsequent surge of Japanese popular cultural products, apart from young fans of Japanese 'trendy dramas'. Indeed, Japanese and Korean producers began to develop formal co-productions. In 2004, MBC collaborated with Fuji TV on the two-part mini-series, *Star's Echo*. Elsewhere in Asia, Singapore's preoccupation with Western culture offered a line of resistance to Japanese television programs (Lim 2004). Japanese programs have not been promoted and supplemented by merchandising in Singapore to the extent that has occurred in Taiwan and Hong Kong.

China's position within the inter-Asian trade matrix is a work in progress. Currently, China suffers from an acknowledged 'cultural trade deficit' in its media and cultural industries. According to the deputy director of the Culture Market Department within the Chinese Ministry of Culture, 'The market share of Chinese cultural products in the United States is close to zero' (*People's Daily* 22 August 2005). Nevertheless, an increase in co-productions between China and Taiwan, and between China and Hong Kong, means that China is moving more directly into the local circuits of production that are undermining the authority of Western programming. The result of China's integration will inevitably mean stronger market synergies, more mainland Chinese product aimed at neighbouring regional markets, and a shift to a more entertainment-focused and apolitical style — already apparent in entrepreneurial stations, best exemplified by Hunan Satellite Station in south China.

3

Rethinking Structures of Dominance, Translation Effects, and Export Models

How does creative content from East Asia find its way into world markets? How can the East Asian cultural imagination transcend domestic containers and move into international markets?

These are crucial questions for media industries in East Asia. Influencing the balance of audio-visual flows through export success is important for producers — for some, more important than how national governments might legislate to artificially restrict foreign content. When sold at prices that local markets can afford, imported programming displaces local content and becomes an impediment to local industry development, as well as a source of nationalist discomfort. Imports — whether these be top-of-the-range quality programming *(The X-Files)* or recycled sit-coms *(Friends)* — reduce incentives to compete in the same genre. Export of creative content is therefore important, not so much for its material dividends, as for its intangible outcomes. Exports bring multiplier effects: they promote confidence, provide openings for others to follow, and help to reduce the rhetoric of cultural protectionism.

Industry protection policy has been applied successfully to stimulate film and television industry development in South Korea, Australia, France, Canada, and China. The protection of diversity through encouraging local voices is promoted by many industry spokespeople as an antidote to Americanisation and, in South Korea and China, Japanisation. But is there a more effective strategy than erecting barriers? Perhaps the best example of export success combined with low protectionism is Japan, which provides East Asia with a model for assimilating Western (primarily US) techniques of quality control, marketing, and management. Iwabuchi (2004) writes that Japan has 'localized US influences by imitating, emulating and appropriating, rather than being dominated and colonized by American products' (2004: 22). Japan has also used franchising strategies to build television exports. The most internationally licensed examples are *Exciting Animal Land (Wakuwaku)*, *Happy Family Plan (Shiawase Kazoku Keikaku)*, *Future Diary (Mirai Nikki)*, and *Iron Chef (Ryouri no Tetsujin)*.

In this chapter, we examine preconditions for export success and the role of TV franchises and formats in extending audio-visual markets. In contrast to top-down media imperialism models that constitute the substantive theoretical toolkit of political economy, our approach identifies bottom-up tactics of East Asian media producers. The chapter begins with a discussion of some of the inherent problems within the political economy of media tradition when it is applied to East Asia. Following this, we offer new ways of thinking through processes of cultural translation and exchange. This leads to a five-stage creative content development framework, suggesting that the TV franchise serves as a mid-range strategy for East Asian television producers. Are TV formats a temporary phase of development or a long-term model for creating capacity in East Asian television?

Cultural Imperialism: The Return of the Repressed?

Since the 1960s, governments, academics, producers — and often concerned ordinary citizens — have extolled the threat of cultural and media imperialism. In 1977, Tunstall defined cultural imperialism in the following way: 'authentic, traditional and local culture in many parts of the world is being battered out of existence by the indiscriminate dumping of large quantities of slick commercial and media products, mainly from the United States' (1977: 57). The political economy scholar Herbert Schiller, perhaps more than anybody, was responsible for the internationalisation of the concept of media imperialism, modifying its US-centrism to account for the diversification of ownership and control into transnational corporate culture (H. Schiller 1989; 1991). If we follow this assessment, East Asia's integration into the global economy goes hand in hand with transnational foreign direct investment into Asia — a point emphasised in Dan Schiller's reflections on 'digital capitalism'. Schiller constructs a bleak scenario of global media integration with new power structures emerging from state-assisted media industries in China. Digital capitalism is the inevitable end point of new networks of influence (D. Schiller 1999). Examples of such transnational media consolidation are not difficult to instantiate: they include Taiwan's multinational-dominated music industry (Lee and Huang 2002), the Hong Kong advertising industry

(Ma 2005) and the international satellite television industry of Singapore (Abel 2005).

It is a widely held tenet of political economy that global media are relentlessly inducing corporatisation and conglomeration, and closing down avenues for democratic voices and cultural diversity. This top-down view of transnational media, however, sidesteps a crucial point about the nature of innovation in media industries: most breakthrough ideas emerge from small and medium enterprises or from individual creators. Indeed, more than ever before, communications media companies are looking at how audiences and users are redefining innovation. The 'pull' of the market and a corresponding churn of products are driving forces of change rather than the 'push' of large media corporations. This is a point to which we will return throughout this study.

In approaching the question of how East Asian content can compete against global structures of dominance, we need to be aware that academic approaches are embedded within disciplinary conventions. While this qualification may seem unnecessary, a great deal of analysis within the Marxist political economy field is captive to axiomatic conceptual structures that are grounded in dialectical class-based relations, such as capitalism versus socialism, neo-liberalism versus egalitarianism, and corporate management versus producer autonomy. In short, this approach sees dominant interests controlling the media which, in turn, act as vehicles for ideological control. The inevitable domination scenario unfolds. Cultural homogenisation reduces diversity *across* societies, while diversity *within* society suffers because of excessive media concentration. In addition, labour is exploited to accumulate profits for capitalist managerial classes. And, further negating the possibilities of grass-roots agency, the consumer-driven content of commercial media distorts relations between the media-rich and the media-poor: the latter are socially disadvantaged because the programming — and the advertising that supports it — doesn't reflect their identities.

Consolidating this view of structured dominance are regular pronouncements that Asia is a new frontier for Western media business (see *Fortune Magazine*, 4 October, 2004). That is, with the right approach and knowledge, the Asian market is there for the taking. Of course, this is a reinforcement strategy used by the capitalist media: create confidence in the market and investors will respond accordingly. In short, the digital capitalism thesis offers a persuasive account of global structures of dominance. However, while the United States — and Hollywood in particular — assumes a dominant position in English-language markets, we need to be wary of reading the domination scenario too literally in East Asia. The strength of political economy is its marshalling of information. Indeed, the best research on Asia in the English language comes from Asian scholars, many of whom have graduated from journalism and communication schools in the United States, the United Kingdom, Hong Kong, Australasia, and Singapore.

Notwithstanding the rigor of a few leading scholars, a persistent weakness of the field is over-reliance on trade journal literature. In researching China, Downing and Cao (2004) find 'speculation and sweeping assertions' in academic research. They argue that researchers need to 'cease relying so much on US-based trade magazine sources of information which inevitably tend to explore what they know best, and so often overstate the US role to the exclusion of Japanese, Taiwanese and Korean roles in participation' (Downing and Cao 2004: 19).

Reporting in trade journals and business journalism is marked by three tendencies. First, accounts frequently register activities of large media companies — for example, between Viacom and Shanghai Television, between News Corporation and Phoenix, or between China Central TV and News Corp's Channel V. Second, there is little reporting in the English press of the influence of domestic programs and genres, and when this does occur the information for the story is often provided by the publicity department of the producing organisation. According to Granada, the Chinese remake of the English *Coronation Street* series *(xingfu jie)* experienced a receptive market — so much so that a panel was convened at the Edinburgh Television Festival in 2004 entitled 'Cracking China' (EITF 2004). The evidence came from Granada, not from any actual audited ratings analysis. As we discuss in Chapter 5, this program barely registered a ripple in the Chinese market.

Reliance on trade journal reporting can lead to unsubstantiated claims surfacing in academic publishing. In many reports investment and sales figures don't tell the real story — and they just don't add up. Freedman claimed with some authority that, 'The beneficiaries of British imagination now include the 400 million Chinese who watch *Joy Luck Street*, based on the UK's most successful soap opera, *Coronation Street*' (2003: 34). In fact, the only program in China likely to reach anywhere near 400 million viewers is the China Central Television (CCTV) national news broadcast at 7.00 pm nightly, and this reach is only guaranteed because it is a mandatory broadcast on all of China's channels. In the process, a myth of demand is sustained — that is, Asian audiences yearn for sophisticated Western content, or in this case, 'British imagination'. The reality is that much of what is presented as evidence for success is, in fact, promotional spin, a perceived need to talk up the market.

English-language evidence for the internationalisation of Asian television is less visible than reports of cinema export success, except for occasional academic articles. Within journals and edited collections, the focus is predominantly on cultural globalisation, political ideology, ownership, resistance and case studies of subject formation (Erni and Chua 2004; Curran and Park 2000). Invariably, such studies focus on particular countries. It is only in the past decade that we have seen a focus on regional dynamics. A few studies have looked at flows of culture within East Asia — and from Asia outwards to the West (Iwabuchi et al. 2004: Hu 2004; Yeh and Davis 2002; Cunningham and Sinclair 1999; Moran and Keane 2004; Lee 2004; Cooper-Chen 1994: Fung and Ma 2002: Lee 1998; Curtin 2003; 2005).

The third tendency in reporting in trade journals and business journalism is that stereotypical attitudes often prevail with regard to Asian culture. Failure to differentiate across Asian cultures damages credibility. As the international advertising industry has discovered, the Asian consumer market is segmented and heterogeneous (Li 1998; Wang 2005). There is a further irony in political economy's reliance on the business press. Trenchant critics of the media's distortion of reality depend on the veracity of evidence presented in 'capitalist' publications such as *Variety*, *The Hollywood Reporter*, *The Wall Street Journal*, *The New York Times*, and *The Economist* to critique the dominance of neo-liberalism and the threats to democracy and cultural diversity. While a convincing argument for the power of capitalist media can indeed be construed from the reports issued to subscribers of trade presses, a diminution of cultural context is inevitable. Decontextualisation of production from cultural specificity inevitably leads to claims that Western scholars misunderstand and misrepresent the field of Asian media production (Erni and Chua 2005). Non-English-language reports that address the consumption and stories behind popular indigenous forms and genres seldom find their way into publications such as *Variety* and *The Wall Street Journal*. In the entertainment press, stories about the successes of familiar conglomerates and Western shows in frontier markets appeal more to subscribers than facts about largely unfamiliar Asian media companies and their programs.

The Problem of Believing What You Read

The problem of information inconsistency is inevitable in English-language accounts of Asian media. There is an inherent difficulty in presenting the sheer value of figures as *prima facie* proof of trends towards greater concentration and conglomeration. The mismatch between reportage and reality might be evident in the aggregate sales value within Asian markets — if those sales figures were available and were able to be proportionally disaggregated.

Adding to an under-valuing of market activity is the practice of bartering content for advertising space or trading content at low prices among under-capitalised Asian media companies. For many international companies trying to land sales in Asian markets, indigenous bartering practices make accounting difficult, while intellectual property enforcement is complex and long-term planning is problematic.

Another variable that contributes to the slipperiness of statistics is black market activity. While cinema — particularly US big-budget productions — is saleable across cultural boundaries in Asia, this value of the market is undercut by rampant piracy. The Motion Picture Association (MPA) claimed that its members reportedly lost US$718 million in revenue due to illegal Asian video piracy in 2003 (Young 2004). Again, these figures are extremely difficult to verify. Widespread discrepancies in the amounts of piracy parallel the high incidence of program boosting that is evident in the ratings practices of Chinese media organisations. There is a palpable lack of transparent, audited media research. The result is that Western companies working in these huge markets are often as culpable as local companies of misrepresenting truth when it comes to reporting (see Gutmann 2004). In drawing attention to the issue of the black market, we should also note that piracy of DVDs and other electronic media retards domestic industry development in Asia to a greater extent than it does the Hollywood 'majors', who have the capacity to absorb the damage of illegal copying. For instance, the bootlegging of *anime* by fans within Asia is detrimental to the success of many small developers. For domestic industries, piracy is poisoning their business models and their competitiveness (Montgomery and Keane 2006).

Another Way of Looking at the Field of Asian Production

While media industries in many parts of the globe have attempted to copy US genres, formats and organisational models, there are ways of making programming, assuring finance and securing distribution that devolve from local knowledge. The focus on the global — and on the activities of international conglomerates — obscures the diversity of production activity in these 'peripheries'. The reality is that entrepreneurial activity is active at all levels of business, from the micro-level to the mega-conglomerate. With local media industries competing more vigorously and investing in content that can be traded domestically, the amount of imported content diminishes or is rescheduled to dead viewing zones (Compaine 2000). This is a productive outcome for local production and a positive externality of market forces. We note the president of Sony Pictures International lamenting that, 'Whereas American TV shows used to occupy prime-time slots, they are now more typically on cable, or airing in late-night or week-end slots' (cited in Kapner 2003: 1). The highest rating show in South Korea in September 2003, for instance, was *The Era of the Abandoned Hero*. This locally produced drama attracted 22.7 percent of viewers, while at the same time the highest ranking non-Korean show, *CSI* (CBS) managed just 2.7 percent (Kapner 2003, 2). As we saw in the previous chapter, local production in Japan registers an average of 95 percent of broadcast time. While American dramas — such as *Beverly Hills, 90210, ER,* and *Ally McBeal* — have attracted young female viewers, their popularity is minimal compared with Japanese television dramas (Iwabuchi 2004).

While arguments about Hollywood's influence are persuasive, there are strong counter-arguments to suggest that local culture is reaching out to wider publics. The rise in cultural consumption in East Asia is reflected in the film industries of Hong Kong and South Korea. In music, Canto-pop and Mando-pop — and more recently J-pop and K-pop — are generating massive sales, while Japanese *manga* and *anime* have influenced local production fashions and styles. Asian cinema has also achieved positive gains in world markets during the past few years. Movies such as China's *Hero* and *The House of Flying Daggers,* South Korea's *My Wife is a Gangster, Shiri,* and *Musa,* and Taiwan's *Eat, Man, Drink, Woman* and *Crouching Tiger Hidden Dragon* testify to the confidence of local production outside the established Hong Kong movie and television industry (Berry and Farquhar 2006; Curtin 2007). The East Asian influence in Hollywood has also grown, with directorial debuts by Ang Lee (Taiwan), Chen Kaige (China), and John Woo (Hong Kong). Also, Hollywood films are being shot in East Asia, increasingly incorporating local culture and using high profile actors.

Ethos, Flows, and Translations

The need to 'catch up' (and compete) with the developed West has been a concern for East Asian governments since the 1970s. Hitherto culturally conservative governments now embrace foreign investment while supporting businesses that offer a future beyond manufacturing. But economic liberalisation brings new challenges to old cultural traditions. King and Craig note:

> The problem for authoritarian governments is that modernization is a
> package deal: cultural values sneak in on the coat tails of industrial and

technical marvels; wealth creation is accompanied by alluring products to spend it on; television screens sought for their educational value are also illuminated by fantasies of greed and its gratification; hardware comes fully loaded with software. (2001: 5)

National governments in Asia face difficult decisions about balancing preservation of traditional values with selective importation of cosmopolitan consumer society. In evaluating East Asia's accelerated integration into global culture and its strategies to engage through exporting its own culture, it is necessary to reconsider how cultural exchange occurs. Along with global trade and more rapid flows of information, ideas, technologies, people, and media during the past decade — to use Appadurai's well-known description of 'disjuncture' in the global economy (Appadurai 1990) — formerly regulated cultural spheres in Taiwan, South Korea, and China have opened up. With the shift from restricted archives of officially sanctioned content towards a marketplace in which content flows within and along new audio–visual trade routes, we propose a flexible model of cultural exchange. This model contrasts with the oft-cited post-colonial motif of cultural hybridity. In particular, accounts of resistance have tended towards a sometimes uncritical celebration of hybridity, echoing Hall's notion of 'the aesthetics of the hybrid, the aesthetics of the cross over, the aesthetics of the diaspora, the aesthetics of creolization' (1997: 38–39) As applied within post-colonial theory, hybridity is an effect of colonial power, 'a strategic reversal of the process of domination' (Bhaba 1985: 154). While hybridity catches the spirit of appropriation, bricolage, syncretism, creolisation, and even user-led consumption — and is helpful to describe the music industry — it is less useful in showing how ideas are transferred in television industries, particularly through processes of adaptation and formatting.

That is not to deny that television formats are indeed hybrids. They incorporate other formats and genres in an evolutionary cycle. But, at the level of the televisual text, the trope of resistance is diffuse. Of course, resistance is calculated in another form when the economic power of the imported program is reduced through appropriation and translation into local versions. In framing cultural exchange, moreover, we need to bear in mind that television program formats are both textual commodities and material artefacts of trade. The process of cultural translation that occurs when formats are introduced into new locations alerts us to the importance of origins, and the tensions between transfer and uptake.

The Russian semiologist Yuri Lotman (1990) has introduced the concept of *sending* and *receiving* cultures. Lotman wrote that all cultures proceed through stages of absorbing and sending ideas. He nominates the Renaissance in Italy and the Enlightenment in France as periods where ideas were absorbed from the whole of Europe: 'the ideas of the Reformation from Holland, Germany and Switzerland, the empiricism of Bacon and Locke and Newtonian mechanics, the Latinism of the Italian Humanists, and the Mannerism of the Spanish and Italian Baroque … ' (Lotman 1990: 146). Obviously, periods existed throughout history when nations exported their ideas through trade routes. Spice, opium, and cotton were the valued commodities during the eighteenth and nineteenth centuries. The period of 'pax Britannia' saw British culture, values, ideas, and capital circulating through colonial expansion, extending into India and South-east Asia and finally taking root in Hong Kong. The decline of the British Empire and the ensuing 'pax Americana' coincided with the twentieth century technologies of information dissemination — the motion picture, television, video technologies and, in the last decade of the century, the internet.

In contrast to these modern periods of information and cultural globalisation, there have been many great periods of creativity in antiquity in which countries and regions assumed pre-eminence as senders of ideas. Cowan writes about the concept of 'ethos', an unpriced, untraded input into production that is collectively produced by the actions and attitudes of people in periods of great social interaction (2002: 49). The Tang dynasty in China (618–907 AD) is considered to be one of the great periods of invention and the arts. It saw an unprecedented *ethos*, a flow of ideas into Chinese cities and a flowering of creativity in many fields, stimulated by contact with India and the Middle East. Buddhism, which was introduced from India, became thoroughly sinicised. Block printing was invented, and this made the written word available to wider audiences. The period was indeed the golden age of literature and art.

In other parts of Asia, the Chinese influence extended outwards. Both Korea and Vietnam imported and indigenised Taoism and Chinese forms of Mahayana Buddhism. Eventual decline and the collapse of the Chinese dynastical system in 1911 led to a long period in which China closed down to international ideas, except for a relatively brief period of cosmopolitanism in China's treaty ports (Peking, Tianjin, Shanghai and Canton) during the first four decades of the twentieth century. By the mid-twentieth century, threats posed by Western capitalism eventually led to complete isolationism under the Communist regime, apart from trade in culture and ideology between China and Russia. China was officially closed off to most outside influence between 1949 and 1978. When the Open Door Policy was announced after decades of isolation, the nation became a receiving culture as people consumed new ideas and sought to make up for enforced cultural deprivation.

In the period in which China declined as a receiver of foreign cultures, Hong Kong rose to prominence. Hong Kong was a British colony from 1842 until 1997. During that time, the locale absorbed cultural influences from abroad, particularly from the United Kingdom and mainland China, but also from international business and expatriate culture. From the 1950s, Hong Kong rapidly became an international finance centre (Ma 1999: 23). Popular media displaced political culture, and Hong Kong began to produce its own unique film, TV, and music, and export these — first to South-east and East Asia, and then to international markets (Curtin 2007).

Translation and Adaptation of Popular Culture

In these periods of suddenly accelerated idea transfer — including ideas about business, lifestyle, morality, and success — the appropriation and translation of foreign concepts often became a form of cargo cult. In China, an ongoing love-hate relationship with America fed critical denunciations of its military aggression along with sometimes uncritical acceptance of *laissez faire* markets. A recent story illustrates the desire to think American. The *New York Times* records how a visit by the relatively unknown author, Chester Elton, to Harbin in north China verged on hysteria. Elton, the author of the management handbook called *The 24-Carrot Manager*, dispensed real carrots to the audience while popular music played in the background. Echoing the same fervour, a lecture tour by Jack Welch, former chairman of General Electric, to China in 2004 produced mild pandemonium as cameramen jostled with audience members who had paid huge sums of money to get close to him (Barboza 2005).

Such stories, while stereotyping Chinese as reaching out and grasping towards the 'pax Americana' ethos of success and prosperity, reflect a widespread tendency to appropriate anything that has the aura of 'the new'. In other words, foreign forms, ideas, and styles are not so much absorbed as window-shopped like new commodities. In times of unprecedented change, processes of translation are applied to commercial culture with sometimes unusual results. For instance, the gay disco anthem *YMCA* by the San Francisco group *Village People* appeared in a 1990s Chinese TV drama, completely stripped of its association with sexual politics (Keane 1998). Where cultural markets have been exposed to a variety of commercial culture — for instance, in Japan, Hong Kong, and Taiwan — the translation is less problematic and transparent. In particular, the reception of Japanese culture in Hong Kong and Taiwan is mediated by proximity and a sense of shared modernity.

In re-theorising the adaptation practices of East Asian television production, we can draw on Lotman's characterisation of how foreign texts are received and host cultures subsequently restructured (Lotman 1990; see O'Regan 1999 for a discussion of this in relation to film). Lotman's first stage of exchange is where the foreign text holds an aura and is valued as somehow true and beautiful (1990: 146). In contrast, the texts (or programs) of the host culture are devalued; they are considered inferior or coarse. The local fades in comparison with the brilliance of the highly valued and authentic foreign product. In many cases, the foreign product remains in its original form. In print culture, the possession of original foreign books bestowed prestige and status. Such a story is recalled in the Chinese film *Balzac and the Little Chinese Seamstress* (2003), a tale of youth sent down to the countryside during the Cultural Revolution (1966–1976). The possession of a work by Balzac endows two youths with a certain reflected aura, at least in the eyes of a young girl. In the electronic media, early US programs were the models that shone brightly. When television began in Japan in the 1950s, American programs such as *I Love Lucy* and *Superman* were attractive because the production techniques were superior (Kato 1998). The 'foreign' television program, with its superior production aesthetics, was regarded as superior and 'beautiful'.

The second stage, according to Lotman, is where the 'imported' texts and the 'home' culture restructure each other. In this stage, 'translations, imitations and adaptations multiply' (Lotman 1990: 146). It wasn't long before the American mode of production was incorporated into Japanese television. Watching American programs allowed Japanese producers insights into how to make more sophisticated television. The dominant impulse at this stage 'is to break with the past' — to idolise the imported worldview. In Taiwan, a similar process occurred with news programs heavily dependent on US formats (Liu and Chen 2004). Hong Kong also began importing Japanese language cartoons from the 1970s with little modification in content. In comparison, when the popular *Pokemon* cartoons were sold into the US market, content was heavily modified to neutralise elements of cultural incompatibility (Fung 2005).

The third stage is where the higher content of the imported text is reinscribed in the local, reinvigorating the meaning of the imported texts by its association with the purer local version. For instance, when a foreign text, philosophy, or policy is adopted by China, a standard phrase is 'the imported idea' with 'Chinese characteristics', the implication usually being that the idea has been improved in the process of adaptation. As the producer of the Chinese copy of *Who Wants to Be a Millionaire? (kaixin cidian)* confidently asserted, the local pure version represented a big improvement over the expensive foreign product (interview by Keane, 2002). 'Chinese characteristics' are portrayed — particularly by Chinese commentators — as dominant genes. In the Chinese *Millionaire*, such characteristics reflect traditional family sensibilities, such as allowing family members to be incorporated into the game, in contrast to the UK original which only allows the 'significant other' or partner to speak (producer, interview by Fung 2003). The phrase 'with Chinese characteristics' has become a way of asserting sovereignty in an era that has seen an unprecedented influx of global products, theories and ideologies. Hence 'Chinese characteristics' not only celebrates adaptation, but more importantly, its application becomes a normative strategy to ensure economic reforms do not become automatically associated with an ideological drift towards liberal governance and celebrations of a consumer society.

The fourth stage is where the imported texts are entirely dissolved in the receiving culture. Lotman notes that, 'the culture itself changes to a state of activity and begins rapidly to produce new texts; these texts are based on cultural codes which in the distant past were stimulated by invasions from outside, but which now have been wholly transformed through the many asymmetrical transformations into a new and original structural model' (1990: 147). For instance, the Korean video game *The Legend of Mir* had become a huge success in China by 2002. The licence fees paid to the Korean company forced Shanda, the leading Chinese game developer, to commission local games that drew on the myths and legends of China. Likewise, in the television industry, a period of time elapses and programs or formats are recognised as pure — as was the case with the quiz variety show, *Zhengda zongyi* (see Chapter 11). The longevity of this popular show ensured that it was recognised as 'local'.

The fifth stage is where the receiving culture becomes a sending culture. The foreign text is absorbed, cleansed and localised. The host culture then becomes an originator. It can now export the renovated product.

Export Growth and Strategies for Mid-size Markets

How, then, might new models of production and distribution, typified by formatted or franchised culture, impact upon global media trade? In the first decade of the twenty-first century, a new global model of integration has emerged. While fewer companies control ownership of culture, digital technologies have reduced production costs. This reduced cost, combined with advantages offered by the rapid transfer of information, allows accelerated catch-up. According to Ozawa et al., 'any successful developing economy climbs a ladder of growth' (2001: 290). The catch-up is facilitated by a proliferation of global and regional production networks, which have, in turn, acted as conduits for knowledge diffusion outside the developed economies. Television industries in middle-sized markets such as South Korea, Taiwan and Hong Kong have been affected by changes in the world economy. The increase in flows of global ideas — and the growth of inter-regional trade due to falling protection barriers — provide greater opportunities for cultural exchange and local networks of cooperation. This environment of culturally assisted global integration destabilises media imperialism models. It also sets up opportunities for new players, such as China and Korea, to work their way up the ladder of growth, offsetting the competitive advantages of incumbent media centres such as Hong Kong and Hollywood.

The optimum model for creating high-value cultural exports is the transnational media corporation. This organisational form allows content producers to exploit cross-promotion and vertical integration strategies (Scott 2004). As Schiller has pointed out, mergers and acquisitions deliver further competitive advantages — and, in some cases, deliver monopolies (D. Schiller 1999). The metaphor of mother ship and flotilla captures what is at stake here. Large mother ship oligopolies include CBS/Viacom and Vivendi/Universal, Disney, Sony, Viacom, and News Corporation with smaller studios and companies such as Dreamworks, HBO, and MTV forming an affiliated flotilla.

The clustering of media companies in geographical locations adds to network advantages, even taking into account the tendency to outsource to global locations. Fishing from a clustered pond of talent allows majors to make more informed decisions based on superior project development (Cowan 2002: 88). Distribution agreements, along with economies of scale and scope, further compound the difficulty faced by small media organisations competing in the same language pond. In other words, large companies can control both content production and content distribution. Being a mega platform owner with global brand awareness or a critical mass of subscribers (for instance, pay TV) also brings 'capital complementarities' — in other words, the ownership of technologies and content, combined with global status, produces cumulative effects. Producers want to get their content on to successful channels. In China, CCTV is the national broadcaster and commands the greatest advertising rates. In Brazil, Globo has assumed a dominant position in the market because of its economies of scale. This advantage has also allowed it to develop an export industry based on its strengths in fictional television — namely, telenovelas (La Pastina et al. 2004; Sinclair 1999, 2004).

Elsewhere, many media organisations are forced into different production models and into different ponds in order to achieve export success. Freedman talks about problems that confronted British television exports during the 1990s. Faced with increasing difficulty matching competitively priced US content in overseas markets, many British companies opted to pursue success in television formats and to target satellite and cable sales (Freedman 2003: 33). This example illustrates the relationship between competitive advantage and comparative advantage. The *competitive advantage* of Hollywood's position as a creative cluster and a world centre for film and television means increasing returns to specialisation. Such specialisations, and the branding and distribution network synergies that accompany clustering, assure a dominant presence in global markets. These large clusters produce a great deal of specialised product (cinema, television, and ancillary merchandising) that is sold into multiple markets. On the other hand, *comparative advantage*, a principle of neo-classical economics, would appear to dictate that other countries look for success in areas where they have expertise and trade in these commodities. In many cases, these are lower-value markets. For British companies such as BBC and ECM, the format business model opened up such a market; it not only rescued the local industry, but created interest in English production within the competitive Los Angeles cluster (Freedman 2003: 33).

Hollywood's dominance in the English-language markets, and Mexico's Televisa and Brazil's Globo in the Latin American markets, would seem to diminish the chances for newcomers, except as providers for these large companies. Likewise, Hong Kong's success as a television centre and exporter of martial arts films during the 1980s and 1990s has been well documented (Curtin 2003, 2005; Yeh and Davis 2002). Tokyo has established a reputation as a centre for new media, *manga*, animation, and electronic entertainment industries, while Seoul has become a production centre for video games and film. One of the positive benefits of globalisation, however, is increasing trade between regions and the 'discovery' of traditional cultures. The globalisation of film and television, and the search for the next breakthrough, provide some optimism for East Asian cultures. Breakthrough hits occur from time to time, although East Asian cinema hits are usually a combination of timing, marketing, and financial support from major media investors and studios. In the previous chapter we discussed the surge in original content within East Asia. Movies such as *Crouching Tiger Hidden Dragon* are essentially new versions of old stories, tapping into traditions and folklore. The international development of these 'kung-fu' stories, already well established in East Asian media markets, has been built on the reputation of directors who have already experienced initial 'breakthroughs'. In the case of Ang Lee, the crossover breakthrough was achieved in the film *Wedding Banquet* (1993).

Greater availability of information due to the internet means that consumers of cultural products and services are increasingly knowledgeable and demanding (Cowan 2002: 103). Niche markets, fans, and the constant search for the 'next big thing' in the global marketplace puts a premium on innovation. For industries moving up the value chain, niche markets — both global and local — provide alternatives to the kind of parasitic imitation of global products that often leads to charges of cultural homogenisation. New niches have appeared as a result of the globalisation of media channels — for instance, the surge of Bollywood and Chinese-language content has allowed international satellite and cable providers to acquire inexpensive programming for broadcast (Griffith 2003: 143). In other words, these programs are relatively cheap in their local markets. Many of these programs are subsequently presented as premium subscription content within the international television landscape.

The important point about breakthroughs like this is that they undermine the conventional media industry logic of promotion. The success of hit shows creates its own momentum. Much niche content is also appearing on subscription digital channels, where ratings are less important. For broadcasters in East Asia, international channels and distribution through video outlets provide sales income. If these sales are secured in US markets, the returns are significant for the seller; on the other hand returns from Asian Diaspora video markets are often incremental and subject to copyright infringement (Cunningham and Sinclair 1999). In some cases, access to lucrative international channels is conditional on allowing international broadcasters into the local market. This has been the case in China. Landing rights (that is, permission to broadcast in certain areas) for News Corporation's Star TV platform and its Mandarin language channel *(xingkong weishi)* have led to China Central Television's international channels, CCTV-4 and CCTV-9, being carried on some US cable networks.

Culture provides employment and attracts international investors. In the mid-range growth segment we call formatting, industries can also move up the value chain by various forms of 'learning by doing'. In other words, intangible notions about value creation, branding and marketing are brokered through partnerships. The international co-production constitutes a strategy to build value while promoting local industry development. The anticipated pay off from joint ventures with international production companies is stimulation of local industries through training, employment, expertise and infrastructure. Pooling of resources, as well as access to foreign government's incentives and subsidies, and to desired locations, are all advantages associated with co-productions and formats (Hoskins, McFadyen and Finn 1999; Goldsmith and O'Regan 2005; Elmer and Gasher 2005; Miller et al. 2001). World cinema is where we mostly celebrate successful co-productions. Markets without the financial muscle of Hollywood fall back on co-production activity as a means of pooling resources. In television, however, the franchise model is increasingly evident. The practice of licensing or franchising television formats shows how technologies and ideas can be transferred (see Chapter 5). In such cases, consultancy and expertise is the valued commodity. The production of the television game show *The Weakest Link* in Hong Kong, for instance, involved a complicated process of training and supervision by the BBC format owners prior to being broadcast locally as *Yibi OUT xiao* (Fung 2004).

Japan has been a leader within Asia in reversing the flow of television programming, most notably through international formats *Happy Family Plan*, *Iron Chef*, and *Future Diary*. TBS, the leading exporter of TV programs and format in Japan, has sold more than a hundred program formats to more than forty countries. TBS started in the format business with its sale of the format *Wakuwaku Animal Land* to the Netherlands in 1987 (Iwabuchi 2004). In turning the tables on the Americanisation of culture thesis, Japan has successfully achieved international distribution through the franchising of its formats — a business model that allows Japanese creativity to circulate without visible traits of Japaneseness that might undermine reception in many parts of East Asia, where the memory of Japanese imperialism remains strong.

A further rung down the value ladder is imitation. Cloning someone else's success is a business model that provides short-term rewards, but brings with it the associated problems of intellectual property infringement. Imitation is also an effect of globalisation, which simultaneously promotes flows of products and knowledge of how to copy products in different continents. As Bonabeau writes, 'This greater knowledge is a result of a proliferation of feedback loops, mechanisms for collecting, sometimes aggregating other's thoughts, opinions, or preferences and then communicating them back to the public' (2004: 44). Imitation has obvious benefits. It is 'the natural mechanism for both inspiration and aspiration' (2004: 46). Where intellectual property control is loosely administered — for instance, in countries such as China, India, Malaysia, and Indonesia — it is a relatively simple matter to make identical or similar products and services, usually at lower cost. This applies to software (content) as much as hardware (applications). Television formats have become templates for low-cost replication across countries and within domestic markets. Where this activity is unlicensed and opportunistic it exacerbates a cloning culture. And, while such follow-the-leader activity provides economic benefits for under-capitalised producers, it produces diminishing returns as more and more take the same route. This applies at the level of the firm as well as that of the national industry. As we argue later, the cloning of television programs has negative effects on the development of export content.

At the base of the export development model is low-cost production. While there are parallels between low-cost fabrication and co-production, the former applies particularly to cases where cost saving is the bottom line and there is little or no sharing of intellectual property (Keane 2006). Outsourcing in cinema is perhaps the most celebrated example of (cultural) de-territorialisation, drawing upon more advanced skill-sets than routine manufacture of artefacts. Most productions are lower end (smaller budget, made-for-TV movies and TV drama), although there are some notable examples of blockbusters produced offshore. For developed economies like Australia, New Zealand, Canada, South Africa, and, more recently, Romania; for the newly industrialised nations of Malaysia and Thailand; and even developing countries, such as China and Mexico outsourcing combines with the aspiration to grow media production centres or locales — to emulate the success of global production districts. In the short term, this form of production results in competition to attract international players. In order to attract these high-value creative industries, governments — both national and local — provide incentives such as tax relief, waivers of location fees, equity investment, and a range of subsidies (Goldsmith and O'Regan 2005; Elmer and Gasher 2005; Miller et al. 2001). For countries and localities that rely on the outsourcing of cultural production, their chief asset is reserves of surplus low-paid labour. For countries that outsource their production, and in Miller et al.'s New International Division of Cultural Labour (NICL) thesis, this is primarily the United States — the loss of local jobs to foreigners is a significant issue. Miller et al. claim that by the end of the 1990s, Los Angeles was losing US$7.5 billion in multiplier effects, plus 20,000 jobs (2001: 58).

For the offshore location, this race to the bottom can retard the development of local design and talent. The ubiquitous 'made in China' label reveals a deep-seated problem — and not just for home industries undercut by cheap labour. Offshoring is most evident in electrical component manufacturing. Standardised components for electronic devices (mobile phone handsets and computers) and entertainment software are produced at race-to-the-bottom process in India and China; call centres remain a growth industry in India with its competitive advantage of English-language fluency.

As Taiwan, Singapore, and Hong Kong refocus on becoming information 'hubs', more standardised production is outsourced as wages increase due to the absorption of excess labour.

Concluding Remarks: Creativity, Networks and Export Growth

In this chapter we have looked at strategies for export growth that counter the commonly perceived idea that globalisation is a one-way street. While 'foreign' programming is an obstacle to local industry development and a source of nationalist discomfort, a resurgence of local content in East Asia during the past few years provides a renewed sense of optimism. This local content has absorbed and *translated* international flavours, styles and influences. Within this environment, formatting has played — and continues to play — a key role in assisting less-developed industries to achieve sales of programs in international markets.

As well as the de-territorialisation of production and capital, the export growth model provides evidence of a 're-territorialisation of creativity'. In media industries talent migrates towards capital. This migration takes a couple of forms. First, talented individuals (producers, scriptwriters, designers) move to locations where they have better chances of employment. In Asia, this may be Hong Kong or Tokyo, or more globally, Hollywood and Silicon Valley (Florida 2005). From a national perspective, such leakage of talent is detrimental. However, this movement of talent is increasingly flexible and short term. Hollywood is no longer the only centre of production. While it serves the English-language world and extends its influence globally, there are now many competing media capitals whose viability is enhanced by global integration and network capitalism (Curtin 2003, 2007; Keane 2006).

The export growth model also alerts us to the fact that transnational media corporations are not the only lens through which to view media globalisation. The bottom-up approach achieves traction through formatting (including copying and franchising) and through exploiting the networks of exchange and skills transfer that are available. This five-stage model of export growth (clusters, niche, franchising, cloning and de-territorialisation) destabilises the dominant paradigm in which structures of dominance erode cultural uniqueness. To draw an analogy from Sun Zi's *Art of War*, 'there are no fixed forms or inflexible rules in military tactics. Only those who are able to vary their tactics according to the changing manoeuvre of the enemy and win victories have miraculous skill' (Sun Wu 1996: 61). In other words, while outflanked by the capital and distribution networks of the majors, East Asia is building on comparative advantage in cultural and linguistic products.

Formats allow ideas to move more rapidly than in the past. Does this mean, therefore, that formats reconstitute cultural imperialism in a more benign way? Freedman argues that the so-called distinctive local identities expressed in formatted programs are 'less about the articulation of cultures than the re-presentation of dominant voices in new market disguises' (2003: 36). Of course, the rise of formatting within television systems requires consideration within a wider socio-political context. The television format allows ideas to migrate across national boundaries and within television trading networks. With its capacity to circumvent domestic content quota standards and censorship regimes, it might well be a 'Trojan Horse' — a means by which foreign values and ideas are repackaged in local environments. To understand these questions, we now turn to look more closely at the formats in question.

4

Formats, Genres, and Engines

Formats are the cost effective key. It is the format that will even increasingly offer a reliable map to the highways and byways of the new production landscape.
– Michel Rodrigue, CEO of Distraction Formats (2000)

There are a whole bunch of key engines in *Who Wants to Be a Millionaire?* that made it unique. Most other formats have two or three. *Millionaire* has six or seven, which made it a huge hit, and it spawned all those copycats.
– Mark Overett, producer, cited in Adair and Moran (2004: 24)

Adaptation is a critical component of global television production, but it is conspicuously under-represented within media studies critique. Television formats are templates for adaptation. They move fast, mutate, and replace previous versions. While the expanding scale of television adaptation is a global phenomenon, there is an important local dynamic. To use a common phrase in media studies, it is 'where the global meets the local'. However, more than just 'glocalisation' — a term coined to explain the mutually constitutive elements of the global and the local (Robertson 1994; Kraidy 2005) — the TV format adaptation process is a mechanism of flexible, leaner production and a response to evolving industry practices. In addition, the format generates greater traction for television producers. By this statement, we mean that formats can provide new ways of connecting with audiences. We call these 'engines'; they include million dollar prizes, the prisoner's dilemma, lifelines and immunity, built-in potential conflict, voting-off, exotic or familiar locations, gladiatorial elements, renovation and care of the self, and authenticity testing.

The chapter begins with a definition of the format. We differentiate format from genre in order to show how the television format business has generated innovations that extend the product life-cycle of concepts. In this sense, the flexibility of the format is tailored to the rapidly shortened shelf-life of television programming — a consequence of evolving audience demand for new services. By brokering closer awareness of viewer tastes, new television formats anticipate industry evolution. Using strategic adaptation to spin out the currency of ideas implies incremental innovation. Attracting and maintaining audiences is about exploiting familiar concepts expressed in different forms (or formats).

Defining the Format

In a forum on television formats published in February 2000, the IDtv International producer Harry de Winter commented that it was time to redefine the meaning of the format, in order to avoid Jerry Springer claiming ownership of what might be called the 'wild talk show'. This tongue-in-cheek comment illustrates the need to clarify what has become a rapidly evolving segment of the media industry. What constitutes a format, and why has this mode of production become so important in the past decade?

Observers of developments in the history of film and television might argue with some degree of conviction that 'genre' and 'format' are interchangeable. Certainly, there is category confusion evident in much contemporary critique. We are more particular in identifying the differences. For instance, a show in which people are introduced from behind a curtain to renew acquaintances with a guest is a format if the show is replicated by other television stations with obvious sequential similarities. This forms our operative definition of a format: it is industrial first and foremost, and influential as a mechanism of cultural exchange.

In considering the comment attributed to Harry de Winter above, a show that copies the *Jerry Springer Show* concept of confessional sex and confrontational relationships is more appropriately located within the genre of 'talk shows dealing with sexuality'. A talk show that features celebrities happily reminiscing about old times is an example of the more universal 'celebrity talk show' genre (*The Wit* 2003). Neither the 'talk show dealing with sexuality' nor the 'celebrity talk show' becomes a true industrial format until it is licensed, sold, or copied by another production company or network.

Definitional confusion resides in a relative abundance of similar television programs. It is also possible to use the term 'format' as loosely as 'genre'.

Indeed, the practice of formatting has existed since television industries began looking for creative ideas — and even longer if we include other media and cultural forms. So asking the question 'What is a format?' may indeed be the wrong direction to take. The term 'format' has meaning not so much because of what it is, but because of what it permits or facilitates. From our examinations of the motivations for producing formats, hybrid versions, clones and generic imitations of international successes in East Asian media industries, we can endorse the view that the format is indeed functional and generative.

A clear analytical foundation for our study is necessary, however, particularly in regard to cataloguing the reasons for widespread mimicry of programs in East Asia. Aside from genre there is no single agreed-upon critical term that describes the ever-expanding phenomenon of adaptation of narrative and other content across different media. Within the international television industry, broadcasters and producers have been quick to embrace both the term and the practice of adaptation, although critical researchers have been slow to acknowledge such developments. Until 1998, the only book on the subject of the television format was a legal handbook published in Dutch (van Manen 1994). There is no entry concerning the television format in the *New York Times Encyclopaedia of Television* (Brown 1977), while only a short note appears in the *Museum of Broadcasting Communication Encyclopaedia of Television* (Fiddy 1997). A more recent addition to the literature is an entry of 'Format sales, International' in the *Encyclopaedia of Television,* second edition (Newcomb 2004). At the same time, however, there have been several discussions of specific program recycling — even if the researchers involved have not paid any conceptual attention to the general phenomenon of format adaptation (Heinderyckx 1993; Cooper-Chen 1994; Gillespie 1995; Pearson and Uricchio 1999).

The TV format is now a crucial mechanism in regulating the recycling of program content across different television systems in the world (cf. Heller 2003; Moran and Keane 2004). In contradistinction to the general use of the term, and even its specific application in radio (cf. Johnson and Jones 1978), a TV format is understood as that set of invariable elements in a program out of which the variable elements of an individual episode are produced. Or, as a more homely recent explanation for would-be format devisors would have it:

> A format sale is a product sale. The product is a recipe for re-producing a successful television program, in another territory, as a local program. The recipe comes with all the necessary ingredients and is offered as a product along with a consultant who can be thought of as an expert chef. (Bodycombe 2002)

Although international television industries talk confidently of the format as a single object, it is in fact a complex abstract and multiple entity that is typically manifest in a series of overlapping but separate forms. At the point of programming and distribution, a format takes the cultural form of different episodes of the same program. Meanwhile, at the *production* end, these different industrial manifestations include the paper format, the program Bible, a dossier of demographic and ratings information, program scripts, off-air videotapes of broadcast programs, insertable film or video footage, computer software and graphics, and production consultancy services. These various illustrations underline the point that a format is not a single or a simple entity. The TV format has become one of the most important means of functioning industrially in the era of multi-channelling.

Formatting, Historically Speaking

Bill Ryan (1992) argues that the origin of formatting can be traced to the nineteenth century and the emergence of the craft workshop system that saw creative entrepreneurs establishing partnerships with independent artists. The role of the designate artist-manager was to preside over the division of labour. Ryan says that with the advent of the film and television industries, the managerial aspect of production became a means of mediating the irrationality of creativity (Ryan 1992: 151–153). As creative personnel were often considered to be less prone to the logic of the marketplace and inclined to indulge in 'free flights of imagination', it was important to administer the logic of repetition and standardisation around both work practices and creative output to ensure that commercial goals were realised.

In the contemporary media environment, the functional aspect of commercial success remains much the same, despite the obvious standardising economies that flow from the efficiencies of mechanical reproduction. Moreover, it is customary to assert that the commercial mass media live or die on audience satisfaction. A causal link thus exists between techniques of presentation and strategies designed to capture sufficient audience numbers to generate advertising revenue or subscriptions. The early broadcasting industry illustrates the relationship between formats, technology and audiences. In the formative years days of radio in the United States, the technology of sound recording did not allow the broadcasting of music. Radio stations would often have their own orchestra standing by to render musical broadcasts. Technological limitations of the medium at the time determined the kind of content that could be broadcast. With the advent of the forty-five-single technology in the 1950s radio became the popular music medium with disc jockeys 'spinning' vinyl discs. Radio, in turn, became more industrialised as music became a mass medium for youth expression. Eventually radio stations diversified into niche formats — classical, easy-listening, golden oldies, sports and talk formats.

In film industries, formatting began as early as the arrival of talking pictures. Bill Grantham reminds us of the utility of the silent picture form by which a Chaplin movie could be shown in many countries. Likewise, 'a German picture could be shown in Japan or a French picture in America' (Grantham 2003: 42). When the technology of sound recording became available, the problem of adapting film for multiple markets became more complex. One solution was to simultaneously shoot films in different languages. For instance, there were two versions of the Josef von Sternberg film *The Blue Angel* made in 1930, one in English and one in German.

In journalism, production has long been organised around a specialised division of labour. Aside from the relations between sub-editors and specialist and general reporters, journalism made use of production formats such as the 'nut graf', the 'soft lede', and the narrow column — stylised conventions that were adopted as standards (Kleiner 2001). Magazine production is also format driven. It draws upon technologies of representation that have accumulated success and recognition in the marketplace. When a magazine's editors consciously adopt a new presentation style or modify an existing format, they risk alienating their readership. Likewise, sticking with a convention can lead to creative rigor mortis and eventual desertion by readerships. All kinds of media need to balance the payoffs between establishing successful formulas (including content and design) and ensuring that this doesn't become too predictable. This is increasingly the case in the emerging multi-channel, multi-platform broadcasting environment. Content might be king, but content is extremely disposable — and, as we maintain in this study, adaptable.

Formats and Genres

Despite the very clear understandings of formats within the television industry itself, there are different understandings of the term within television critique. The question that needs to be raised at this juncture is: why are formats so misunderstood within cultural and media studies? Indeed, media academics all too often conflate formats with genre. This was the case in a special issue of the journal *Media International Australia* entitled 'New Television Formats' (Hawkins and Roscoe 2001). Formats in this instance were construed primarily as hybrid genres, which included docu–soaps and reality TV.

The distinction between format and genre is an important one for the purposes of our study. In the pure or true sense of a format, we are referring to the television format business — although as we shall see — many of the examples in this study are indeed clones or generic variations on successful programs. Whereas the format is a local adaptation of a program produced under licence, a genre is a representational convention. As mentioned earlier, a television format embodies the formalisation of elements that make up a television program. These elements can be codified in more or less detail: the concept, the order of events, the mechanics, the scene, the presentation, the music, the type of presenter, and the duration.

The term 'genre' is directly associated with narrative structure and types of programming. O'Sullivan et al. described genres as 'recognized paradigmatic sets' that allow the viewer/reader/ critic to orient their reactions — in other words, to make sense of the text or to 'limit the meaning potential of a given text' (1983: 99). The genre represents a process of categorisation marked by conventions, features, and norms. Within film and literary theory, genre usually applies to narrative forms. The problem with genre, however, is that it deals with enclosure of forms within standardised conventions. In television today, there is an unprecedented degree of change in the mode of production, the planning of product lifecycles, and the predilections of consumers, who are increasingly migrating to interactive and themed choices.

The generic framework of understanding cultural forms as conventions — or paradigmatic sets — ultimately depends on reception over time and critical evaluation. Genres are essentially understandings shared by theorists, readers and viewers. The idea of genre, as understood by theorists, is arguably under threat as lower-cost programming disrupts established conventions. First-order generic conventions apply to drama or tragedy, while second–order conventions devolve to the teleplay, the telenovela, the soap opera, the western, the police series, the teen series, or the hospital drama. Limits on generic categorisation are, however, constrained by the nature of television in a multi–channel environment. While genres are expanding, they are also converging. As Hawkins and Roscoe (2001) point out, multi–platform 'event television', such as *Big Brother* and *Idol*, is bringing about a convergence of genre and technologies.

Where does the mutability of genres leave the television producer? It is evident that creative teams consider generic conventions in their appraisal of what will work commercially. With the migration to multi–channel digital platforms, it is increasingly problematic to reduce programming to a limited stable of genres. The diversification of second-order categories illustrates the profusion of categories — the docu-soap, the fly-on-the-wall documentary and the 'mock documentary'. For instance, do the producers of *Survivor* construe their production as a reality game show with certain generic conventions? We contend that the conceptualisation of reality game show television as a genre in its own right, while accommodating schools of textual critique, misses a salient point about production. Formula production has become more transparent as models for adaptation within the multi-channel environment. As viewers, we identify the formula at work. This brings us back to the image of televisual *déjà vu* when we encounter variations in different countries. Adaptations are produced across different cultural locations with minimal adjustments to local tastes and values. More often, the television format does fall within an existing genre, be it first-, second-, or third-order convention.

The recent history of television formats is evidence of the fragmentation. For instance, within the genre of factual television there has been an never-ending supply of formats (*Who Wants to Be a Millionaire?*, *The Weakest Link*, *The Fear Factor*, *The Bachelor*, and so on). The short history of docu-soap has resulted in programs such as *Popstars* and *Airport*; and, within the genre of reality television, *Survivor*, *Big Brother*, and *Temptation Island*. Indeed, the concept of genre is less useful than the format in talking about processes of cultural exchange in television industries. Furthermore, while genre implies imitation, it doesn't make sense to talk of a television genre business. A genre is not produced under licence in the same manner as a television format, which in the terms of our discussion is created in order to re-create value in different incarnations. A genre is thus a more qualitative, descriptive concept. Formalisation and formulaic attributes are linked to genres, but this is a result of producers pre-empting the reading strategy of the audience based upon existing conventions. Where a genre is copied or even localised, there remains a sense of obeying grammars of film and television that have been developed and ordained by critics. The grammar is a loose one, and not as structured as most elements of formatted productions.

We can therefore distinguish between genre imitation and adaptation of a successful format. The late-night variety show, made famous by Johnny Carson during the 1950s and 1960s, spawned any number of imitators. It had a standardised order of events, but its content was constantly changing. Imitators added to a genre — rather than simply re-versioning a format. Despite having many common elements such as funny-man host, interviews with celebrities, and so on, the imitation of the late-night variety genre does not constitute format appropriation in the purest sense. The original format has been in existence for some time and its formulaic attributes have become generic (see *The Wit* 2003).

Categorisation according to genre is a way of explaining how programming is produced, distributed, and consumed by audiences. Genre categorisation applies to television industries in East Asia. When we speak of television programs, we generally locate them within broad programming classifications, often imposed by regulatory decree. For instance, Taiwan has four broad program categories: news and propaganda; education and culture; public service; and entertainment. The People's Republic of China has similar categories. As in most international schedules, we can identify first-order genres, second-order genres and a range of new mutations that are a response to industry commercialisation. For instance, within most programming classifications in East Asia, we observe recognisable 'universal' production genres such as news, infotainment, talk, prime-time drama series, and game shows.

Travelling Templates: Global Forms

Adaptation of TV program ideas from one territory to another as a means of producing a new series is not novel. Replicating experiences in radio, television broadcasters and producers in many parts of the world have for many years looked to both the United States and the United Kingdom for program templates that would guarantee the production viability of new content ideas and help ensure the success of the finished program.

And of course, the fact that these ideas had been indigenised or vernacularised within local cultures was one important step towards that success. In the past — and especially in the Anglophone countries — this borrowing mostly occurred in a series of lower-cost genres, including news and current affairs, game shows, variety programs, and children's programs. Historically, these adaptations were usually not paid for (and often not even explicitly acknowledged) — a practice shared by producers from Latin America, Europe, Asia, and the Pacific (van Manen 1994; Moran 1998; Straubhaar 1991). The practice of unauthorised adaptation is far from dead: it continues as a matter of course in large television markets such as those of India and China (Thomas and Kumar 2004; Keane 2004). Additionally, as legal disputes and even court cases attest, it also arises from time to time in the West (see Brenton and Cohen 2003; see also Chapter 11 in this volume).

Prior to the formalisation of the television format business in the 1990s, when payments were made at all, they were often in the form of a compliment or a gesture of goodwill rather than as a tariff or fee. At least three factors were at work in this situation. First, the original producer was frequently unaware of a recycling taking place elsewhere. Much more significant was the fact that most program devisors and owners lacked the international reach that would have enabled them to pursue legal action against format appropriation in other territories. Under the Berne Convention, legal action against perceived infringement must take place in the jurisdiction of the territory where this occurred. Finally, these borrowings — no matter how frequent — tended to be *ad hoc* and one-offs, so that devisors and owners did not organise long-term international legal protection. The net result of these elements was that international TV program idea transfer occurred in a milieu of apparent benign ignorance and indifference.

Historically, this pattern of transfer was one means among several that helped make television production economically viable in many different parts of the world. Adapting successful overseas programs (mostly from the United States or the United Kingdom) meant that local broadcasters and producers saved the expense of the relatively costly research and development (R&D) work involved in the first production of a successful TV program. Adapting a popular program that had been on air in the United States or the United Kingdom therefore meant that a local producer or broadcaster was accessing a template that had already withstood two rounds of R&D — first to survive development and trialling before broadcasting executives; and second to survive further testing before viewing audiences. Recycling notable TV program ideas took much of the guesswork out of local television production in many lower cost genres. After all, these were not endowed with the more costly, quality production values that would make them highly desirable and exportable. In English-speaking markets such as Canada or Australia, more expensive genres such as fiction were rarely imitated or adapted, precisely because the original US or UK programs were imported. In markets such as Russia and India, which are shielded by language or other cultural barriers, adaptation certainly takes place in fiction (Thomas and Kumar 2004; Heller 2003; Iwabuchi 2004).

In recent times, this process of international adaptation of TV program ideas has consciously been routinised and formalised through a series of related measures. These include a deliberate generation of value-adding elements (such as the format Bible), format marketing arrangements (industry festivals and markets), licensing processes, and a form of self-regulation within the industry administered by a new industry association, the Format Recognition and Protection Association (FRAPA). TV program ideas are now claimed as intellectual property (with constant industry rhetoric about 'piracy').

Meanwhile, there has been a concerted international attempt to formalise and commodify program ideas under the label of 'format'. In turn, this has produced a degree of regularity in the licensed adaptation of program ideas to other producers and to other places. Additionally, the format commodity can also circulate within any particular multi-channel system, generating income from a variety of cross-platform sources.

Clearly, this new situation and arrangement formalises what was once casual and spontaneous as a means of deriving financial benefit — most especially from overseas adaptations. TV programs are not now simply devised and produced for local buyers with the (often faint) hope that they might sell elsewhere in the world. Instead, they are consciously created with the deliberate intention of achieving near-simultaneous international adaptation. Additionally, increased communication and company linkages around the world have meant that unauthorised appropriation of TV program formats is less and less likely to go unchallenged. This reconfiguration of the international circulation of TV program ideas has facilitated the emergence of new national sources of TV formats.

The TV format often referred to as event television, and exemplified by *Big Brother* and *Idol*, has an important historical antecedent. Since the 1969 televised moon landing, one kind of global television program has prevailed. This is the television public event, other forms of which have included major international sporting encounters, ceremonial events, and the outbreak and pursuit of wars (Dayan 1997). This kind of program is constituted by the simultaneous transmission of the same live event to different audiences in different parts of the world. The recent era, moreover, has seen the emergence of a new type of television — namely, the globally local program (Lie and Servas 2000; Moran and Keane 2004). Here there is not a single live event being transmitted simultaneously. Instead, there are a series of parallel events being transmitted in the same proximate time to a series of audiences who might, cumulatively, be said to have seen the 'same' program. Although people worldwide watch *Big Brother*, the audience is made up of a series of smaller audiences who have seen, or heard about, a succession of adaptations (*Big Brother US* Series 1, *Big Brother UK* Series 2, *Big Brother Australia* Series 3 and so on) based on the *Big Brother* format (Mathijs and Jones 2004). In other words, we encounter a program that is abstract and international in type while also being local and concrete in its particular manifestations. Formats thereby generate regional, national or pan-national series, even while the program itself is international or global.

Engines and the Role of Innovation

New formats have provided producers with a licence to experiment with ideas that may be inimical to the legacy of the national culture or the brand of the network. The format from abroad may indeed be a kind of Trojan horse that enters into protected and conservative organisational environments. In China, for instance, new television formats began to be introduced in 1998 and have subsequently expanded the grammar and the vocabulary of Chinese television, as well as changing the visual appearance. A television industry that was dominated in the 1980s by staid propaganda documentaries and stern newsreaders is now abundantly provided with reality game shows featuring flashy set designs and hosts that freely ad lib and interact with audiences. Likewise, Japanese game and variety formats were localized in South Korea and Taiwan during the 1990s, providing new creative inputs into indigenous production practices. While these aspects of cultural borrowing and cultural technology transfer are dealt with in more detail elsewhere, we argue here that a refashioning of the relationship between producers, participants and viewers is key to understanding the uptake of new television formats globally. As Roscoe and Hawkins point out, while it may be pleasurable 'to ponder the textual peculiarities of new formats, their emergence also demands a close consideration of how meaning is implicated with money, policy and technology' (2001: 5).

Notwithstanding the various ways of defining adaptations and re-versions, the key point to bear in mind is that formats have brought about new developments in television production and injected new life into sterile forms. The documentary has received a make-over as reality television (see Chapter 9), the quiz show becomes an information challenge (see Chapters 6 and 7), and the variety show gets 'real' variety from audience participation (see Chapter 8). Documentary genres such as wildlife and animal shows that have been 'female' now cross over into reality, injecting adventure, novelty, and the element of surprise. The new elements are known as 'engines': they generate interest and interactivity. In showing how these engines provide traction for local industries in East Asia, we can identify several innovations, most of which are recognisable features of global television schedules.

Million-dollar prizes

The most conspicuous newcomer in Asia is the maximum pay-off 'winner-takes-all' quiz show. While quiz shows have been a staple diet of audiences in Japan, China, Hong Kong, Taiwan and South Korea for some time, the sudden emergence and licensing of the international brand format *Who Wants to Be a Millionaire?* (Celador UK) created a new benchmark for quiz show-makers. Quiz shows had suddenly become more competitive. Part of the mystique and attraction of the Celador format is the magic lure of becoming an instant millionaire. Until the arrival of *Who Wants to Be a Millionaire?* large payouts were not permitted on television in China, Japan, or South Korea. In Japan the maximum prize for a single contestant remains two million yen (US20,300) and in China the prize limit is generally set at RMB20,000 (US$2,500) per family (although there are variations on this, with ancillary prizes offered of greater value). While these amounts might appear insubstantial in comparison with UK and US payouts, there is the proviso in Japan that a maximum prize of ten million yen (US$101,500) can be shared among five team members — the person answering questions and nominated 'phone-a-friend' team members. In Hong Kong, where there in no limit on prizes, the success of the Celador 'franchise' was partly attributed to a yearning for material success at a time when the Asian economic crisis had hit hard. With people losing their hard-earned savings in the crisis, the idea of instant wealth created a *Millionaire* fever.

Built-in potential conflict and the prisoner's dilemma

A sub-category of winner-takes-all formats is the elimination reality game show or elimination quiz show. The most high-profile international precedents are *Survivor, Big Brother,* and *The Weakest Link.* While these programs have drawn criticism for being too individualistic and materialistic for Asian audiences, there have nevertheless been several attempts to utilise the fundamental premise on which these shows are based. This is the prisoner's dilemma, a gambit that necessitates contestants forming strategic alliances with other players in order to progress in the game. This makes for a complex game in which viewers can have the pleasure of anticipating alliances. The survival-of-the-fittest scenario is correlated with eliminating strong rivals. However, this elimination of strong competitors is paradoxically offset by the need to maximise chances of progressing through the game or garnering greater economic benefits. A strategic ploy is to keep strong players in the game, as in *The Weakest Link* or *Survivor,* and to obtain their support in order to win rewards and so-called 'immunity' challenges. These ideas of built-in conflict have infiltrated reality shows such as *The Biggest Loser,* in which overweight contestants conspire within teams, and against each other, to remain in the game.

Lifelines and immunity

Lifelines *(Millionaire)*, immunities *(Survivor)*, and audience voting *(Idol)* are engines that allow for uncertainty and build tension in the program. These 'get-out-of-gaol' cards often provide justice and work best where the contestant has developed some kind of empathy with the audience. *Millionaire* was the first show to utilise multiple lifeline engines and, as one producer has noted (Overett 2004), these engines were quickly imitated. Despite Celador claiming a trademark on its '50/50', 'Phone a Friend' and 'Ask the Audience', the Chinese (CCTV) version of *Millionaire* 'borrowed' these key elements (see Chapter 7). Even the background, set design, and use of heartbeat background sounds during questions are strikingly similar.

Voting off is probably the key engine of reality formats and became the central element of game shows like *The Weakest Link*. In their book *Shooting People*, Benton and Cohen (2003) relate how the voting-off engine originated. The devisor of the desert island survivor concept, Charlie Parsons, had considerable difficulty convincing network executives in the United States of the benefits of spending a lot of money developing an expensive programming idea. It was during a brainstorming meeting in the United States that the idea of linking challenges to a process of contestant votes emerged (Brenton and Cohen 2003: 47–48). The rest is history and, as we see in Chapter 10, not without intellectual property dispute. Voting off allows television stations to maximise advertising revenue as viewers are kept waiting until the end of the show, or between episodes, to find out who bows out. In addition, the voting engine captures a range of cross-platform publicity, including television news, magazines, radio, and the internet.

Exotic or familiar locations

The reality game show *Survivor*, the first format to utilise the prisoner's dilemma, achieved great success from its strategy of locating its contestants in 'hostile' oriental settings such as Borneo, Thailand and the Pearl Islands. However, attempts to localise the format in Asia have met with disapproval from audiences. Japanese *Survivor* commenced in April 2002 (Tokyo Broadcasting System) with a great deal of promotional activity, only to struggle with its own survival. Other reality game shows such as *Race Around the World* have further developed the engine of exotic and dangerous locations, while weight-loss programs now combine exotic locations with lifestyle modification.

Gladiatorial elements

Gladiatorial elements are not new to television. But shows such as *The Fear Factor* and *The Weakest Link* add greater suspense and excitement than their predecessors, while reflecting elements of everyday social relations. As we discuss in Chapter 7, there is social recognition in seeing people lose out to contestants who are not necessarily more intelligent or stronger, but who have the just found a way to use the rules of the game to garner votes, whether from fellow contestants or the viewers in their living rooms. The predominance of elimination, winner-takes-all and million-dollar prize scenarios evokes a sense of ultimate contest. The use of pounding heartbeats and the design of flashy sets that reflect computer video games further add to the heightened tension.

Performativity and authenticity

Performativity refers to the processes by which identities are reproduced by repeated approximations of models that are sanctioned by the state (Butler 1990; Yúdice 2003). For instance, racialised minorities or gays will perform their identity, in the process reinforcing social norms *(Queer Eye for the Straight Guy)*. In many instances, the failure to repeat normative behaviour may actually enhance the system rather than threaten it. Performative force is understood differently in different societies, and by different audiences, and these variations impact upon how culture is invoked in different locations. The ritualised performance of difference and similarity is also celebrated as ordinary people take on the responsibility of acting according to what they believe is normative behaviour. For instance, participants on reality shows such as *Big Brother* fall into performing roles that are subtly scripted for them through pre-selection of stereotypes. Part of the attraction of viewing is to 'discover' the degree of authenticity in the performances of contestants.

Renovation, DIY, and care of the self

The kinds of programs amenable to formatting differ according to what we might call social environmental factors. For instance, in the United Kingdom, Europe, the United States, Canada, Australia, and New Zealand, viewers are exposed to a glut of house and garden makeover and rescue programs, even hybrids such as *The Block* (Nine Network Australia 2003) that see elements of reality television combined with 'do-it-yourself' (DIY) advice for renovation. The social landscape of these countries, along with extensive home ownership and promotion of home improvement as a metaphor for success, undoubtedly promotes the relative abundance of DIY. An examination of schedules in Australia and New Zealand in any given week would find programs with names such as such as *Dream Home*, *Changing Rooms*, *Hot Property*, or *Better Homes and Gardens* occupying prominent positions in the ratings. By way of contrast, house or apartment makeover programs are less conspicuous in Asia. That is not to say, however, that home- or self-improvement don't rate. The fact that many people live in apartment blocks in Asian cities precludes major makeovers to some extent. On the other hand, we locate the ethos of self-improvement in shows such as China Central Television's (CCTV's) *Human Resources*, a program that brought together a group of contestants to compete for an ultimate prize. 'Borrowed' from an Argentinean program of the same name, the concept of improvement revolves around the contestants learning the rules of the marketplace so that they can aspire to a better, higher-paying and, ultimately, more satisfying career. Unlike improvement cooking hybrids such as *Jamie's Kitchen* (UK), which attempt to professionalise a short-listed group of long-term unemployed by offering them instructions on how to provide better service in the restaurant industry, *Human Resource*'s participants are all tertiary educated and employed. The winner of the competition walks away with a better job. The ethos of the show, which was first broadcast on CCTV's Economic Channel (Channel 2) in 2004, is to provide information about China's changing economic environment in an entertainment format (producer, interview by Keane, 2004). Likewise, weight loss contests such as Hong Kong TVB's *SlimFlight* (see Chapter 10) engender a sense of striving to achieve socially acceptable norms while providing opportunities for cosmetic and make-over product placement and advertising.

Keeping it in the family

The family participation engine is a core element of many Asian television formats. The Japanese format *Happy Family Plan* (Japan), which was successfully marketed within Asia, exploited collectivism and care for family fortunes. Whereas friends and family appear on international versions of *Idol* and *Big Brother*, the family is mandatory for most reality and information challenges in Asia. In addition, the family benefits from the prize pool. Likewise, heavily copied dating shows such as *Special Man and Woman* (*feichang nannü*, Taiwan) have featured family members offering positive support for the contestant (Keane 2004).

Formats in East Asia

In an article written in 1991, before the terms 'globalisation' and 'hybridity' had become compulsory in academic accounts of cultural exchange, the Hong Kong scholar Paul Lee described the impact of international cultural influences in Hong Kong using a biological metaphor. Lee proposed four patterns of 'absorption and indigenisation of foreign cultures based on the transformation of form and content' (Lee 1991: 64). He called these patterns 'parrot', 'amoeba', 'coral', and 'butterfly'. The first of these is where the foreign cultural product is wholly adopted rather than adapted. The program or music is broadcast in the foreign language. The second variant, the amoeba, is where the content remains the same but the program is repackaged with local hosts — for instance, sports programming such as *Premier League Soccer* (UK) or *Funniest Home Videos* (US). The coral pattern, on the other hand, keeps the form but changes the content. This coral metaphor is the most applicable to television format adaptation. Keeping the form and changing the content also correlates with the 'pie and crust' model that is used within the television industry to refer to formats. Finally, the butterfly pattern describes a final stage of assimilation of foreign culture in which the original form and content are wholly transformed in the receiving culture, so that they are recognised as local and spin off (or fly away) their own variety.

In effect, Lee's four patterns were about cultural exchange. The first two were minimal change models, while the coral and the butterfly were dominant copying strategies in the marketplace. As well as a means of extracting value from the marketplace, copying (or cultural borrowing) represents a strategy of localisation that enables cultures to diversify. It has often been suggested that Japan's business success in the modern era was founded on copying, assimilating, and localising Western models. Iwabuchi (2002) has described this process as one in which Japanese awareness of Western culture resulted in successful adaptation of US cultural forms, in turn allowing Japan to act as a creator of templates by which contemporary popular culture could be re-manufactured and formatted within the East Asian region. In this process, Japanese producers have exploited Japan's knowledge of East Asian sensibilities, including sensitivity to its role as an aggressor and coloniser during the past century. For instance, Japanese popular culture, such as television, music, and cinema, was officially banned in Taiwan until 1992 and has only recently been officially allowed to penetrate Korean households (Lee 2004).

With the emergence of inter-regional cultural flows in Asia — albeit uneven — Japan is reinscribed as a key player, but not solely as a localiser of Western cultural models. It is also a provider of templates. Countries in the

East Asian region have copied, assimilated, and localised Japanese models. The predominance of copying as a business model and as a production strategy is therefore important to understand, and there is a great deal of speculation within the television industry as to the ethics of format adaptation, in particular, the question of creative ownership of ideas.

The television format has come to be viewed as a solution to a creativity deficit. In short, it is easier to copy someone else's success than to take a risk on a new, untested idea. The mindset of copying has become more entrenched in the new era of television as channels proliferate, in turn, creating demand for content that can be packaged and re-packaged in themed channels — for example, reality, lifestyle, and drama. The significant dynamic of the present era in television is adaptation, transfer, and recycling of content. This tendency is not limited to television, but is characteristic across many media and related creative or cultural industries.

In writing about the formatting phenomenon in South Korea, Dong-Hoo Lee nominates three modes of adaptation, which she refers to as 'cloning', 'developing' and 'collaging'. Cloning describes wholesale mimicry of the original concept; developing is where some part of the original program is extracted and used to seed a new format; and collaging represents genuine hybridity, where elements of two or more programs are refashioned to form a new product. These strategies illustrate what Albert Moran (1998) has termed 'open' and 'closed' adaptations. An open adaptation is where there is a significant degree of flexibility in how the original text or format is remade. Most unlicensed formats are open adaptations. It is easy to see that a loose adaptation effectively reduces the likelihood of legal action for breach of copyright. Lee's developing and collaging models are strategies through which some part of an idea is utilised with significant new material being added. There is often a greater degree of creativity involved in this kind of formatting.

The closed adaptation model corresponds to Dong-Hoo Lee's cloning strategy. Cloning may be authorised, whereby the licence fee is exchanged and the format is produced according to set instructions. Agreed minor variations are the norm, as in the case of Beijing Television's remake of the Japanese format *Happy Family Plan*. Japan's TBS *Happy Family Plan* was sold to more than thirty countries. In 2000, Beijing Television (BTV) bought the licence and presented it as *Dreams Come True (mengxiang chengzhen)*, which was then on-sold to forty-three stations throughout China. The terms of the collaboration between BTV (Beijing) and TBS were three years in the making, according to a Chinese producer who had previously seen a version of the program screened on UK television. As the UK network was unable to sell the licence, BTV looked to the format owner, TBS. Licence fees were subsequently exchanged between BTV, TBS, and the Beijing-based production company. The producers cited long-term goodwill with TBS as the reason why they paid fees rather than just copying like other Chinese stations. The original licence fee paid to TBS was equivalent to US$1500, but this was reduced over subsequent seasons as the local stations incorporated greater localisation. In particular, BTV introduced a monthly version that allowed celebrities to participate (producer of *Dreams Come True*, interview by Keane, June 2004).

Alternatively, when there is no exchange of licence fees and the product is a direct copy, we can say that cloning is contravening the copyright of the originating company. Instances of unlicensed copying of *Happy Family Plan* in Korea and Taiwan aroused the ire of the Japanese parent broadcaster, TBS (Lee 2004; Iwabuchi 2004).

If one takes a purely legalistic approach, there is not much that can be done to stop wilful copying. Rights are constructed aspects of the competition between different program producers, local and international, and between different users of program content and 'brands', such as broadcasters, cable, radio, telephone and internet. This emphasis on rights helps secure the general conditions for the process of selling the same content over and over again across a series of different media. This is the new face of media globalisation.

Liu and Chen (2004) have described the formatting environment in Taiwan in a more inclusive sense, using a broad definition of formatting. They nominate several categories of formats in Taiwan: imported programming, licence, adaptation, clone, reproduction, original, syndication and free copy. Five of these can be usefully incorporated in our discussion. The first, imported programs, corresponds to what is typically referred to as trans-border video exchange (see Bates 1998). There are no changes to content as these are finished programs purchased from abroad and rebroadcast in Taiwan utilising subtitles or dubbing. The main sources for imported programs in Taiwan are Hong Kong, Japan, America, and South Korea. In terms of our emphasis on formatting or re-versioning, however, the finished program — even where subtitled — does not constitute a genuine format.

The second category of format described by Liu and Chen is the licensed format — that is, a business agreement where a licence or franchise is traded between two companies to produce an authorised local version. The licence contract in this case covers the use of the entire format, including expertise, props, or scripts. In Taiwan, there has been an increase in this mode of program rights exchange, although most formatting belongs to the third and fourth categories: the clone and the adaptation.

The clone formatting model is by definition unlicensed; it implies replicating the entire format. However, this practice is not easy to prosecute as most producers will make some variations on the copied format (see Chapter 11). Adaptation is where a foreign program is copied, or alternatively, significant elements of it are taken and adapted for local consumption. Based on the degree of imitation we note the above-mentioned distinctions between open and closed adaptation.

The fifth category of formatting nominated is reproduction, where footage is bought abroad and re-edited, often with a local host adding flavour (for example, *Funniest Home Videos*). This format model mirrors the first category of imported program. Another category is what Liu and Chen call the 'original format' — where a producer devises a new format in its own right. From a producer's perspective, this is original content, although that is not to say that 'origins' are expunged. It is very rare to find a program that is so new that it is regarded as cutting edge. The last two categories — syndication and free copy — have more to do with format distribution practices. Terrestrial stations, independent producers or cable television channels, will sell their programs to other local stations or channels after a first run; free copy is where programs are provided by other channels (such as religious channels) free of charge. This is common practice in Taiwan.

The point of this ground-clearing exercise is to determine the incidence of formatting in its various manifestations. Liu and Chen looked at a sample of programs from ten channels in one week of Taiwanese broadcasting (21–27 May 2002), and found no licensed formats. However, 16.5 percent of programs were adaptations of foreign programs. Due to the difficulty of adjudicating clones and generic variants, this statistic included programs that were close copies. In short, the incidence of format licensing is generally proportional to the value of international relations within the global and regional TV network. Format licences are being traded in Taiwan, but the incidence is very low. In Hong Kong, the practice is more widespread — as we shall see in Chapter 7. Few format licences have been brokered in China, the notable exceptions being *Happy Family Plan* and the information challenge show *The Weakest Link*. Japan, meanwhile, continues to produce and sell formats regionally and internationally.

Concluding Remarks: Similarity and Difference within Globalisation

As we will observe in Part 2, most formatting falls under the umbrella term 'generic variation', where the adaptation draws on the key structural elements but adds in local flavours and accents. This high incidence of imitation does not, however, obviate the fact that these open adaptations add to knowledges of production circulating in the East Asian region. In this chapter we have defined formats from several perspectives, but in doing so, have drawn attention to them as cultural technologies. In other words, they enhance the adaptability of a television program already devised and developed elsewhere. Any program can, of course, be copied, imitated, adapted, or used as inspiration for another program. On the other hand, the act of formatting is a conscious and deliberate attempt to facilitate these processes, to speed up and smooth out the adjustment that will result in a new version of the program. Clearly, this kind of operation is, at least for the most part, concerned with producing a general likeness or resemblance to a preceding program. Even though we have reviewed several useful attempts to construct various break-downs of subtypes of adaptation, the point is that the format operates within a domain of similarity and resemblance. Genre, on the other hand, operates within a far wider arena of difference as well as likeness, variation and repetition. With genre, there is never a single master text that contains all possibilities and variations — and against which any particular text can be compared and contrasted. With a format, on the other hand, there is always such an originating text. For this reason, we argue against a loose use of the term 'format' that would see it as coterminous in meaning with genre. Where there is palpable cloning or imitation, we will defer to the master concept of adaptation. Mention of genres, formats, and engines also serves as an introduction to the next chapter, where we take up the idea of cultural resourcefulness and 'imagination' in relation to transfer of television productions in East Asia.

PART II

Formats, Clones, and Generic Variations

5

Cultural Diversity, Trade, and Technology Transfer

> English and Chinese tastes in entertainment are not the same. For instance, European people like to watch the subtleties in people's relationships, the rich, psychological and emotional conflicts that occur. Chinese audiences appreciate more traditional narratives.
> — actor in the Chinese TV drama *Joy Luck Street*

> Soap operas can work anywhere as long as people can identify with the characters. People always want to know what their neighbours are doing.
> — Eugene Ferguson, Granada, consultant on *Joy Luck Street*

In Chapter 2 we examined the characteristics of television systems and categories of programming in China, Hong Kong, Japan, Taiwan, and South Korea. We concluded that there were similarities across these countries as well as comparable structures of feeling that assist the exchange of programs. This chapter and the next focus on the material assets exchanged when programs are traded and techniques of production move across national television systems.

Franchising models play a role in reshaping and restructuring global activity in two ways. First, many transferred formats embody high levels of internationalised 'intangibles': notions about value creation, branding, marketing and consulting routinely accompany exchanges and contribute to establishing a culture of competition and business ethics. Second, the resulting productions are in most cases recognisably local: they draw on local tastes and values, they partner with local knowledge, and in doing so, they generate mutual benefits and cultural technology transfer.

We begin with a proposition that cultural diversity is the economic basis for trans-border trade in television programs. Our point of departure is the paradox of diversity. The pro–free-trade economist Tyler Cowan argues that two models of diversity prevail in discussions about globalisation: diversity *across* societies and diversity *within* a society (Cowan 2002: 1–15). Most globalisation critics attend to the former, particularly how global trade in mass culture products threatens cultural diversity. Fredric Jameson contends that, 'The standardisation of world culture, with local popular or traditional forms driven out or dumbed down to make way for American television, American music, food, clothes and films, has been seen by many as the very heart of globalization' (Jameson 2000). For many critics, formatted television shows add little value to local cultures. A corollary to this view is that consumers in many countries mimic American culture while producers, in turn, mimic Hollywood models of production. The result is a flattening of difference and a reflection of Jameson's dark heart of globalisation.

Advocates of cultural protection in smaller and mid-size media markets regularly contend that diversity is a good thing, although the understanding of diversity in this instance is normally tempered by an antipathy to mass culture and, in particular, US entertainment industries. The argument hangs on the principle of difference — or, to use a biological metaphor, a rainforest of rare species. This rainforest, with all its unique natural endowments, is threatened by standardised and homogenised forms of culture. International trade agreements such as the Agreement on Trade-related Aspects of Intellectual Property Rights (TRIPS) seek to lower nationally erected barriers to international culture and threaten the biodiversity. In the sensitive debate over cultural uniqueness, however, we need to attend to a necessary interplay between tradition and change. As researchers of cultural exchange, we also need to be cognisant of the danger, as Appadurai puts it, of emphasising 'trait geographies' — conceptions of 'geographical, civilisational and cultural coherence that rely on some sort of trait list — of values, languages, material practices, ecological adaptations, marriage patterns and the like' (2001: 7).

Parallel to trait geographies are process geographies: 'various kinds of action, interaction, and motion' (2001: 7). Most particularly, cultural trade brings with it an exchange of material endowments, not just cultural values. To take an economist's perspective, material exchange occurs because there is a demand for the product or service. Sophisticated and successful commercial products from one market, in turn, engender interest from creators and producers looking to emulate success or break free of existing conventions. Furthermore, distinctions between traditional culture and commercial culture require us to recognise the utility of cultural exchange and the kinds of endowments that are traded. In many countries and regions in East Asia, where cultural output has been highly regulated and directed towards approved forms by political decrees, openness to international commercial culture has brought positive impacts. Traditional cultural artefacts, more resistant to hybridisation, often encounter apathy from younger consumers weaned on the web and interactive technologies. At the same time, politically endorsed or state-censored forms — film, documentary, and news — have pushed audiences towards apolitical culture from outside, even if the outside culture is more difficult to understand.

In other words, cultural policy has worked to restrict diversity *within* society. For many years, South Korea resisted Japanese popular culture, erecting quotas and restrictions, while at the same time exploiting Japanese production techniques to effectively produce Korean versions. By 2004 the barriers had all but come down, a process of liberalisation and self-confidence that coincided with a renaissance in Korean media production (Lee 2004; Yoon 2001). In China, the political maxim of 'let a hundred flowers bloom, let a hundred schools of thought contend' celebrates diversity and free expression — on the surface at least. However, this model of diversity applies to a limited field of expression *within* society. Since China opened up to international trade in culture in 1978, the politically correct way of 'doing cultural work' has moved irreversibly towards hybridity, embracing diversity *across* cultures and reinscribing diversity *within* the culture.

From the viewpoint of diversity, both within and across society, trade is imperative. And from the viewpoint of trade in cultural (and creative) goods, diversity is the oil of commercial consideration. Tyler Cowan writes that 'both art consumers and art producers need "otherness" to fulfil their creative wishes' (2002: 19). Cultural exchange and trade drives innovation. Cowan says, 'More generally, the economically poorer nations have used Western technologies and the modern city to drive a host of innovations in fields as diverse as literature, cinema, and the visual arts' (2002: 23). Perhaps this is overstating the case. Nonetheless, frequent interactions among globally connected networks of people and finance facilitate the diversification of ideas and fashions. This, in turn, provides a space for Néstor Garcia Canclini's 'cultural reconversion' (1992), whereby traditional forms and fields of culture that have lost ground are renovated through reformatting, or are 'reconverted' into contemporary expressions. For instance, oppositional or *avant garde* art practices find sponsorship from corporations; traditional analogue forms are reconverted into commercial services through digital technology; and traditional art encounters the international art market.

While the momentum and rate of cultural exchange has accelerated with globalisation, there are many precedents in traditional societies. For instance,

Skinner has written about the impact of market towns in pre-modern China, places where traders from different countries and regions met, where wandering performing arts troupes performed, and where new ideas and technologies were diffused (Skinner 1964). In modern times, cities bring together buyers (now trading in copyrights, trademarks, and patents) that engender networks of supply and training. Static but resilient forms of symbolic capital encounter the commercial ethos of hybridity and mercantilism.

Global culture abounds with examples of how cultural exchange brokers 'capital complementarity' — a term referring to capital goods that increase each other's value. World music has arisen in the past two decades from its roots in Africa (Zaire [now the Democratic Republic of Congo] and South Africa) and the Caribbean (Kingston, Jamaica). Technologies introduced by traders have allowed local artists to break free of traditional constraints. In Trinidad, the distinctive steel band ensemble was made possible by the 'discovery' of the musical potential of fifty-gallon oil drums of multinational oil companies, discarded by American armed forces after the Second World War. These new technologies of production displaced the indigenous percussion technology of bamboo (Cowan 2002: 29). Another pertinent example of how technologies of production cross cultural divides is the introduction of acrylic paints to the Papunya aboriginal community in Australia by a white schoolteacher, Geoff Bardon, in the early 1970s. This technology allowed the sacred art of the Western Desert people to be commercially produced and modified. In this way, a cultural maintenance practice was subsumed into the supply-demand mechanisms of Western art markets (Frow 1997: 136–37). The actual display and consumption of this artwork on a global scale served to change perceptions of Aboriginal culture. The shift from the community-binding 'use value' of culture to the commodity form is also characteristic of the evolving media market.

However, there is a cautionary note to be sounded in celebrating the power of trade to reinvigorate so-called moribund cultural traditions. The indigenous art of Australian Aborigines is a case in point where the imperative to commercialise produces negative cultural impacts by destabilising meaning systems that are embedded in ancient lore (law) over time. In effect, the diffusion of ideas can also lead to new structures of power and domination extending into communities. In addition, exploitation of indigenous symbols by copyists, usually for the benefit of tourists who are ignorant of traditional contexts, leads to an inevitable sense of cultural loss — as the artefact is sold for low value to persons who have no real empathy with the culture. While economists such as Cowan argue that the inevitability of hybridity allows survivors and entrepreneurs to 'cash in' on tradition, there is a need to acknowledge that diversity depends on the maintenance of cultural tradition, ownership and control of copyright by creators, as much as the transnational flow of trade and ideas.

Formats and Technology

The television format trade has impacted upon diversity *within* and diversity *across* cultures. As we have already discussed, the television format is increasingly conspicuous on the international television landscape. Even network heavyweights such as NBC and ABC in the United States have taken to exploiting the economies of production offered by reality and game formats, notwithstanding a refrain of critique echoing Fredric Jameson's views on Americanisation, namely that formats are the latest wave in a global dumbing-down of culture (Jameson 2000). While the cultural imaginations of television producers may be less extended by formatting than originating new content, we nevertheless argue that formats have contributed more to the development of the television landscape than has been acknowledged by academic research.

It is not just representational similarities or differences that make the border-crossing practices of formats intriguing and the lack of scrutiny so conspicuous. Our argument — that the format is both the crust and the pie — indicates logics of production suited to the aspirations of small-scale producers. While television production has always involved imitation of successes, the institutionalised practice of format licensing across national systems legitimises, and even celebrates, imitation. Moreover, along with the format crust comes new ingredients and varying degrees of flexibility in how these ingredients are mixed. This contrasts with finished programming, which is pre-formed, pre-cooked, and far less interactive.

It is important therefore to consider non-textual elements of television format exchange. Although formats have been licensed for some decades, the turn towards formatting as a business model is a response to escalating cost structures, and what Alan Griffith (2003) refers to as the haemorrhaging of free-to-air channels due to falling advertising sales. As multi-channelling creates demand for more varieties of content, flexible and hybrid forms of programming attract the interest of television networks. The globalisation of formats, along with interactive cross-media promotion and production techniques, illustrates 'cultural technology transfer': the television format is a package of technologies and services, delivering growth and profit opportunities for television networks, producers and advertisers.

Indeed, the flexible and modular nature of the television format complicates critiques of cultural globalisation. In its more simplistic variety, globalisation has been associated with the lack of diversity *across* societies — implying a flattening of cultural difference as global audio-visual products and services are disseminated by transnational media channels. The internationalisation of audio-visual markets and corporate consolidation exacerbates fear of homogenisation. For example, Viacom controls MTV, Nickelodeon and VH1, and has ties to Paramount and CBS. In the East Asian region, there are ownership alliances between Star TV (News Corporation) and Phoenix television; there are synergies between Hong-Kong based content providers Sun TV and mainland Chinese internet content provider Sina.com. In many instances, consolidation occurs in order for new markets to be accessed through co-productions. Accessing local knowledge is an important factor in bringing about these mergers and acquisitions.

Arif Dirlik (2001) has pointed to some of the intellectual folly in debates ensuing over cultural homogenisation and heterogenisation. He argues that whether the world is headed for homogeneity or heterogeneity depends on where we look and what meaning we assign to what we see:

> Arguments for heterogenisation no less than arguments for homogenisation are constrained by an assumption of a cultural and intellectual space that presupposes a paradigm (or, more severely, ideology) of globalisation. (2001: 19)

Evoking a somewhat different metaphor of trees rather than the cultural rainforest, Dirlik argues that those who focus on trees see heterogeneity everywhere, with little attention to how the forest may shape the trees. Likewise, focusing on the forest may lose sight of the distinctiveness of the trees.

In short, we argue that it is more helpful to move back and examine the factors that promote new growth areas. As we noted in Chapter 3, Asian directors and scripts are highly sought after by Hollywood as the centre looks to the peripheries for new talent. So a reverse flow of creativity is occurring. The question that is important in this exchange is how global the resultant program or film is. For instance, do Asian directors sell out their authenticity to Hollywood by incorporating elements that appease international audiences?

Meanwhile, studies of television systems regularly tell us that, if given the choice, people will consume local product rather than imported — that is, viewers prefer to watch programs and consume services that are indeed culturally specific (Sinclair et al. 1996). The academic focus on the reach of transnational satellite channels often misses this central point. The availability of multi-channelling does not mean that audiences will be drawn like lemmings to foreign programming; often the transnational channel just happens to be part of a pay-TV package. The global content of such channels needs to be spliced with local content, and this demand for local flavour results in media organisations actively localising, often in co-productions with local interests. The optimum vehicle for localisation is the television format, and the franchising agreement is in effect a form of co-production.

As the evidence from our research volume suggests, along with negative effects such as an increasing network dependency on formats to the detriment of investment in new local content (e.g. dramas, tele-movies), formats stimulate consumption, promote producer-consumer interactivity, and transfer technology. Drawing attention to strategies of utilising local knowledge, Dirlik suggests that the key focus ought not to be about heterogeneity or homogeneity as effects of globalisation, but rather the systematic inroads into local cultures made by marketing companies. He says:

> It is arguable that advertisers and marketers display a greater awareness of what is at issue in these conflicts than academics who seem to drift aimlessly over these discursive terrains with no visible purpose other than adding case after case to the questionable assertions of postcolonial or postmodern criticism concerning hybridization, localization or re-signification. (Dirlik 2001: 15)

Dirlik is correct in suggesting that there is another, largely unnoticed effect of the localisation of foreign products: the gradual bedding down of a Western-style consumer society that is aided and abetted by local elites who have taken on board foreign techniques of management, marketing, and distribution. As we shall see, the format licensing deal is often a joint venture that provides a means for the transfer of techniques across systems, frequently acting as a vehicle for the introduction of a range of ideas, innovations, management styles, and social relations. Whether Western consumer society is ultimately detrimental is a moot point. 'Western' ideas of consumer society include the motto of consumer satisfaction, a concept that regulates the unethical practice of rip-off and fakes in many East Asian markets. The same applies to the spread of Western styles of management and production. They have had a positive effect of introducing best practices, training, and efficiencies in domains where these were absent. Joint ventures, co-productions, and franchises are vehicles for technology transfer. We argue that the transfer of 'international' production and marketing techniques has in many cases empowered television producers long accustomed to operating according to routines bounded by national imaginations and constrained by national policies.

Cultural Technology Transfer

Knowing that a format works in another country does not necessarily translate into market success. A successful program in one locale may be amenable to transfer, or it may be a dismal failure. The reality of today's international mediascape is that television concepts and ideas are swiftly copied, modified and exploited by stations desperate to put together successful programs to keep ratings elevated. The format is a combination of technologies that enables change in media systems. In this sense, technology may be defined as 'simply knowledge about techniques, to which some significant degree of reliability or dependability is attached by those possessing it' (Paul 1997: 14).

Generally speaking, the term 'technology transfer' connotes transfer of materials, designs, scientific papers, and databases. 'Cultural technology' is usually attributed to the work of the Canadian communication scholar Marshall McLuhan (1962), and refers to advances in communication — a continuum from Sumerian ideographs through alphabets to printing, photography, television, the internet and so on. However, cultural technology has a more direct connotation to television content if linked to the idea of 'knowledges' about production, about marketing, and about consumer patterns — in other words, how to make more successful programs that return profits to investors.

Having made this connection between knowledges and returns on investment, we propose that all commercial entertainment media are cultural technologies insofar as they aim to attract your attention, keep your attention and — in the case of commercial television — sell your attention to advertisers. Programming decisions are usually based on market research. In the cultural sphere, innovation entails the application of new technologies, whether these come from overseas or are originated in the domestic industry. Cultural technology transfer provides a shift from text-based explanations. It allows us to take into account the dynamics of flows and the measurable economic benefits that accrue. At the same time, ideas, policies, and organisational practices are introduced into the receiving system.

Cultural technology transfer has two edges. In a material sense, a cultural commodity is formed; in another sense, the success of the commodity — in the case of a television program, high ratings — leads to further dissemination of the technology. The licensing, co-production, and adaptation of television formats demonstrates cultural exchange of a different order than we are generally accustomed to in media studies. Whereas knowledge of audience taste and predisposition garnered by market research is used to originate programs, a package of associated technologies is traded (under licence). Format technology transfer (in the formal sense at least) can include the provision of computer software for program credits, animation sequences, designer blueprints for such things as program sets and studio filming, film footage for insertion in the new program version of the format, and scripts for individual episodes (van Manen 1994). Other technologies may also constitute a part of the transfer package. These include ratings information derived from audience surveys, programming details, and polls associated with the broadcast of the earlier program version of the format. Another technology that is frequently added to the value is a consultancy service, whereby a production executive associated with the earlier program will act as adviser to a new production of the format (Moran 1998).

Cultural technology transfer entails looking at program flows through the pragmatic lens of content internationalisation. The recipient broadcaster is making a decision about the utility and value of the format package: the cost of replication is measured against the technical capacity to accommodate the format and provide local content. The cultural technology transfer model is therefore a way of bridging the gap between modernisation theory that supposes that modern 'Western' technology, and its ways of organisation, contribute to an inevitable transition from tradition to modernity, and media imperialism, which has tended to see foreign programming only as a threat to social values. In effect, the equation is not so straightforward. Like technology transfer itself, the cultural technology transfer of format licensing and appropriation depends on the environment in which it is transplanted. Sometimes it takes, sometimes it doesn't.

This is not to say that the technology transfer model dismisses power relations. On the contrary, the point is that cultural traffic routinely encompasses both textual and non-textual forms of exchange — ideas about government, as well as industrial processes and protocols, which by moving from one locale to another result in intellectual, social, and institutional reconfigurations.

Joy Luck Street

An example of how the introduction of a television format provides recipient industries with technology transfers is the case of *Joy Luck Street (xingfu jie)*, a television series co-production based on the long-running UK melodrama, *Coronation Street*. The Chinese version went to air in 2002, initially paying close attention to its English 'grandparent'. *Coronation Street* began as an attempt to find a larger, more popular audience for the 'kitchen sink' fiction of novel and theatre of the late 1950s associated with the working-class areas of northern England.

The early *Coronation Street* was sufficiently popular that Granada (in conjunction with the ITV network) decided to turn it into an ongoing series that would be broadcast from all stations in the network across the United Kingdom. Originally, one half-hour episode went to air each week. Almost fifty years later, this number has climbed to four half-hour broadcasts a week. Meeting this schedule entailed a large reorganisation of production, including storylining, scripting, casting, scheduling, editing, and so on. It also meant that the series had to be video-recorded, and an integrated system of recording came about.

The remaking — or more correctly, the re-versioning of *Coronation Street* for the Chinese audience — demonstrates how production and consultancy processes are exchanged, albeit with considerable cultural friction. In this case, Granada Media provided production capital through a venture with the Hong Kong-based Yahuan Audio and Video Production Company, with the Beijing Broadcasting Institute acting as a partner and providing local expertise. Granada invested in a production deal for three years. In order to make this production, the Chinese team had to restructure many of its work practices to incorporate continuous scriptwriting and shooting, working in rotating teams.

The Chinese-language *Joy Luck Street* experience was far from a seamless transfer of the original *Coronation Street* format into the Chinese environment. There were a number of difficulties involved in transferring the Manchester narrative to a North Chinese melodramatic idiom. For example, the nuances of English working-class humour were decidedly unfamiliar to Chinese viewers. Producers also had to moderate the interplay of dysfunctional family relations and unstable relationships to accommodate viewers' expectations. By the time the series had achieved fifty episodes, it had acquired a distinctive local feel, but only with the intervention of local writers. Unfortunately, it failed to make any subsequent headway into the Chinese television drama market.

The process of making the Chinese version was a calculated attempt by Granada to move production into China — a foreign market that, according to Granada's representative, Eugene Ferguson, had so far resisted the never-ending soap opera. The producer's pitch that the never-ending soap format could succeed in a Chinese cultural and media environment where all television dramas had beginnings and endings, was, in hindsight, optimistic. The innovation of producing a twenty-five-minute soap, in contrast to the standard fifty-minute serial, was also untested. The producers had also imagined that a 6.30 pm theatre concept, promoted as a 'quality television' window leading up to the national news at 7.00 pm, would present an opportunity to capture the ideal viewer, the Chinese housewife returning from work, and to market this viewer to companies such as Proctor and Gamble. This proved to be a rather optimistic scenario.

The Chinese Production Environment

Coronation Street concentrates on relationships within and between families. Judith Jones (2004) notes that, 'The viewer of Coronation Street is often encouraged to make a moral judgement on a particular kind of character, and it is generally the stronger women characters who set the tone' (602). In contemporary China, the domestic sphere and the concepts of place and neighbourhood — so central to the *Coronation Street* narrative — evoke particular kinds of social arrangements. Indeed, it was cultural differences that complicated this re-versioning of *Coronation Street*. The series encountered strong competition from Chinese, Hong Kong, and Taiwanese dramas that were more attuned to the lifestyle sensibilities of Chinese viewers. Viewer unfamiliarity with the soap opera genre, moreover, can hardly be blamed for *Joy Luck Street's* lack of success. Chinese viewers have been weaned on domestic melodramas, both in cinema and television. More importantly, perhaps, the domestic melodrama in China is normally located in the work unit, the courtyard, the apartment building, and the family home. In most instances, the story revolves around one family unit. The idea of a neutral locale such as the English public house is rare in Chinese drama, although there were some attempts in TV drama production during the 1990s to move out of the confines of the home and the work unit (Keane 2001). Nor is the concept of parallel narrative development — a feature of much BBC entertainment — germane to Chinese drama traditions.

Perhaps the narrative development of *Joy Luck Street* also erred too much on the side of dysfunction. But this is a tale of desperation on the part of the Chinese scriptwriters, who were unused to the pressure of writing as the story itself unfolds. The story centres on two families in an imaginary northern Chinese city not far from Beijing. One of the families is headed by a high-ranking chef, Shi Weitian, who has had the privilege of cooking for

Communist Party leaders. The father of two daughters, Mr. Shi is recently retired as the series opens. Daughter One is a nurse in a hospital and Daughter Two is away in England. In the first episode, a young boy suddenly arrives in Joy Luck Street. It turns out that he is the child of Daughter Two, born out of wedlock in England. Because of the shame associated with the overseas daughter getting pregnant, the patriarch does not accept the boy into the family. Daughter One, on the other hand, is a soft-hearted and honest person but is married to an unsuccessful lawyer who is seeing another woman. Daughter Two returns from England to a frosty reception; soon after that, Daughter One is poisoned by her husband but survives. She then adopts a child who has leukaemia while the patriarch develops liver problems from excessive drinking brought about by the fading family fortunes.

In the other main family in the street, there is a minor celebrity — a football player called Xiao Yang who has also returned from the United Kingdom after featuring in the minor leagues. In Joy Luck Street, the football star's mother runs a small supermarket with the assistance of a village girl. This girl is besotted with Xiao Yang, but he already has a girlfriend in Beijing who works in a public relations company that promotes aspiring movie stars. A friend of Xiao Yang, who runs a bar, happens to be a former lover of Daughter Two when both were young. As well, a flower shop and a chemist play minor roles.

As the above scenarios suggest, there are parallels with *Coronation Street*. A more conspicuous similarity, however, is an ensemble of characters that undergo a series of unhappy life events. By episode 30, despite the best intentions of Granada consultants and local scriptwriters to concoct a credible story, it was clear that the complicated web of diminishing relationships was not connecting with the target audience. This lack of affect was then addressed by introducing another troubled character into the fictional street — an out-of-work ex-convict whose presence in *Joy Luck Street* precipitated a major twist in the somewhat predictable tale of slow disease, bad fortune, and infidelity. Adding another touch of desperation, an escaped killer who knows the ex-convict from his prison days turns up in the street.

Writing in these dangerous characters was a calculated gamble by scriptwriters, particularly when we take into account the title of the serial. As one of the leading actors commented, the concept of the street was misplaced, the characterisation was under-developed — at least in terms of what constituted drama in the Chinese television marketplace — and the foreign producers appeared to underestimate the difficulties in transplanting the format. *Joy Luck Street* would never succeed on the basis of a streetscape and its residents; it needed substantial modification to make it a family-based melodrama. According to this actor, this required localisation with an understanding of the cultural nuances, which was more than the international consultants could provide. Local actors complained that the international consultants didn't understand the subtleties of Chinese narrative form, and that their nominated Hong Kong director spoke Putonghua badly and didn't understand life in Beijing. They felt they were pressured to accept decisions made from afar. The process of referring scripts back to the United Kingdom for polishing also upset the local team whose members believed they had more insight into script development than persons living in a foreign land. By episode 24, the Hong Kong director was replaced by a local director who lasted just several episodes before leaving.

> The whole process was extremely complicated and troublesome: write the script, translate it into English, and send it to Granada for confirmation and their revisions. So the script preparation process was a little unrefined. (*Joy Luck Street* actor, interview by Keane, 5 November 2000)

Nor was the introduction of writing teams seamless:

> Because of the necessity of completing the shooting within a small time frame, we noticed that the script had some problems but there was not enough time to rectify this. This was a relatively obvious problem. Other characters had some revisions and the screenwriters were constantly changing. There were five or six people writing the script and some people had good skills at this, and wrote some good stuff, some others were a little off the mark. (*Joy Luck Street* actor, interview)

Nonetheless, the decision to identify a *Coronation Street* in China and to render this as *Joy Luck Street* is interesting from a number of perspectives. The translation of 'joy luck' into Chinese is *xingfu* — literally 'happiness and well-being'. In fact, Beijing has several streets and housing apartments bearing this name. The serendipitous association of the television street with 'happiness and well-being' would, on the surface, appear to strike a chord in contemporary urban China where happiness can now be openly associated with wealth and status. However, the scenario of events described above is anything but joyful — and possibly this dark atmosphere is attributable to the *Coronation Street* provenance. In addition, the social grouping targeted in the series is not the Chinese working class, but the 'common people' (*laobaixing*; literally the 'the old hundred names'). The common people are a more inclusive grouping than any politicised class segment such as the working class (*gongren jieji*).

Moreover, among China's common people, social status has become a familiar media topic. After all, this is a society that has moved from orthodox socialism to unorthodox capitalism — what the government prefers to now call 'a market economy with Chinese characteristics'. Whereas the period from the 1950s to the 1980s saw the working class regaled as the vanguard of the social revolution, by the 1990s their fate and political inheritance — the promise of full-time employment and political support — had been usurped by the new middle class. The common people are therefore above suspicion; they reflect the idealism of nation-building and form a bridge between the disenfranchised workers and the newly affluent and, sometimes, distrusted middle class. By the mid-1990s, television drama producers had anticipated the shift in sentiment among viewers: stories of uncomplaining role models had given way to stories about enterprising, upwardly mobile urban families. When the producers of *Joy Luck Street* were pitching their ideas to the China market, they were cognisant of a legacy of working-class identification among viewers, but were, in hindsight, guilty of over-estimating the extent to which Chinese viewers would identify with a slow-moving narrative and the tribulations of 'common people' from a much different cultural hemisphere.

Another Street, Another City

A more successful adaptation based upon co-production licensing agreements was that of the children's program *Sesame Street*, which was licensed to Shanghai Television as *Zhima jie* in 1999. In this case, the format — owned by the Children's Television Workshop — was rigorously workshopped in order to tailor it to the expectations of the Chinese child and notoriously conservative Chinese educators. The eventual sinicisation of *Sesame Street* was reported to be of the same order of technology transfer as the Chinese Sangtana motor vehicle, which borrowed German technology, workmanship and standards, and applied Chinese materials and labour (see China Cue Online 2000). The same report further opines that Shanghai Television's reputation, and Chinese pedagogic practice in general, benefited from the collaboration. According to the report, Chinese children's television had, until the advent of *Sesame Street,* been devised by adults:

> We used adult program formats and applied these mechanically to children's content with the result that adults felt it was infantile and children felt it was dreary. The reason for this is obvious: those who create children's shows are adults and they are used to using adult thought

processes to observe and regulate the world of children. (China Cue Online 2000)

The Chinese contributed a team of eighteen child education specialists, headed by a renowned physicist and head of Fudan University, Professor Xie Xide. New characters, such as Xiao Meizi (Little Berry) and Huhu Zhu (Puff Pig), were added to accommodate local idioms. Part of the technology transfer meant sending the Shanghai Television producers to New York to work with their American counterparts. This exchange was funded by the US giant General Electric, which no doubt had its own commercial agenda. The outcome of the pre-production workshop and training was a reference volume outlining in detail the minutiae of production. The program is now syndicated throughout China, as are *Sesame Street* products and the Children's Television Workshop website.

Concluding Remarks: A Fine Line between Innovation and Imitation

As we have argued, there are also compelling arguments to suggest that global culture, including commercial mass culture, can invigorate and spur national cultural production to be more innovative, and not just imitative. The innovation effect is triggered by cultural technology transfer as production, marketing, and distribution strategies of the major media players are adopted in the region. In activating local production, these global shifts of technology and know-how demonstrate that the line between innovation and imitation is not predetermined. In fact, as we will see throughout the examples of new television formats, creativity does not begin at some specific point of origin.

There is nothing surprising in capitalising on a good idea, except that the more a format is copied, the more it loses its uniqueness, the more the cultural identity factor is diluted, and the more it decreases in economic value. Meanwhile, as programs are re-formatted and cloned, they become detached from their original national moorings. The positive side of formats is that they represent a conveyance of ideas and techniques. Many of these formats add value to the system by introducing new production and marketing techniques. A cycle of receiving and adapting formats thus becomes the business model of a television industry desperately seeking imaginative concepts. Having looked at a format licensing failure, we now turn to an indisputable success story.

6

The International Currency of *Who Wants to Be a Millionaire?*

If you were to ask residents of Hong Kong, Singapore, or Tokyo the question 'do you want to be a millionaire?' it is likely that the answer would be in the affirmative, with a passing acknowledgement of the popularity of the TV program *Who Wants to Be a Millionaire? (Millionaire)*. With millionaire-ship now effectively packaged as popular culture, few people — with the possible exception of religious zealots and hard-core socialists — challenge the morality of instant wealth. Fascination with the televised exploits of ordinary people winning great cash payouts supports a core tenet of neo-liberalism — the idea that anyone can succeed with luck, skill, and hard work. In recent times, the opportunity for ordinary citizens to prosper from intelligence has also received endorsement from political leaders in the People's Republic of China.

This chapter looks at the genesis of the format of *Millionaire* and its global franchising. In contrast to high-cost brand formats whose internationalisation has suffered from copycats, *Millionaire* is a model format: its copyright has been managed successfully and localisation has been accommodated incrementally — that is, without moving too far from the original concept. That is not to say that the show has achieved domination of all territories. In the second half of the chapter, we explore some conspicuous unlicensed variations of the *Millionaire* format.

Quiz shows have had a long association with the broadcast media in all countries. As we discuss in the following chapter, most of the early quiz shows in Asia observed the ideal of knowledge acquisition. Prizes were minimal — the opportunity to be on TV — or were commodities provided by sponsors. When large amounts of money began to be factored into the prize pool, the audience swarmed to watch. This trajectory replicates the international development of quiz shows. Following a series of 'leaking of answers' scandals in the United States in 1958 (one incident from the show *Twenty-one* was later made into a movie directed by Robert Redford called *Quiz Show*), quiz shows moved away from high culture and factual knowledge to shows that featured both factual and everyday knowledge. Olaf Hoerschelmann (2004) alerts us to that fact that, prior to the quiz show scandals, there was no differentiation between quiz and game shows. *People are Funny* and *Truth and Consequence*, which contained minor quiz elements, were called quiz shows. Of the few dedicated quiz shows, the most notable was CBS's *$64,000 Question*, the first program to use the idea of the jackpot. It also introduced other visual elements to good effect: 'an IBM sorting machine, bank guards, an isolation booth, and neon signs' (Hoerschelmann 2004: 1872). Quiz shows took on flashy sets, loud music, and genial hosts. During the 1970s, widely syndicated shows such as *The Price Is Right* and *Sale of the Century* introduced elements of market knowledge. Knowing the price of household consumer items became a bankable asset.

Despite the pre-history of the quiz show, the advent of *Millionaire* marked out a new stage in the history of both the quiz genre and the international format trade. *Millionaire* was an innovation in the genre. With multiple complementary 'engines' and interactive elements, one format producer has appreciatively commented: 'They're giving away a million dollars, a prize we've never seen before. Secondly, they're giving away the answers. Thirdly, you've got three lifelines: phone a friend; 50/50; ask the audience. We haven't seen these engines before in a game show' (Overett, cited in Adair and Moran 2004: 23).

The global success of the *Millionaire* format is indicative of the role that TV formats have played in redefining genres. In blending audience participation, a gladiatorial atmosphere, and intense psychological pressure to choose between similar answers, the show reinvigorates the myth of the heroic challenger. Moreover, while *Millionaire* has multiple engines, the million-dollar prize, more than anything else, brands the show. The strategy of offering a fairy-tale financial enticement has provided the format creators with a first-mover advantage — that is, the show established a new benchmark that others emulated, often unsuccessfully. In a strategic sense, the production of *Millionaire* was a calculated investment. The program was one of several high-profile international formats that were genuinely novel — that is, they were not just about product differentiation. Initial sunk costs of production, including time spent in development, were high; however, these were strategically offset by ancillary merchandising, sharing of revenue with telecommunications companies, and the potential tradability of the format across television borders. The million-dollar prize format, in fact, illustrates an old strategy. Heavy investment in production is not new in the creative industries. Another example of driving up investment costs in order to create dominance is the US film industry. In the early twentieth century, a small number of entrepreneurs realised that the escalation of production costs in cinema had the effect of disproportionably increasing revenues. Other companies joined in, with many eventually going bankrupt (Bakker 2003). The few that survived this cost war became the leading production studios that eventually dominated the landscape

The built-in lifelines of ask the audience, 50/50, and phone a friend allow new levels of interactivity. The studio audience is seated in close proximity to the contestant and quiz master, facing towards the virtual audience. The use of the lifelines is key to success, and illustrates a principle described by James Surowiecki (2004) as 'the wisdom of crowds'. If the contestant is unable to answer, she is allowed to eliminate two of the four multiple-choice answers (the 50/50 lifeline); to place a call to a trusted friend, an expert selected in advance by the contestant; or to consult the studio audience. Drawing data from the US *Millionaire*, Surowiecki claims that while the selected friend/ expert produced correct answers 65 percent of the time, the studio audience performed even better, selecting correct answers 91 percent of the time (Surowiecki 2004: 4). In effect, the studio audience of non-experts is a direct link to the virtual audience.

The Genesis

Taking its title from a Cole Porter song of the 1950s, when becoming a millionaire meant colossal wealth, the program has taken advantage of economic inflation in a series of countries across the world to offer its contestants the same kind of monetary dream. In spite of the allure of the ultimate jackpot, surprisingly few have actually managed to win the prize. In Australia, for example, the program has been on air for seven years at the time of writing (1999–2006), yet only two contestants have actually ever won the million-dollar prize. Similarly in Chile, only one contestant has ever won the hundred million pesos that formed the major prize. The average prize in the United Kingdom is a modest £32 000 (US$60 000), while many contestants leave the program having won little or nothing.

Another significant element is that *Millionaire* originated in the United Kingdom rather than in the United States — long the source of many highly successful formats such as *The Price Is Right* and *Family Feud*. In fact, the story of the origin and development of *Millionaire* is an object lesson in how long and sustained the research and development (R&D) process is in the assembly of a format that will appeal to producers in other parts of the world. Hoerschelmann credits Michael P. Davies as creator of the United Kingdom-originated program format (2004: 2537). However, the origin according to Celador, who own the format, was a proposal devised by David Briggs in 1995. Briggs had worked at Britain's Capital Radio in various senior positions from 1972 to 1994, including as Head of Competitions and Executive Producer of the *Chris Tarrant Show*. From 1994 to 1996, Briggs was Head of Marketing at GMTV where he was responsible for promoting competitions, many of which included the use of premium-rate telephone lines. In this context he devised a new game show idea. Briggs's proposal was a quiz program entitled *The Cash Mountain* in which contestants would answer multiple-choice questions with the value doubling with each successful question. After each round, the contestants had the choice of leaving the game and keeping the money they had won or staying in, with the risk that they would forfeit their winnings if they gave a wrong answer. The prize money was to be substantially funded by revenue from calls on premium lines from prospective contestants seeking to enter the quiz show.

The project received a boost when Briggs floated the idea to Michael Whitehill and Steven Knight, who since 1988 had been contracted to provide writing and other creative services to Celador, a well-known UK independent television production company. Whitehill and Knight had worked on numerous projects, including devising and developing game shows. Briggs saw the program as an ideal vehicle for the British TV celebrity, Chris Tarrant. In mid-1995, Briggs had lunch with Whitehill and described his proposal, which was later submitted in writing to Paul Smith, the Chief Executive of Celador. Smith liked the concept and ordered further work on its development.

The R&D process included decisions on the top prize (£1 million), allowing contestants to view questions before deciding whether to answer them, providing a guaranteed level of prize money for answering a certain number of questions correctly, and allowing contestants three forms of help. The written concept for the program was revised accordingly and Celador pitched the concept to ITV early in 1996. Although a middle-ranking executive was enthusiastic, the network director was interested only to the extent of commissioning some qualitative market research which concluded that audience reactions were good — although the concept needed a new title. There was a suggestion that including the term 'million' in the title would work better than 'cash mountain'. ITV passed on the chance to commission a pilot and Celador had no immediate response from the other UK television networks. Throughout 1997, *Cash Mountain* was decidedly cold as far as network investors were concerned. However, a change of management at ITV reopened the door and a pilot was commissioned. The title became *Who Wants to Be a Millionaire?* and the question structure was modified. The pilot was aired in August 1998, followed by some further incremental changes, and the first episode was finally broadcast in the United Kingdom in early September 1998.

Altogether, this story is highly instructive about the complicated process of negotiation that occurs in the devising and development stages of a new TV format. Typically, many television executives were involved in the process — which is hardly surprising given the large number of elements. At the same time, as the story tells us, it is clear that an emerging format meets a series of organisational gatekeepers at different levels of a television institution. Their decisions influence whether or not the process of development goes forward or is stalled. It is important to note the succession of documentations of the paper format that are recorded. Clearly, these were important stages in the evolution of the format and would later turn out to be vital for Celador's case in the High Court against a number of claimants.

The program was enormously successful in the United Kingdom, and Celador immediately set about licensing the format around the world. By summer of the following year, the ABC network in the United States had taken up the format and enjoyed high ratings. During 1999 the format moved through most of the territories of Western Europe. Altogether, up to the time of writing, the format has been licensed in sixty-seven territories across the world, ranging from Argentina to Vietnam, making it the most simultaneously viewed quiz program of all time. Local versions of *Millionaire* have been seen in Latin America (Waisbord 2004) as well as in Middle Eastern countries that prioritise tradition and religious austerity. For instance, the Middle East Broadcasting Centre, located in Dubai City, broadcasts an Arabic version which is available in Kuwait, Egypt, and Saudi Arabia (Khali 2004; McKenzie 2004).

There are several clear reasons for the spike in popularity. While game shows are cheap to produce (the enumeration of prizes counts as program content while constituting a form of product marketing), *Millionaire* has never been about giving away holidays, cameras and cars — it is about hard cash. *Millionaire* has an enticing allure: it promises to make a contestant wealthy in a short time. This is central to the program: wherever the format has been remade, the title continues to stress the possibility of sudden great fortune. In France, the title is *Qui Veut Gagner Des Milliones* (*Who Wants to Win Millions?*); in Turkey the program is *Kim 500 (besyiiz) milyar ister?* (*Who Wants*

500 Billion?). At the same time, the actual dynamics of the program wherever it is remade restrict the million pound, peso, deutschmark, or lira prize going off too often.

Successful rapid takeoff of the franchise has also much to do with outflanking unauthorised and unlicensed clones and look-alikes, vividly illustrated in Australia when a competing game show appeared on air at the moment of its first appearance. In early April 1999, the relatively smooth waters of Australian commercial television were ruffled by mid-season decisions at the Nine and Seven networks. A month earlier, the Nine Network, in conjunction with Grundy Television, announced that it was giving its most popular and long-running game show, *Sale of the Century*, a brief two-week respite. In its place the network planned to broadcast twelve half-hour episodes of a new game show, *Who Wants to Be a Millionaire?*. Grundy would make the Australian version. Eddie Maguire, a Melbourne businessman, president of the Collingwood Football Club and host of the high-rating *Footy Show*, was selected as host of *Millionaire*. McGuire had established a reputation in a short time as a celebrity through his high-profile presidency of the most popular Australian Rules football team. Almost a month before the launch on 18 April 1999, Nine began a saturation on-air promotion campaign. However, in the week before *Millionaire* began its initial two-week nightly season, the Seven Network announced its own launch of a new game show. *Million Dollar Chance of a Lifetime* was licensed from a British producer, Action Time. Hosted by Frank Warwick, a grey-haired schoolmaster-like newsreader, the would-be competitor began its broadcast on 14 April 1999, four days before the Celador format. Each program was successful in its first short season and Seven decided to run *Million Dollar Chance of a Lifetime* as a strip program in its weekday 5.30 pm timeslot. Nine counter-programmed *Millionaire* in the same slot. Within four weeks, Seven was forced to pull its million-dollar game show off the air as it was being trounced in the ratings.

This ratings competition between the million-dollar shows was accompanied by claims of format plagiarism. Depending on your point of view, the two programs were either similar or distinctly different. As their names imply, both offered a total prize of a million dollars. Similarly, contestants on both were given several 'lifelines' to help answer their questions correctly. Additionally, both groups of contestants were selected by means of similar systems based on telephone registries. The visual styles of the two were also substantially alike. In reality, however, *Who Wants to Be a Millionaire?* and *Million Dollar Chance of a Lifetime* were marked by some important engine differences. For example, despite the telephone registry system, the programs selected their contestants in quite different ways. There was disparity between the two in terms of the number of questions that a contestant faced to win the total prize of $1 million — ten in the case of *Million Dollar Chance of a Lifetime* and fifteen, later reduced to eleven, in the case of *Millionaire*. The lifelines also functioned differently in the two programs. Most importantly, though, the cash value of each question was set in advance for *Who Wants to Be a Millionaire?* while contestants on *Million Dollar Chance of a Lifetime* had a 'bank' and could wager on each question.

Asian *Millionaires*

In Asia, *Who Wants to Be a Millionaire?* was first broadcast in Japan in 2000. Two versions followed in Singapore in 2001, first in English, then in Chinese Mandarin. A Cantonese version of *Millionaire* was unveiled in Hong Kong in May 2001, while other versions followed in India (Hindi) and Indonesia (Bahasa). In India, the show, licensed by Rupert Murdoch's STAR Plus as *Kaun Banega Crorepati*, and hosted by the leading Hindi actor Amitabh Bachchan, generated unprecedented quiz show fever. Thomas and Kumar (2004) tell of how the phrase 'lock it in', spoken in cultured Hindi by Bachchan, found its way into everyday conversation. The program is easily transferable to local idioms elsewhere in Asia. In Indonesia, the format debuted in 2002 on Jakarta's RCTI channel. When Channel 13 in the Philippines licensed *Millionaire* it was translated into Filipino, even though English was well understood by the upper and middle classes, the obvious target audiences for the program. However, it was the re-versioning of *Millionaire* by the leading local network ABS-CBN which demonstrated that no international format has a guarantee of success. The local version, *Are you Ready for the Game* (*Game Ka Na Ba*), offered greater prizes — as well as a smart modernistic set (Santos 2004). In Singapore formatted quiz shows were successful at prime time in 2002/03. The local version of *Millionaire* even precipitated political controversy in Singapore. The production, first in English, and then in Mandarin Chinese, provoked passionate outbursts from Indian and Malay Singaporeans, who claimed that the show was pitched at the highly affluent Chinese majority (Lim 2004).

Millionaire achieved instant success in Japan, a country long conditioned to quiz shows, but resistant to imported formats. Fuji Television bought the Celador licence in 2000 and soon afterwards followed this with *The Weakest Link* (Iwabuchi 2004). The success, particularly of *Millionaire*, reflects a Japanese penchant for quiz formats. In May 2001, Asia Television Hong Kong

(ATV) licensed the first million-dollar quiz show in Hong Kong. The network outlaid US$3.8 million (HK$30 million) to acquire the licence for forty-eight episodes in the first season, starting on 29 April 2001. Before this, horseracing and Mark 6 — the only legal lottery in Hong Kong — were the fast tracks to instant wealth for ordinary people. Stripped of the dubious connotations of gambling, *Millionaire* became a legitimate and alternative means of acquiring a fast fortune. Its audience skyrocketed to 1.42 million in its seventh week and its success instigated a trend for acquiring global formats (Fung 2004).

The most notable modification under this franchising arrangement was that the local station was allowed to rename the program using a simpler Chinese name *Millionaire*. ATV program director Kai-yip Leung confirmed that the British head company Celador sent delegates to Hong Kong to ensure that Hong Kong's *Millionaire* complied with the original format — for instance, sets, musical effects, lighting, host, question design, graphics, audience dynamics and even the design of the cameras (*Ming Pao*, 3 July 2001: A3). While the ten participants in each episode were allowed to choose their dress and clothing, they would be asked to reshuffle seats if the Celador delegate felt that the colour of their outfits clashed with the colour of the stage. As in other national instances of the format, local flexibility pertained to the nature of questions. According to Leung (*Ming Pao*, 3 July 2001: A3), while the questions in the United Kingdom were more academic, the Hong Kong version allowed a wider range of questions, incorporating local tastes and entertainment.

On average, the hourly production cost of *Millionaire* in Hong Kong was low (US$80 000; approximately HK$624 000) compared with TV dramas (the hourly production cost of these is up to US$100 000 (HK$780 000) (*Sing Tao Daily*, 16 June 2001: B5). Despite paying licence fees to Celador within this cost package, the prime-time economics gave ATV an advantage over TVB, its competitor. And, despite the licensing requirements, the Hong Kong production was considerably cheaper than in many other countries. For example, in the United States, CBS's production cost an average US$700 000 per episode (which included prize costs and salary of the host) (*Oriental Daily*, 25 April 2001: International page). Likewise, there are scale economies in relation to the profits generated. It has been estimated that the US version generated a net profit for CBS of up to US$2 million. The profit of ATV was considerably lower due to market size (HK$1 million which is about US$130 000 per hour).

Send in the Clones

The dilemma of whether to purchase format rights from foreign providers or to simply localise and be damned exercised the minds of Chinese producers in 2001, a time when *Who Wants to Be a Millionaire?* fever swept the globe. Hunan City Television (Channel 5), a broadcaster in southern China — and, coincidentally, the home province of the great revolutionary leader Mao Zedong — was quick to seize the opportunities quiz formats offered. The Hunan station had taken heed of its younger cousin, Hunan Satellite Television, which had established a growing reputation as a risk-taking media consortium, even though the risks were generally about trying out ideas that had been successful elsewhere without paying for the rights. While some of Hunan Satellite's more interesting ideas, including weather reports delivered by sexy female presenters reclining on sofas, were eventually consigned back to the filing cabinet, the station was proactive in its policy of imitation. On 25 October 2001, the Hunan City station launched *Superhero* (*chaoji yingxiong*), a quiz challenge format that bore a striking resemblance to ATV Hong Kong's *Who Wants to Be Millionaire?* In true entrepreneurial spirit the Hunan producers dispensed with the problem of paying rights by simply making a clone. With a prize worth RMB500 000 on offer — a substantial amount of money in China — *Superhero* soon claimed the number one spot in regional ratings.

Meanwhile, China Central Television had been noticing the tumult down south and the worldwide impact of *Millionaire*. In an attempt to revitalise the freefall ratings of its economic channel (CCTV2), the network unleashed its own variant called *The Dictionary of Happiness* (*kaixin cidian*). According to the producer of *Dictionary*, a team at CCTV had looked far and wide for a format that suited Chinese audience tastes (interview by Keane, 21 June 2002). Rejecting the offer and the costs of the ready-made Celador format, they set to work to replicate it. To all intents and purposes, *Dictionary* and *Superhero* are Chinese adaptations of the Celador format, with all the accoutrements of interactivity, such as phone a friend, ask the audience, and the 50/50 elimination of choices. The calm demeanour of hosts is also influenced by the international version, as is the thematic music. The idea that success is based upon opportunism is flatly rejected, however. According to the producers of both shows, the Chinese versions were influenced by the 'foreign' formats — that is, the content is different and there are minor modifications and refinements.

In *Dictionary*, contestants proceed through three stages, worth RMB1000, RMB5000 and RMB10 000 respectively (US$1 = RMB8). It is noteworthy that the contestants on China's national broadcaster receive prizes and not cash, as in *Millionaire*. Contestants are recruited via an online testing system which filters out the weak (analogous to the political system). In contrast to its European precedents which allow a greater cross section of performers, the Chinese version focuses more on the super-intelligent. In addition, before proceeding to the actual contest, prospective contestants are screened for obvious defects that would make this less appealing to audiences; the successful ones are then given instructions on how to 'perform' — for instance, how to present to the audience when introduced. These introductory vignettes where contestants assume a slightly outrageous pose to camera, mimic the introductions of *Millionaire*. Again, according to the producers, this *may* be coincidence. The eccentric gestures to cameras, such as thumbs up and big toothy smiles, diminish the nerdy stereotypes usually associated with quiz shows.

Apart from a lower prize threshold, another important modification that characterises the Chinese show is the nomination of family members who will receive the prizes on offer. The family members are brought on to the stage, not just as significant others of the contestant, but as a family unit. In this way, winning represents a family dream (*jiating mengxiang*). The proceedings are moderated by the attractive Wang Xiaoya, who superseded a number of male quiz masters to become the visible celebrity icon of *Dictionary*. In justifying the bona fides of the Chinese show, the producers of *Dictionary* argue that the questions asked in *Millionaire* are trivial, while the Chinese questions constitute socially useful knowledge (interview by Keane, 21 June 2002). The questions, which are available on China Central Television's (CCTV's) website, have a distinctly pedagogic and often governmental flavour:

Example 1 (used in the final selection round)

If you have to turn in fake money to the authorities you should go to:
A: police
B: Bank of China
C: a shopping centre
D: a branch of a bank
E: any public bank

Answer (A, B, D, E)

Example 2 (used in round three)

Which of the following animals is the symbol of Chinese ancient law?

A: dragon
B: tiger
C: turtle
D: leopard
E: unicorn

Answer (D)

(Xie 2001: 51)

CCTV has been at the forefront of format imitation in recent years. When one of the authors spoke with the producer of another high-rating CCTV show that had blatantly copied a UK game format, the response was that 'now we are now in the World Trade Organisation we know the rules of the game'. In effect, this means that justifying the 'influence' of international programs is no longer necessary because international law doesn't protect formats. This is a dilemma that we will ponder in more detail in Chapter 11.

Concluding Remarks: Quiz Shows on Steroids

Celador's *Who Wants to Be a Millionaire?* provides an exemplary case of how the format movement of the late 1990s disrupted the conservatism of broadcast television, in the process, changing the rationale for licensing content across territories. *Millionaire*, like the reality game show *Survivor*, evolved through successive iterations and unsuccessful pitches to networks, finally hitting the ratings target (see Chapter 11). Old-style quiz shows were dispatched to the margins of programming, while nerdy contestants received make-overs and media training. Echoing the moment in the 1950s in the United States when *$64,000 Question* blew away competitors, *Millionaire* again raised the bar, introducing new engines, interactivity, and ancillary merchandising rights.

While *Who Wants to be a Millionaire?* might seem like a 1980s quiz show on steroids, its emergence is part of a wider movement towards independent production that has allowed new ideas to contend for producer interest. In fact, the venerable quiz show has received an even more radical makeover. These 'information challenges' are the subject of the following chapter.

7

Knowledge, Economy, and Government

Even if a man is bad, how can it be right to cast him off?
– Chinese saying attributed to the sage Laozi, 604 BC

Good-bye, you are the weakest link.
– attributed to Anne Robinson, the host of *The Weakest Link*

In the penultimate round of a Chinese quiz show, three contestants remain. The rules of the contest call for the nomination of an opponent who will be cast off, leaving two in the final round. In this episode, broadcast in 2002, two of the participants collude to cast off the strongest challenger (that is, the person who has answered most questions correctly). In the ensuing final round, the weaker of the two finalists jumps to an unexpected lead and takes the jackpot.

As the final credits roll on this Chinese version of *The Weakest Link* (suitably titled *The Wise Rule*), the winner reveals the successful strategy. For her, the contest is like a 1500-metre distance race: 'If you run quickly to the front, you are likely to be overtaken, so it's best to bide your time and wait for the opportunity to strike.'

Following the winner's disclosure in the above contest, her tactical manoeuvre attracted the scrutiny of critics. 'Why is it that the strongest is eliminated in the early rounds but the less smart contestants aren't?' asked one academic. 'It's because everyone has their own self-interest. The strongest contestant has the power to win the final prize so it's better to eliminate him. The program explores the dark side of people's psyche and should be called "the stupidest rules"' (Yuan 2002).

The Wise Rule was first broadcast in 2002 on Nanjing Television (NTV), the main city channel in Jiangsu province, north-west of Shanghai. In this well-known accumulation/elimination format, the participants work as a team to build up a bank balance. This accumulation process takes place when a quota of questions is answered correctly within a time limit with each correct answer effectively adding another link to the chain of accumulation. However, when a question is answered incorrectly, the chain is broken and the process begins again — hence the concept of 'the weakest link'. The chain also restarts if a player calls out 'bank' before their question. When this happens, the accumulated money is safe. In Taiwan, *The Weakest Link* (localised as *The Wise Survive [zhizhe shengcun]*) failed to survive, with some critics suggesting the host's demeanour and her abstruse questioning were culturally insensitive and inappropriate (Liu and Chen 2004). However, the concept of the 'weakest link' and the show's cultural appropriateness were interpreted more positively in mainland China and Hong Kong.

In China, the UK distributor ECM initially approached Shanghai Oriental Television, one of the country's largest networks. The concept of paying for a foreign franchise failed to appeal to the pragmatic local broadcaster, which later produced its own imitation, *The Examination Room of Wealth (caifu da kaochang)*. According to a spokesperson from the Shanghai production company, a quiz show needed atmosphere, local flavour, and audience involvement — all features that they claimed were conspicuously lacking in the UK format. Heading off suggestions of plagiarism, the spokesperson was quick to opine that television producers were all cooking in the same big pot, an interesting take on the standard format business metaphor of the 'pie and the crust' (Wang 2002).

The subsequent sale of the ECM licence to Nanjing TV, operating through a Beijing-based production company, the Beijing Eastern Cultural Broadcasting Company, represented a calculated gamble by the local station. However, in a significant concession to local sensitivities, the format's licensors permitted modifications within the host–contestant relationship. In contrast to the bitchy, cajoling Anne Robinson prototype in the UK version, the Chinese quiz mistress was an attractive journalist, Shen Bing, who encouraged rather than belittled contestants. With structures of feeling more attuned to Chinese society, contestants entered into the spirit of elimination, contending to the end for the ultimate pay off and even taking 'the walk of shame'.

In this chapter we explore the relationship between quiz formats and economic development. We begin with a brief discussion of the penetration of such shows within Asia. Following this, we examine the social impact when traditional understandings of knowledge intersect with contemporary knowledge capitalism. We then look closely at how imported formats, particularly *Who Wants to Be a Millionaire?* and *The Weakest Link*, refashion the relationship between government and entrepreneurship, and between ethical values and expediency. In particular, we encounter perceptions that these two shows reflect different but similar value systems. In the parlance of television production, we might say that they work on different 'engines'. Difference resides in the fact that the *Millionaire* engine reflects a tradition of accumulated intellectual capital that can be exchanged for economic capital. To assist this transaction, there are the lifeline engines: phone a friend, ask the audience and 50/50. The game provides rewards to a small minority of the educated class, in contrast to *The Weakest Link* format, which reflects a more strategic use of intelligence and fast-thinking to win the prize. In this latter struggle for knowledge, the prisoner's dilemma engine is built in, allowing competitors to work together to undermine a stronger opponent. In the context of contemporary social relations, the latter has greater relevance. However, similarities exist in the newness of these formats, their use of modern sets and moments of great tension, all skilfully moderated by popular hosts.

More recently, the format boom of the last decade has precipitated a new generation of quiz shows in which the challenge is more than answering questions or guessing the price of commodities. Anne Cooper-Chen's analysis (1994), *Games in the Global Village*, offers a comprehensive typology, nominating 'mixed' and 'interactive' formats as ways of structuring analysis. It is instructive to note that her core proposition is that these are game shows (Cooper-Chen 1994). Taking a middle-road approach, we use the term 'information challenge', which connotes a tension between pure information or knowledge and other kinds of life-skills, including negotiating, forming alliances and presentation of a positive self-image.

Quiz shows proliferated on East Asian television for many years, often with a schoolteacher host interrogating brainy students. The information challenge is more of a sudden-death format, often with elimination built into a narrative of survival. More recently, internationally syndicated information challenges have appeared in Asian television schedules — whether as early evening commodity contests *(Wheel of Fortune)* or prime-time winner-takes-all and elimination contests *(Millionaire, The Weakest Link)*. There are a number of reasons for this. First, such shows are relatively easy to produce and have historically received loyal support from audiences. Fascination with celebrity and money regularly out-rates political issues, and such popular formats allow 'ordinary people' to appear alongside celebrities.

Information challenge shows are pedagogic by definition and are popularly received by content gatekeepers in countries with authoritarian and communitarian regimes. In contrast, winner-takes-all reality game shows, such as *Survivor,* have not found the same kind of audience acceptance in parts of Asia, compared with their success in the more individualist American, European and Australasian markets (see Chapter 6). Finally, the offer of lucrative cash prizes has helped these shows to achieve success, forcing the many low-budget quiz shows out of the ratings market.

Overall, we observe that both information challenge and quiz shows endorse prudentialism and family asset management, both core values in East Asian society. In addition to these traditional ideals, such formats reproduce ideologies of development and economic reform. Ideological reproduction occurs on two levels. First, the answers to questions — which in most cases are either multiple choice or true/false — accord with approved history, closing down the opportunity for alternative knowledge that might challenge the status quo. Second, information challenge shows cash in on the long process of knowledge acquisition that reproduces Confucian hierarchies of authority and deference. Information challenges reward intelligence, diligence and common sense; in doing so, they reinforce the idea that investment in education brings remuneration to the family.

Coalitions and Contestations: Social Relations in the Modern City

In contrast to the more conventional quiz format of Celador's *Who Wants to Be a Millionaire?*, the 'peer' elimination format of *The Weakest Link* epitomises capitalist accumulation. In a transitional society like China, it might be fair to assume that such values meet with disapproval. However, whereas displays of 'bourgeois individualism' and self-interest were a punishable offence during the 1960s and even socially divisive during the 1980s, it is now acceptable to enrich one's bank balance by correctly answering general knowledge questions and undermining challengers.

In another twist on the program's anticipation of social norms, both the viewing public and participants are subject to the will of the majority decision. This follows the logic of many political contests where the party machine often chooses leaders who are most likely to support factions. In China, a country with a long history of internecine struggles, strategic coalitions are critical for social mobility and economic advancement. It is not surprising that Chinese viewers are able to identify with these strategies. The process of elimination and alliances also reflects business hierarchies where promotion is often a cut-throat affair and merit is not always the indicator of success (see Fevreir and Linnemar 2002).

Information challenge shows further resonate with Chinese sensibilities. In extolling the traditional virtues of conscientiousness and diligence, they draw on the Confucian tradition of the superior man — the idea that anyone can ascend to a higher social rank through learning. In this way, they accentuate meritocracy, the basic premise of which is that the better you are, the more you stand to gain. In reality, however, a fully liberal and meritocratic society is not realisable. Nor did Confucianism provide many social climbing opportunities for women. Giddens (1998) has argued that meritocratic societies are unequal on the level of income distribution. Indeed, *The Weakest Link* is far from meritocratic. There is a sub-text of survival. Under dim blue lights, the contestants are cast into a complex competitive environment. The calculating self-interest of neo-liberalism surfaces as the end-game strategy echoes social reality. Knowledge is essential, but shrewdness, cunning and pretence are just as important. Quite often it is a mediocre contestant who remains standing in the final stages.

According to one Chinese viewer's bulletin board posting, 'When I first saw *The Weakest Link* I couldn't understand why it concerned itself with these kind of struggles, but when I think deeper I realise it is more innovative than standard quiz shows (like *Dictionary of Happiness* and *Lucky 52*). It demonstrates real intelligence whereas the others are just dealing in the kind of knowledge you learn from books.' The writer goes on to say, 'I like this show because you can see a variety of different personality types, and you can see people who are really wily but who appear slow-witted *(dazhi ruoyu)*' (Wang 2002).

Normalising the Knowledge Economy: The Will to Power

The question of why these shows resonate with audiences in East Asia is more complex and deep-seated than in their Western countries of origin. In addition to the core value of *renqing* (the importance of human relationships) that works against some, in the more individualistic shows like *Survivor*, there is a strong connection between government and the people in East Asia that has historically been mediated by the 'knowledge economy' — albeit a different transactional form from the one celebrated within contemporary capitalism. In traditional Confucian society, the scholar-gentry class administered the provincial and central organs of government. This scholar-gentry class had authority to interpret the *Five Classics* (the Confucian books of knowledge) and to use this authority for personal aggrandisement. The longevity of the classical Chinese tradition is testimony to the gentry's reluctance to tamper with a symbolic order that preserved their own social ranking.

Inherent in this ordering of society was a pedagogical concern with proper conduct and the idea that through attainment of a high canon of learning, one would be elevated to a superior rank. In addition, a superior ethical disposition was said to be achieved through education in the classics. This superior state, although attainable by a person (male) of the lowest rank, was considered out of the reach of the 'common people', who were held by Confucius *(Kongzi)* to be lacking in ethical refinement. The Confucian *Classics* also had little to say about money, apart from the fact that the merchant class was ranked lower than the scholar-gentry class and needed the latter's support. In other words, knowledge was a form of power, such that a 'knowledge economy' predated the modern period. Alexander Woodside notes that from the end of the 1500s in the Confucian societies of China, Korea, and Japan, a concern emerged with economic management. This so-called 'practical learning' was articulated as 'order the state and save the world' *(jingguo jishi)*. The abbreviated form of this — *jingji* — now translates into the Western concept of economy in Chinese (Woodside 1998; also Woodside 2006: 57).

The importance of knowledge is further regulated by scarcity. By the late nineteenth century, China was open to various forms of scientific and technical knowledge (Spence 1991). Like economic capital, knowledge capital — particularly technical knowledge — was in short supply until well into the twentieth century. Intellectuals, the traditional disseminators of knowledge, have played a key role in China's modernisation since the 1980s. However, learning has not always been accepted as conducive to government. There were periods under Chairman Mao Zedong's stewardship in the 1950s and 1960s when both educated and business classes were on the receiving end of shaming (ironically, anticipating *The Weakest Link*).

In the first decade of the twenty-first century, the importance of knowledge has further been accentuated by privatisation of education, which in countries such as China, Hong Kong, Korea, and Taiwan, has created great pressures on students to deliver returns on investment — that is, the investment by the family in the education of the children. Accordingly, educational investment is value that is added. In the Chinese contemporary lexicon of development this essence is termed *suzhi*, roughly glossed as 'quality'. Andrew Kipnis (2006) has written of this mysterious commodity, noting how educational reform is justified in terms of quality. Ann Anagnost (2004) writes that *suzhi* sets up a contradistinction between the low quality of the uneducated rural body and the accumulated competencies that are often prescribed in children by middle-class families. In other words, the labour of parents in providing children with resources to be successful is emblematic of the production of value in contemporary China. Since 1990, private institutions have provided 70 percent or more of tertiary education in Japan, Korea and Taiwan (Yusuf 2004). China has likewise also introduced reforms into its educational sector, allowing more private colleges to contend with state education providers. It is now estimated that 98 percent of Chinese government provincial officials have a tertiary education, compared with 20 percent in 1982. Among younger leaders — the so-called 'fourth generation' — two-thirds hold masters or PhD degrees (Ramo 2004: 20). The new focus on knowledge parallels discussions of the knowledge economy, bringing the acquisition of knowledge in line with economic development and entrepreneurship. Knowledge is the currency of development and its dissemination in new forms legitimates the prizes on offer in modern quiz shows. In short, knowledge is power. Despite the knowledge frenzy, one critic commenting on *The Weakest Link* argues that even though the knowledge economy is presented as support of such shows, the questions are too trivial to uphold this association. Rather, it is the interrelationships between contestants that attract viewers, often in a cruel way (Wang 2002).

Hong Kong: The Information Challenge Format and Political Stability

The relationship between government, economy, and knowledge comes into finer focus as we investigate the popularity of information challenge shows in Hong Kong. The former British colony's reunification with the People's Republic of China (PRC) in 1997 promised a new epoch for a population which had lived under uncertainty and instability in the period leading up to the transition of power. Likewise, the new millennium offered hopes for advancement, opulence and rejuvenation following the Asian financial crisis of the 1990s. However, neither the return of Hong Kong nor the turn of the century brought relief. In 2000, Hong Kong was in economic disarray and the government seemed to have no solutions to the downturn. The city's annual budget deficit was eating into the reserve. During this period, Hong Kongers waited anxiously for the economy to rebound. Prior to the handover to China in 1997, many had already left for countries such as Canada or Australia — where governments provided welcome mats for economic migrants. In the new Hong Kong Special Administrative Region, consistently depressing news on employment, salary reductions, and the plunging stock market and estate property values was producing a crisis in confidence, which was impacting upon the former colony's psyche. People needed reassurance for their future.

Prior to the economic downturn, the quick path to prosperity in Hong Kong was stock and property investment markets. The ongoing pessimism over the bubble economy, along with cynicism towards profiteers, normalised economic citizenship by redirecting attention to a more traditional path of wealth acquisition. This was the Confucian ethic of diligence and perseverance — a hard and slow trajectory that stood in contrast to the myth of the Hong Kong entrepreneur willing to take risks. In the time-honoured tradition, knowledge acquisition was again paramount.

While the early shows were modest, low-budget affairs that were attuned to the ethos of development in Hong Kong, the information challenge formats that took the television world by storm in 2001/2002 were flashy and ostentatious. Nevertheless, there is a common reference point: the message of the early shows was that intellectual capital could eventually be exchanged for economic capital. In the new millennium, this was a message that made sense.

The internal logic of quiz and information challenge shows filled a kind of spiritual void. Knowledge was redeemable for wealth. These shows were correctives to the over-emphasis on opportunism: they reinstated the value of knowledge and the idea that, by acquiring knowledge, people could achieve success — and Hong Kong could regain its dynamism. The paradox, however, was that the ethic of risk taking in the economic sphere was transferred to a mediated reality. In short, success packaged with celebrity status became good television in bad economic times. Positive and generally uplifting, these shows pointed towards a way out of economic hardship, if only for a clever minority.

The prime-time phenomenon of ATV's *Who Wants to Be a Millionaire?* prompted competitor Television Broadcast Limited (TVB) to take the unprecedented step of licensing *The Weakest Link* in August 2001. Even the traditional conservative government television station Radio Television Hong Kong went with the flow, repackaging existing junior school quiz shows to regain popularity. Upping the ante, TVB acquired *Russian Roulette* from Colombia TriStar International Television in mid-2002. And, after the first series of *Who Wants to Be a Millionaire?* finished at the end of 2001, ATV bought Celador's *People Versus* (one of the BBC's highest-rating programs in 2000) and *Vault* from an Israeli production company in 2002. In addition to this buying in of ready-made formats, Hong Kong broadcasters also created indigenous information challenge formats, *Brainworks* and *Knowledge Is Power*. The latter was launched by Asia Television at the end of 2001. The title and theme of this program coincided with the government's focus on the knowledge economy, further promoting the idea that following the yellow brick road of knowledge acquisition would lead all the way back to economic stability.

The Knowledge/Money Dialectic

Much of the mythology of Hong Kong's rise to power during the 1950s and 1960s notes a celebration of the intersection of capital and international knowledge. The knowledge/money dialectic, however, is not indigenous to Hong Kong, but is rather deeply embedded in colonialism. Rey Chow (1995) has argued that efficient colonial regimes contained political activism by diverting people's energy to the realm of economics and money making. This is, in contrast, to mainland China during the 1950s and 1960s, where the Communist Party sublimated people's energy into altruistic nation-building and prohibited economic aggrandisement (Ci 1993). The stronger the Hong Kong colonial government's focus was on market activities, the more democracy was neglected. Prior to the transition back to China in 1997, the colonial government de-emphasised civic participation — even deleting significant coverage of modern Chinese history from the Hong Kong education syllabus. Knowledge acquisition was thus contained within the sphere of economics and markets.

It is important to point out at this juncture that the dialectic of knowledge/money — the foundation of information challenge quiz shows — is culturally compatible with the dominant ideology and indirectly serves to stabilise the status quo. Quiz shows prescribe knowledge with standard answers. An exemplar of the new 'knowledge economy' discourse brokered through quiz shows was *Culture* (*Chong Wah Chong Yuen Hung*, literally meaning Chinese cultural ambassador). It targeted educators and high-school students in Hong Kong, Macau, China and other South-East Asian cities. The show was sponsored by the Global Foundation of Distinguished Chinese Limited, a semi-official, non-profit organisation founded by tycoons and patriots with headquarters located in the Xinhua News building (*Three Weekly*, 30 June 2001: 48). The stated purpose of the program was to develop Chinese culture, although it should be noted that this is an endorsed version of Chinese culture. Broadcast by TVB and sponsored by the Hong Kong Education and Manpower Bureau and the Leisure and Culture Service Department, the program provided its own standardised answers. They were drawn from a book published by the Global Foundation of Distinguished Chinese in 2001 entitled *Chinese Culture: Common Knowledge and Standard*. Furthermore, there is only one version of the answers and these are listed on the TVB webpage.

Some questions specified that the enduring values of the Chinese people are harmony (that is, they are peace loving) and respect for multi-ethnicity; other questions even specified who can be regarded as national heroes. Obviously, the standard answers present a politically correct, official view of China, including Taiwan and Tibet as part of China. Such prescriptive questions and answers are a subtle refinement of propaganda; they uphold the official ideology of the state and show the Hong Kong government's complicity with Communist Party historiography.

As mentioned earlier, the forerunner to the contemporary information challenge show was less politicised and less global in its reach. The first quiz shows of note in Hong Kong were broadcast in the 1970s. TVB's *Fa Wong Kui Lok Bo* (Fa Wong Club) enjoyed much popularity at the time. In this program, the host, Wu Cheung Chiu, asked simple, common-sense knowledge questions, often helping the participant with hints. The winners were often offered a choice between gifts and money, one of which would be more valuable than the other. Quite ostensibly, the show was about 'testing' knowledge. However, it also distributed wealth, a strategy that attracted and interested local audiences. In these early days of quiz shows, the message was simple: only by working hard and acquiring knowledge could people earn a living in the developing industrial economy.

Despite the success of the television quiz, the value of intellectual capital was downplayed. The boom economy of the 1980s and 1990s meant that the monetary awards of television programs paled in comparison with the real revenues people could acquire in other financial activities. The bubble eventually burst. The post-economic crisis environment of the mid-1990s was the catalyst for a rethink of boom capitalism. From an institutional perspective, Hong Kong's government sought to transform an industrial economy to a knowledge economy. Inscribing Hong Kong as a knowledge economy to some extent lessened the blame of government for the high unemployment rate and poor economic growth, as the sluggish economy could be attributed to the temporary effect of restructuring (Grammaticas 2001). Similar official discourses also prevailed in many parts of East Asia as governments attempted to replicate Silicon Valley prototypes of the new economy/knowledge economy. One essential element in the blueprint for a new knowledge economy is a psychology that 'creative entrepreneurs' are willing to take risks (Mok 2003). The association of a new economy with a knowledge economy provides television quiz formats with credibility: they bridge the divide between pure knowledge and the institutional milieu of Hong Kong that celebrates entrepreneurship, and they create an atmosphere of tension and excitement in which people have to evaluate their risks, gains and losses.

The high tide of quiz fever ended in about early 2002. In Hong Kong, ratings of both *Who Wants to Be a Millionaire?* and *The Weakest Link* had deflated by late 2001. However, the information challenge format still lingered. ATV suddenly relaunched *Millionaire* in September 2002, and TVB responded by re-launching the celebrity version of *Brainworks* in May 2003 after terminating its quiz show *Russian Roulette* in October 2002. This durability indicates that, despite over-familiarity with the format, viewers still value the discourse of knowledge/money. The knowledge/money complex, however, is not ephemeral; it is widespread in Asian developing countries and complements the mode of governmentality that produces economic stability and social order (Foucault 1977; Hindess 1996; Rose 1999; Bennett 1998).

Mainland China: Competition for Knowledge

The knowledge economy discourse had a flow-on effect in mainland China. In December 2001, the *People's Daily* published an article that accepted a World Bank report arguing that China needed to make a substantial readjustment of its development strategy and to take its place in the knowledge revolution (*China Daily*, 14 December 2001). This view was supported in another account of China's position in the world of knowledge where the author also echoed the World Bank's directive that China needed to develop a knowledge development strategy for the twenty-first century through strategies that included improving the capacity of the general public to assimilate and use knowledge (Hu 2003: 261).

The evolution of information challenge formats in the PRC is evidence of the increasingly competitive society that began to emerge during the 1980s as the country embraced economic form, and with it, a breakdown of the egalitarian society, the 'great society of the communist ideal'. While games were part of socialisation, even during the high tide of Maoist orthodoxy (1950s–70s), the concept of 'winner takes all' was contrary to the stated goals of socialism, namely social equalisation. Games were intended for developing group consciousness, whereas spare time was an opportunity to read political works (Wang 1995). Even though televised quiz shows began to appear on the small screen during the 1980s, it wasn't until 2001 that significant prizes were permitted.

From the time of television's rapid development stage, beginning in the early 1980s, the quiz show played a key role in educating and informing Chinese citizens about their nation and the world outside that was gradually opening up to scrutiny. In comparison to today's new hybrid information challenges featuring flashy set designs and interactivity, 1980s quiz shows were directed at children and young adults; teams from schools provided the contestants with simple prizes such as stationery as a reward for excellence. The design of sets was uncomplicated: two rows of facing desks for contestants, a host who also acted as mediator and judge, and live audiences made up primarily of school students and teachers. The early shows focused mainly on factual and academic knowledge, reflecting a notion that the media had an educative rather than an entertainment function. The television stations often organised these quiz shows around special events — for instance, Children's Day (1 June) or May Fourth Day (the celebration of the Chinese intellectual rebellion in 1919). In 1980, Guangdong Television in southern China produced the *June 1st Knowledge Prize Competition (6.1 you jiang zhili jingcai)*, and the following year Beijing Television commemorated May Fourth with the *May Fourth Television Knowledge Contest (5.4 qingnian jie dianshi jingcai)*.

During the 1980s, Beijing Television launched a regular program called *The Family 100 Second Knowledge Contest (jiating baimiao zhishi jingcai)*. This was hosted by Wang Ji, who later achieved celebrity status playing a feisty Taiwanese businesswoman in the 1993 television series, *Beijingers in New York* (Keane 2001). In 1988, Shanghai Television launched a segment of its variety show *Zhengda zongheng*, as *The Great Knowledge Tide (zhili da chonglang)*, introducing an early participatory format in which a panel of celebrities fielded questions while allowing involvement from members of the audience. Audience participation contributed to television's democratisation, allowing ordinary people to have their brief time in the limelight (Yang 2000). In 1990, China Central Television (CCTV) took over production of the *Zhengda* (or *Chia Tai) Variety Show*, which incorporated many of the features of the Shanghai prototype, but aspired to become a window on the world for China's viewers, in turn, drawing on the Japanese model, *Naruhodo the World*, produced by Fuji TV. In this infotainment format, onstage participants, ranging from actors to teachers, would examine social customs, travel destinations, and nature footage that was either filmed by presenters on location or bought by the co-producer, the Zhengda *(Chia Tai)* Consortium.

The information challenge is a more recent hybrid. The merging of game and quiz elements has been a gradual process in China. In November 1998, CCTV opted to buy the licence rights to *Go Bingo/Lucky Numbers* from London-based distributor, ECM. The Chinese version was broadcast as *Lucky 52 (xingyun 52)* and created a precedent for fast-moving quiz shows featuring modernistic sets and idiosyncratic hosts who were capable of ad-libbing rather than just reading out questions. The format for *Lucky 52* was modified several times over the next few years, responding to the need for high-rating brand programs to keep several steps ahead of imitators.

The success of the information challenge formats reveals a great more about contemporary society than the format's predecessor, the humble 'quiz show'. The first point we should note is that these new programs have taken the *edutainment* concept to a new level. Not simply a pedagogic display of bright young minds, these shows open the stage to people of all ages, with different perspectives on celebrity and fame. The expected rash of imitations that has followed in the wake of successful new formats has, in turn, produced a 'race to the top' of the prize sweepstakes, anticipating a positional arms race. In order to offset cheap imitations, television channels invest more money in prizes, including straight-out cash incentives. The Chinese version of *The Weakest Link (The Wise Rule)* provided a prize jackpot of RMB50 000. These significant rewards for intelligence send a message to the community about the value of education and the gambles of living in a competitive society. Moreover, the change of emphasis from the weakest to the wisest — and ironically, to the wiliest — sends another message about skill sets required in the market economy. 'Ruling' in the contest means eliminating opponents who are threats; likewise, ruling in the market means getting an advantage over your opponent, whether by cleverness or skill. *The Wise Rule* is a contemporary version of Chinese society. It normalises the kinds of structural inequality that were the foundations of communist revolution and which continued through the decades as Chinese Communist Party leaders *(lingdao)* were anointed through factional struggles. Now the struggle is different. The market is the barometer of success. Viewers recognise that success is not measured by how good you are, but by how well you play the game — in other words, how well you form alliances and build relationships that enable you to ascend the ladder of success.

It is perhaps too early to judge whether the kinds of knowledge/money discourses promoted within information challenge shows are an indictment of late capitalism or a sign of East Asia's full integration into the global marketplace. Certainly, the choice of knowledge topics in these information challenges is more reflective of contemporary social relations under a market economy than the pedagogic science model characteristic of quiz shows of the 1980s and 1990s. The cultural phenomenon of information challenges brings together elements of performativity and normalisation. The social imperative to perform, as seen also in reality television, impels people to act according to norms. Here the rules of the game (the norms) are less negotiable than unscripted drama where there is greater scope for improvisation. Likewise, performative force is understood differently in different societies, and by different audiences, and this variation impacts upon how culture is invoked in different locations. This difference does not imply national cultural traits, but rather the institutional forces in different locales that guide the performance (see Yúdice 2003).

It is serendipitous, indeed, for governments in East Asia that the knowledge/money development strategy is aided by the discursive vehicle of quiz and information challenge shows. In most of the adult versions of information challenge shows, the 'power' of knowledge is directly equated with material rewards. However, information challenges did not invent the knowledge/money discourses; they acted as catalysts to expand and amplify what previously existed in traditional culture within a family context, but what had in the modern history of Hong Kong's colonisation been reduced to a more individualistic pursuit of wealth.

Concluding Remarks: On Governing Knowledge

Foucault (1977) has also warned of the problem of equating reason with freedom: in the case of many Eurocentric formats, freedom is reduced to the sovereign individual. Both audience and participants of these edutainment formats are subject to the purview of expert knowledge, administered by a genial host, but adjudicated by abstract authority. Moreover, when people are playing along with 'the rules of game', either as participants or as audience members, they are complicit in reproducing *the* reality that is framed by the expert knowledge of the authorities, in its various manifestations: elimination, children's quiz shows, *Wheels of Fortune*, instant millionaire-ship and so on. The eventual effect of such cultural technologies is the reproduction of knowledge that erases irregularities and produce 'docile' subjects.

On a more local level, there are positive outcomes. The answers to questions may be closed down, but the use of the popular discourse is open to all. The catch phrase, 'It is a popular wish that you should leave', uttered in *The Weakest Link* when the majority cast one of their members out of the competition, has found its way into the popular lexicon. In 2003, this popular phrase was used in a different context to compel senior secretaries of the Hong Kong government to step down (Lau 2003). This example sets the scene for our next investigation, in which mass participation talent shows provide platforms for ordinary people to step up and achieve extraordinary instant celebrity.

8

Super Girl and the Performing of Quality

When *Time Asia* magazine chose the winner of the Chinese TV talent contest *Super Girl* (*chaoji nüsheng*: literally 'Super Female Voice') for the cover of its annual 'Asian Heroes' issue, the story headline read 'Li Yuchun: Loved for Being Herself' (Jakes 2005). Tens of thousands of fans of the *Pop Idol* 'clone' had responded overwhelmingly in voting for the spiky-haired music student from Sichuan province, who some claimed resembled an animation character more than a standard Chinese pop star. Significantly, Li Yuchun's entry in the CNN–Time Warner consortium's parade of Asian heroes was not listed under entertainers, but icons. In spite of carrying off the biggest prize in the Chinese entertainment market, Li was regarded as iconoclastic, but *not* as an entertainer. Nevertheless, *Time Asia* seemed a little unsure. In explaining the icon's unavailability for an interview with the magazine, the report noted that 'one of her agents' feared such publicity 'would portray Li as more than just an entertainer' (Jakes 2005).

This exposure added more spice to a media frenzy about *Super Girl* within China. Viewers and fans endorsed *Time Asia*'s depiction of the winner as iconoclastic, expressing admiration that her 'brave' performance embodied more than just singing. The twenty-one-year-old Li's demeanour throughout the contest was ambiguous, challenging the conventions of Chinese television celebrities. Androgynous in looks, she was described by some as 'both male and female' (Xiao 2006). Rumours and malicious stories continued to circulate about her supposed lesbian tendencies; an internet blog even posted look-alike pictures that appeared to depict Li, bare-breasted, embracing a woman. On another plane of criticism, scholars entered into debates on distinctions between 'national heroes' and 'pop idols'. Obviously, with national hero status normally designated by the Ministry of Culture, the front cover publicity offered by a US-owned media conglomerate was tantamount to imperialism. Cultural sovereignty had been deviously breached by a foreign media company with an agenda of undermining China's democratic reforms. Elsewhere, *The Economist* announced 'Democracy Idol: A Television Show Challenges the Authorities' (*The Economist*, 8 September 2005). Drawing attention to the hubris, Chinese critics opined that if the *Super Girl* pop democracy model were to be extended to the political process — as some international reports audaciously suggested — then China's elected leaders would be as lacking in political skills as Li was deficient in vocal range. The fact that HSTV, an upstart southern China network, was complicit in promoting such a process further demonstrated the need for China Central Television (CCTV) to reassert its authority in popular programming. Leading CCTV personalities were among the most vocal critics of Li and *Super Girl*.

However, this animated debate may actually reveal less about Chinese aspirations for democracy than it does about the diminishing gap between high and low culture — and between high politics and everyday life. Television in China is not immune to the current wave of populism that sees individuals seeking to claim a temporary piece of fame. With the attribution of instant celebrity a defining currency of popular culture, amateur performers now assume an important role as gatekeepers of popular taste. Something akin to this occurred in another historical epoch long before the age of digital reproduction. From 1966 to 1976 amateurs took centre stage in China's Great Proletarian Cultural Revolution. Under Chairman Mao Zedong's attempts to reassert control of the nation, non-experts debunked the authority of teachers and professionals. Many persons of high social rank were reformatted as 'cow demons and stinking number nines' — abusive terms for intellectuals. While not ersatz media celebrities of the kind now regularly manufactured for popular cultural consumption, these amateurs nevertheless showed that ordinary people could perform the same tasks as professionals. The great upheaval of the Chinese Cultural Revolution is deemed by most writers to be a monumental and tragic mistake. Of course, this was adhocracy gone mad. It was anarchic and vengeful. The prize for nomination by neighbours was ritual public humiliation and, perhaps, a trip to the Chinese countryside to countenance a reality of corn bread and cabbage while learning about the truths of Marxism-Leninism from peasants. The inversion of fame in contemporary reality TV is a far more democratic and apolitical affair. The worst that can occur to contestants is public embarrassment — but even this is more often an attraction for aspiring pop stars or celebrities.

This chapter looks at fascination with *Idol* formats, and includes industrial formats as well as generic variants and clones. With media observers and pundits drawing attention to aspirations for democracy on the part of formerly repressed Chinese masses, expressed through the popular cultural ballot box, it is interesting to observe how the democratisation of participation has occurred in liberal democracies. Indeed, the 'engine' of audience adjudication has become a mainstay of popular TV formats globally ever since 2000. In particular, the *Big Brother* format has been a vehicle for the democratisation of celebrity, the secularisation of cultural production, and the participation of viewers. But what do these processes say about their viewerships? In an important study of *Big Brother*, Coleman (2003) found that avid viewers (termed BBs) were more 'ordinary' in terms of occupation than self-confessed critics of the show (political junkies, or PJs), who were twice as likely to be professional workers or managers. Moreover, the BBs felt disengaged from the political process. According to Coleman, 'The most persistent and overwhelming message from BBs concerned authenticity. They regarded politics and politicians as somehow "unreal" and believed that the opaque and devious construction of political imagery could be exposed through the lens of transparent media' (Coleman 2003: 25).

The concept of mediated democracy and contested elimination has taken off in East Asia, along with a boom in SMS and internet usage. Avid users of new technologies and their applications are more likely to be aged below thirty. China has over one hundred million internet users, while mobile phone ownership had exceeded 350 million by mid-2005 (CNNIC 2005). In examining the evolution of *Idol* shows in China and Hong Kong, we note audience familiarity with global formats and the idea of 'watching as if participating'. Moreover, there is a sense that these shows may well represent a challenge to the way we theorise identity politics in China. In liberal democracies, individualism is ideologically construed as a core value, and this includes the right to express one's sexuality and bodily appearance. In the mainland Chinese example, self-presentation has reached new levels of deviance from formally accepted television norms. Performativity (Butler 1990) — the manner in which people conform to or transgress norms — is embedded within an ethos of 'quality', which in the contemporary Chinese lexicon is expressed as *suzhi*. Andrew Kipnis (2006) has drawn attention to the increasing incidence of discourses pertaining to quality in China — from population quality *(renkou suzhi)* to quality education *(suzhi jiaoyu)*. According to one media educator interviewed, there are concerns to reform the *suzhi* of television anchors and presenters within Chinese broadcasting institutions (Chinese Communication University academic, interview by Keane 2005). In other words, presenters are being 'dumbed down', along with the content of reality and quiz shows. Some fear that the increasing commodification of media, the trend to clone television programs, and the appeasement of popular 'taste' have already eroded the authority of 'legitimate' role models. In writing about the *Super Girl* phenomenon, Xiao Hui (2006) sees neo-liberal discourses functioning as a sub-text in discussions surrounding quality and individuality/ the individual self *(ziwo)*. In the case of Li Yuchun's victory, the performativity of gender is subject to debate across media and in internet blogs. Modifications to accepted norms are, in turn, inscribed in new gender politics.

Image Presentation and Attributed Celebrity

In her discussion of reality television, Holmes (2004) points out that many reality shows 'make a claim to "reveal" or "expose" the process of fame construction — whether in terms of following "ordinary" hopefuls from the audition stages to their entrance into the media world, or by claiming to offer us an unprecedented "access" to existing celebrities ("stripping" away the celebrity façade)'. Celebrity stripping certainly occurred in the reality game show *I'm a Celebrity: Get Me Out of Here* (ITV, UK) in which a group of willing participants were stranded at a *Survivor*-style remote location. The subject of a legal dispute by the original devisors of *Survive!* (see Chapter 10), *I'm a Celebrity* offers an ironic take on celebrity by offering up a mix of minor celebrities and ex-celebrities seeking to revive flagging careers.

Whereas *I'm a Celebrity* enlisted people who self-identified as celebrities, the *Idol* TV format is a carefully constructed process of celebrity packaging from the backlots to backstage, and eventually to centre stage. Holmes (2004) writes that participants undergo a process of image transformation, yet the audience retains the memory of where they came from. Along with the actual discovery of talent is the suggestion that the *Idol* format may bring out some more real, more special self that is hidden. The road to becoming a media celebrity is mapped out with the aid of intermediaries, while the program ostensibly condenses 'the dues' that must be paid in the entertainment business into a TV ratings period. Hartley notes that in this format, 'Expert advice is still seen as necessary, not least perhaps because the successful contestant wins a recording contract, so attention needs to be paid to commercial realities' (2006). In the process, professionalism skews to amateurs and celebrity is created from bare aspiration. Rojek (2001) writes about three kinds of celebrity: ascribed, achieved, and attributed celebrity. The first of these refers to inherited celebrity, as in the case of the Japanese or British royal families. Achieved celebrity, on the other hand, connotes accomplishment in 'open competition' — the kind of status earned by actors or sports stars — while attributed celebrity refers to achievements that are not necessarily a fact of individual skill (Rojek 2001: 18).

Marshall has located the front-stage exploits of celebrity within the conceptual frame of governmentality which, in broad terms, suggests that the rational activity of the market and professionals combine to legitimatise certain forms of subjectivity that, in turn, enhance the value of individuality and personality (Marshall 1997, cited in Rojek 2001). The idea of 'can do', so central to US-flavoured neo-liberalism encounters expert guidance; in the *Idol* format, these are industry angels who have 'been there' and warn neophytes of pitfalls and offer advice. Psychologists and personal style consultants are also invited to participate.

A shift from ascribed and achieved celebrity to attributed celebrity represents a significant transformation in film and television industries within East Asia since the 1990s. Yeh and Davis (2002) point to the East Asian celebrity complex illustrated by Japanese film stars who, echoing a more institutional perspective, are 'flexible, high-end resources'. There is an almost production line quality to the continual reformatting of stars and celebrities. A critical theory perspective on *Idol* show formats would no doubt construe participants as mere products that are produced for mass consumption. However, it needs to be pointed out that such commodities are subject to evaluation by audiences that are conversant with the concept of 'image' construction (Holmes 2004).

The Youth Market

For advertisers and programmers alike, the youth market is the cash cow of program development. Avid consumers of fads and fashions, young adults are inclined to spend heavily on ancillary merchandising, while functioning as free promotional vehicles through electronic word of mouth. Whereas the married-with-children group, the professional class, and the retired are predisposed to television serial drama, hooking the sixteen to-twenty-nine year-old demographic has much to do with manipulating niches. In this environment, the breakthrough cult hit is king. During the 1980s and 1990s, when free-to-air networks ruled the broadcast world, quality television drama and sit-coms dominated prime time. Producing a blockbuster in the media remains a key to success, but even blockbusters like *ER* and *Big Brother* are not immune from plagiarism. The trend towards replicating other people's successes is aided by limited (international) copyright protection and comparatively short production lead times (Aris and Bughin 2005: 83). In this 'hit-and-run' industry, a hit show is more likely 'a serendipitous combination of a broad appeal to a mass audience and appearing on the right channel at the right time' (Griffith 2003: 102).

The viral hit program is an important development in the age of channel abundance. Such hit shows have appeared conspicuously in China. As discussed in Chapter 2, entertainment-based genres and formats came much later in China than elsewhere in East Asia. Ideas from Hong Kong and Taiwan were significant factors in the renovation of Chinese television from tedious propaganda to trendy variety formats. During the early stage of television development in the 1980s, south China set the benchmarks, although success was more often a case of fortuitous imitation. These southern stations had the advantage of proximity to Hong Kong and distance from the more politically and culturally conservative north. The example of Hunan Satellite Television's (HSTV's) *The Citadel of Happiness (kuaile daben ying)*, first broadcast in 1996, demonstrates how successful format adaptation, combined with self-reliant management strategies could build a youth-programming brand. The show consisted primarily of apolitical entertainment content based around social issues, youth lifestyle, and popular music. It drew closely on similar entertainment formats in Taiwan.

Echoing the current dispute between China's national broadcaster and HSTV, *The Citadel of Happiness* attracted criticism from Beijing. The producers were subsequently forced to justify its origins. According to management at HSTV, the show was of domestic origin, conceived in response to viewer dissatisfaction with the overly pedagogic tone of existing variety formats, a subtle swipe at CCTV's stable of national icons. Confident that it had a winning concept, the station invested substantially, promoting the show by bringing in celebrities from Hong Kong and Taiwan. The show was successful within a short time, with advertising rates exceeding even the most optimistic expectations. Within a matter of months, the program's own format had been cloned into multiple local variants within China itself, none of these attaining the heights of the original — a fact attributed to its youthful hosts Li Xiang and He Jiong, and its constant evolution in order to distance itself from its imitators.

Idols and New Heroes

The success of shows involving the participation of ordinary citizens created new expectations of what can be achieved with less money. In September 2004, China's Premier Wen Jiabao, in one of his frequent visits to CCTV, issued a directive for producers to create more programs focusing on ordinary people. In the normal course of events, this would entail more positive documentaries or 'main melody' dramas invoking narratives of good socialists overcoming hardships. However, the speech coincided with the launch of CCTV's talent show *Special 6+1 China Dream (Feichang 6+1 mengxiang Zhongguo)*, a seventy-minute program featuring average people vying for a chance at stardom on the program through various live acts.

CCTV was desperately trying to catch on to a new wave of programming. From the beginning of that year, shows featuring amateur singing stars had broken out across Chinese and Taiwanese television screens. The international success of the *Idol* formats had already spawned franchised copies and spin-offs in countries including the United Kingdom, Australia, Canada, and Malaysia. In reality, these shows were refashioning a format that had long featured on television in East Asia. Talent search programs were popular in Taiwan during television's formative years. These included TTV's *Five Star Prize (wu deng jiang)*, which ran for thirty-three years from 1965 to 1998, producing several superstars, including Jacky Wu (Wu Zong-Xian) and A Mei (Chang Hui-Mei). In 1997, two programs appeared that anticipated the arrival of the global *Idol* format: they were *Super New Idol (chaoji xin renwang)* (ETTV) and *The Great New Singing Competition (xinren gechang dasai)* (San Li TV). In 1998, MTV introduced *The New Karaoke Station (xinsheng kawei zhan)*, a singing competition with contestants from all over Asia. In 2004, the program *Super New Idol* received a new lease of life due to the global popularity of the *American Idol* format which was televised in Taiwan.

On the Mainland, the HSTV *Super Girl* was the market leader. Like other Hunan hit shows, it was a calculated approximation of foreign successes. It closely imitated ITV's *Pop Idol* (UK) and *American Idol* (Fox Network USA). The formula is much the same, while the rhetoric of viewer democracy is even more appealing in a country where voting for politicians is not endemic or central to social relations. According to the publicity, the Chinese program aims at manufacturing an idol 'from among ordinary people with the assistance of ordinary people'. Whatever the ingredient, this format performed rating miracles for HSTV, which had previously launched *Super Male Voice (chaoji nansheng)*. The male version had failed to excite, but the fact that 3000 people applied to be on the show within two weeks of its debut alerted its producers to something special. After repackaging by the Hunan Satellite TV (HSTV), *Super Girl* was promoted nationwide in May 2004. Soon after this, the station collaborated with other regional TV stations and the production company, Shanghai Tianyu Company, to create a more national edition called *Happy*

China Super Girl (kuaile Zhongguo chaoji nüsheng). This was broadcast on stations in Wuhan, Chengdu, and Nanjing.

Meanwhile, the popularity of an unsuccessful American-Chinese contestant on *American Idol* in 2004 helped to guarantee the success of the format in Hong Kong. In the US show, William Hung mimicked Ricky Martin, performing 'She Bangs' with a Chinese accent during his January 2004 audition. Hung quickly achieved 'attributed celebrity' through his presentation, which featured bizarre comic dance routines and a strained vocal performance. Nevertheless, his sincerity and earnest, but obviously flawed, renditions endeared him to both judges and audience. Soon after the show concluded, Hung earned a recording contract from Fuse Music Network and KOCH Records. His debut album made headline news on CNN while his celebrity status swept across Asia, with concerts in Singapore, an acting role with the 'real' celebrity Nancy Sit in Hong Kong, and even opportunities for advertisements in mainland China. Hung's popularity even increased to the point where internet rumours circulated that he had succumbed to the celebrity lifestyle and overdosed on heroin (Krupto 2004).

Despite the popularity of *American Idol* and Hung's attributed celebrity, the Hong Kong television industry was not tempted to acquire the international *Idol* licence. Stephen Chan, the General Manager of TVB, explained this reluctance as a function of the costs involved, as well as negative cultural compatibility (interview by Fung, 11 March 2005). Whereas the global *Idol* format emphasises aptitude, skill and diligence through self-improvement regimes, TVB considered these elements inimical to Hong Kong audience taste. On the other hand, post-modern pastiche — expressed as ridicule, laughter and audacity — has experienced success in the former colony, which now confronts a more sober and uncertain political reality. Hong Kong's TVB broadcast a talent show in February 2005 called *Minutes to Fame* (in Chinese, *canku yi ding*: literally 'the cruel bell'). This format follows the well-known NBC *Gong Show* model (1976), and has direct antecedents in shows such as the long-running *Red Faces* segment on Australian television which featured celebrity judges and a large gong (Channel 9). In *Minutes to Fame*, two presenters with an invited celebrity artist act as judges and 'ring away' performers who fail to impress. Participants can show their skills not only by singing, but by demonstrating skills in dance and juggling, and performing kung-fu and magic illusions. 'Singers' or performers will do almost anything humorous, nonsensical, and attention-grabbing to restrain the judges from dragging them offstage (two muscular, oversized guards escort the performers off stage when judges decree it is time to go). The contest is about how long the presenters and judges can tolerate the act. The winner in each episode — the one who remains the longest time on stage — proceeds to another round and receives financial gratification calibrated at HK$100 per minute.

Although some educators and religious organizations expressed outcry that the show was selling people's dignity for money, it was highly successful with a high-ratings mark of 2.5 million. The question remains: why was this kind of program so successful, and why did so many parents encourage their children to participate? Perhaps the underlying essence of this ridiculous *Idol* phenomenon in Hong Kong is epitomised by William Hung's 'legendary' words: 'I hope I've shown everyone in the world that regardless of success or failure, just keep trying. Never give up ... because only then can you say to yourself that you tried your best and had no regrets.'

What is more ironic than the show itself is its influence on the Chinese mainland and the background that framed the transfer of ideas. CCTV's *Feichang 6+1, Dream China (mengxiang Zhongguo)* adopted the *Minutes to Fame* format in order to challenge HSTV's *Super Girl* in July 2005. On 24 July, Alan Tam, the renowned Hong Kong singer, and Hacken Lee, one of the presenters of *Minutes to Fame*, were invited on to *Dream China*, suddenly inverting the language of the show from official Mandarin to non-official Cantonese. Even though the producers repeatedly emphasised that they rejected overt inanity, condescending attitudes to performers, and ridicule, the hybrid phenomenon gave an impression that only by annexing post-modern 'non-sense' into CCTV's serious format could the show attract back the national audience lost to *Super Girl* (*Beijing Morning Post*, 26 July 2005). Meanwhile, ATV (Hong Kong) also launched a similar idol show called *Instant Fame (yiju chengming)* in response to *Minutes to Fame*. In comparison to *Minutes to Fame*, however, performers were allowed to finish the songs and the audience could send SMS messages to vote for their favourites. And, extending its arms to China, participants were recruited from Guangzhou, the capital of Guangdong province.

Super Girl

While these various talent formats sound familiar in the light of the global *Idol* franchise, they were a new phenomenon in mainland China, attracting the attention of cultural and industry critics who proclaimed a new stage of development in TV culture. *Super Girl* took south China by storm, with huge numbers of applicants registered in Changsha (16 000), Nanjing (11 000), Wuhan (10 000) and Chengdu (10 000). The director, Peng Zhijian, admitted that the program took similar overseas programs as reference models, but he also claimed that the producers tried every possible means to localise the formula. This included a more complex system of adjudication in which selected audience members get to pass comments directly to the three judges, including adjudication on the judge's own performance (Duan and Deng 2006).

According to some critics, the success factors of *Super Girl* indicated a road ahead for entertainment programs. Three success factors, in particular, were advanced in support of the format: the ordinary nature of the entertainers, simple sets, and interactivity. The engine of *Super Girl's* success in the Chinese market is 'the ordinary idol' phenomenon *(pingmin ouxiang)*. Much more than just a substitute for popular aspirations for political democracy — albeit via SMS and not the political process — the show taps into widely held attitudes towards power and authority. The ordinary people formed the substantive core of the national project within the Chinese Communist Party's constitution. However, their role in film and television had been primarily as heroes and heroines in narratives of progress, while celebrities had cashed in on the entertainment market. The so-called non-elite *(pingmin)* character of shows like *Super Girl* confirms the everyman aesthetic that resonates with a previous era of unadorned fame: there is no dazzling stage, participants audition for thirty seconds with no musical track, and they face a highly critical and even satirical jury. Audiences then vote for their favoured participants; the rest are eliminated and end up either as blooper material or 'worst of' out-takes that contrast with the careful grooming of the new idols.

Involving the masses in such a quasi-democratic fashion reflects a change in the ideology of TV entertainment. Chinese TV had used the star formula *(mingxing biaoyan)* during the 1980s and 1990s. In the transition to a commercial media model, stars were the focal point of entertainment shows and audience members were merely onlookers — with the notable exceptions of benchmark shows like CCTV's *Chia Tai Variety Show (zhengda zongyi)*, which at least interrogated the audience members. The audience is now not only the viewer but also the content of the program. In reinventing the socialist mass line in this manner, *Super Girl* — as well as other contemporary mass participation shows — reflects a trend by which popular culture destabilises the hegemony of elite cultural forms, echoing global critiques of subsidised state culture (see Carey 2005). Hedonistic fun-seeking and gamesmanship undermine the solemn models of cultural development once espoused by the Ministry of Culture.

Points of substantial similarity with *Idol* are numerous. Like the franchised international versions the three judges in *Super Girl* are strong personalities, they are frequently rude, and they refrain from too many facial expressions. Also like the international versions, interactivity adds value through internet sites and is accounted for by SMS voting. Cross-platform collaboration with internet service providers helped *Super Girl* to maintain consistently high ratings. Enticing prizes also contribute to ratings: the package for the champion includes a car, a contract, and an album especially designed and tailored in their image. The production company likewise follows the international model of using such talent shows to sign successful participants to recording contracts. In short, the process generates a relatively low-cost form of talent scouting.

The economic benefits from *Super Girl* were extraordinary in the context of Chinese television history. People who opted to vote were charged one renminbi (US$0.13) for the privilege. In the semi-finals, each contestant received an average of three million votes with a limit of fifteen votes per day for each phone number. Fans overcame this ruling by multiple voting on their parents and friends' phones. The company responsible for marketing the performers and aggregating ancillary rights such as merchandising, concerts, and CDs — the aptly named *yule baozhuang gongsi (The Entertainment Package Company)* — accrued RMB78 million in revenue. Telecom carriers associated with the show — China Telecom, China Netcom, and the Telecommunications Operations Company — recouped RMB9 million, receiving 15 percent of each SMS call. The other 85 percent from SMS was apportioned among Hunan Satellite TV (HSTV), the producers, and other interests. Altogether, HSTV earned RMB68 million while the producer, Shanghai Tianyu, reaped RMB27.5 million. Other big winners were the internet service providers, Tom.com and Zhangshang Lingtong, which provided constant updates and gossip to SMS subscribers. They recouped RMB21 million. A further one million renminbi was earned by companies who advertised on dedicated *Super Girl* web and chat sites (Duan and Deng 2006). The biggest winner, however, may well have been the show's sponsor, Mongolian Cow Yoghurt, whose income from its products associated with the TV show totalled RMB550 million.

Social Benefits

Critics have claimed that *Super Girl* and other copycat programs cater to vulgar tastes and low culture *(meisu)*; they are low-quality productions; and they rely too much on copying (or cloning) foreign programs with insufficient localisation. The former political dissident Liu Xiaobo, who was central in the post-1989 Tiananmen Square denunciations, provides a dismissive line on the quasi-democratisation of the show. Liu points to a spiritual crisis in China where 'vulgar entertainment' programs are allowed, but serious public figures are banned from discussion (Liu 2005). The mimicking of some Western ideas, regardless of different cultural and social contexts, has likewise provoked critical outcry — for instance, the strategy of making competitors cry from shame or embarrassment in the face of harsh comments from the jury.

Another hit show following hard on the heels of *Super Girl* was *Lycra, My Way*, produced by Shanghai Dragon TV, a broadcaster within the Shanghai Media Group. It was first broadcast in 2004. The winner took away one million renminbi and a recording contract, even managing to sell 100 000 legitimate copies of his debut album in a country where 20 000 sales are considered high (Ryan 2005). While many critics have expressed concern about the proliferation of global talent show formats, there are many international instances in which idol and reality shows have demonstrated positive cultural impacts. In November 2004, a twenty-five-year-old Indian Christian girl was elected by judges and audiences as the champion of the show *Malaysia Idol*. This success was widely reported in the Malaysian newspaper *New Straits Times*, which eulogised the result as a milestone for remedying short-sighted racism (Malaysia was troubled by racial conflict with the dominant Islamic Malay population). The winner of the contest, formerly a singer in a bar, commented, 'They [the Malays] wanted Indians to go back to India; Chinese to go back to China. Many people impeded me [to participate in the event].' Finally, she gained 76 percent of the votes (*Ming Pao*, 26 November 2004). Similar unexpected results featured in *Australian Idol*. The winner in 2004 was an Indigenous Australian. Far from being a glamorous personality, Casey Donovan was a quiet, shy girl with an apparent weight problem. Upon succeeding on *Australian Idol* and drawing votes from across the country, she became a role model to many young Indigenous artists. These results are consistent with active audience arguments of Tincknell and Raghuram (2004) who examined the cultural implications of *Big Brother*. They argue that agency is constantly inscribed, constructed, and reiterated by program presenters who reinforce the role of the television audience, using phrases such as 'You decide' or 'This is how you have voted' (Tincknell and Raghuram 2004: 263). In other words, this format draws heavily on audience participation, allowing viewers to intensively engage with the text and possibly offer a discursive encoding different from the dominant norms. Indeed, in the realm of ethnic and racial problems, *Idol* formats offer a space for 'safe multiculturalism'. Ethnic differences were presented not as radically conflicting, but as consensual.

High/Low Quality; High/Low Culture

The English literary scholar Carey (2005) writes that transcendental experiences often attributed to the finer works of civilised culture are, in fact, overstated by those who seek to perpetuate social divisions on the basis of taste. He cites the French sociologist Pierre Bourdieu, who believed that it was an impossible task to divulge 'legitimate' culture to the uncultured (2005: 119). What is legitimate and real, however, is often a moot point. Is the pleasure obtained by listening to a Pavarotti comparable to that obtained from listening to a *Pop Idol*, for instance, a William Hung or a Li Yuchun? Obviously, the social distinction attached to the former would seem to indicate a more valued experience, but how can this be measured? One thing we can say is that the proliferation of *Idol* formats encounters a clash between celebrity and ordinary values. In 2000, well before the high tide of television formats in East Asia, a Chinese media critic wrote that 'gold collar' consumption would move inevitably towards mass consumption and participation: 'Under normal conditions only certain types of talent can ascend the television stage — leaders, heroes, model workers, literary celebrities, expert scholars and celebrities' (Yang 2000: 16). A mood of boredom was emerging within the Chinese audience towards the procession of sanitised celebrity. Somewhat ironically, in light of what was to follow, this tedium extended to many non-professional performers, such as announcers and TV newsreaders, who were encouraged to perform in gala events and New Year's Eve concerts.

What, then, does the success of *Super Girl* say about the cultural sphere in China? Does it open up greater participation in a common culture from within the newly constituted masses — those who are willing to claim a brief moment of celebrity, as well as those who own mobile phones and are capable of voting? Or does it signal an erosion of popular taste? To understand these positions, it is useful to briefly assess the role of cultural activities in China. In the socialist past, pronouncements relating to culture in China were underwritten by its function of educating and moulding populations. The official model of culture was normative in its mission. During the revolutionary period of the 1950s to the late 1970s — and even during the 1980s and 1990s — cultural representations operated in two ways. First, they established models purporting to represent an ultimate (socialist) human nature. Such models were benchmarks. Cultural producers were entrusted to use these models to raise the consciousness of the population. Second, cultural activities — which included television variety shows featuring pop stars — were used along with other more disciplinary methods of social policy to resolve, or at least attempt to resolve, imbalances and abnormalities within society. Accordingly, one of the principal functions of culture was to act on sectors of the population considered backward, dysfunctional, or recalcitrant. In contrast to the contemporary era, the idea of backwardness was a positive virtue that could be used to advantage, a point stressed by Mao Zedong in his well-known speech of 1958 where he attributed to the Chinese masses the virtues of being 'poor and blank'. As Meisner writes, the 'blankest' were the youth of China who were subsequently the most virtuous and the most revolutionary (1982: 102).

One of the important objectives of cultural activities during the heady revolutionary period of the 1960s and 1970s was raising the political consciousness of the Chinese masses. Again, the youth were the vanguard. The mechanism of dialectics, as a trajectory of development, was offered as a science of progress, explaining the materialist view of history and justifying class struggle. This expediency is illustrated in Mao's vision of a progressive proletarian culture opposing decadent bourgeois views. The manner in which oppositions were posed constituted a mechanism by which approved culture would perform its roles. In other words, such oppositions were not necessarily antagonistic; they were utilised with the intention of changing the beliefs and regulating the conduct of the masses.

Are these oppositions still relevant and how do they apply to the cultural field today? In other words, what is the distinctiveness of new cultural technologies and formats? In the Chinese show *Super Girl* the most commonly articulated themes by both judges and audience were individuality *(ziwo)* and quality *(suzhi)*. Individuality has now become an indicator of cosmopolitanism and youth consciousness in contemporary China, in contrast to the Maoist period (1949–78) when expressions of individuality were liable to attract unwarranted attention. Even after China opened its door in 1978, individualism was still regarded as a Western value. In 2005, at the time of the broadcast of *Super Girl*, China was still far from a society of individuals taking full responsibilities for themselves as autonomous liberal subjects, although the Chinese government has become more tolerant of diversity and sees the value of permitting greater avenues of social expression. Xiao (2006) notes that the term *ziwo* is incorporated into contemporary usage — along with terms such as *zhenwo* (the true self), *dute* (unique), *gexing* (personality), and *geti* (the individual).

In *Super Girl*, the term *ziwo* ('individuality/individual self') is incorporated into the opening credits as well as the promotional videos of competitors. When the winner, Li Yuchun, triumphed in spite of her 'average' performance, many attributed the popular verdict to her individuality. At the same time, her quality was moderated by a unique *(dute)* presentation of self and a conscious decision not to conform. For instance, whereas her competitors resorted to singing revolutionary songs, Li persisted in performing songs written and performed by male artists. This, is turn, contributed to a sense of androgyny and a re-gendering of performative aesthetics. To illustrate this, we draw on the concept of performativity from the work of Butler (1990). She defines performativity as the processes by which identities are constituted by repeated approximations of models that are sanctioned by the state. Performative force, moreover, is understood differently in different societies and by different audiences, and these variations impact upon how culture is invoked in different locations (Butler 1990). In Chinese television, role-model pedagogy was enshrined in dictates and proscriptions as to how presenters addressed audiences. As Yúdice (2003) points out, performative difference does not imply national cultural traits, but rather the institutional forces in different locales that guide performance. What will work in Rio de Janeiro, for instance, will be different to what is effective in Beijing. Of course, we might surmise that pop music iconography has potential to cut across national boundaries, but in reality, the effects of culture are mediated by the dialectic between the status quo (norms) and transgression (failure to repeat loyally).

Here the concepts of *ziwo* (the individual self) and *suzhi* (quality) are reinforcing. Whereas *suzhi* indicates a state of development — in an almost evolutionary sense — *ziwo* points to a capacity to assume personal responsibility for self-improvement. Kipnis (2006) notes that by 1999, *suzhi* had been translated into thirty-two different English terms. While the most cited translation of *suzhi* is 'quality', a more conventional and straightforward understanding of 'quality' is *zhiliang* which refers to the non-human dimension, such as the quality of a product or a service. Both renditions of 'quality' have appeared frequently in social discourse since 1978. However, the pervasiveness of *suzhi quality* has, in many respects, superseded the quality of material commodities. The link between this (a positive concept) and a *lack of suzhi* (a state of ethical incompleteness) evokes the function of culture in both Confucian society and in the communist era. The key point in the contemporary era of economic reform, moreover, is an association of individualism with social distinction. But how are these distinctions normalised? In short, the quality of people is linked into a hierarchy — some people have quality, others don't. The latter are often the poorly educated or people from rural areas.

For Bourdieu (1984), the concept of *suzhi* would have made perfect sense in his hierarchy of distinction. Bourdieu surmised that the purpose of taste is to recognize difference from those below — or above you — in the social order. In effect, this was a sophisticated analysis of the divide between high and low culture as it played out in French society. While arguments about high and low culture persist today, a newer distinction is a disappearing divide between professional and non-professional. The introduction of non-professionals into the television landscape disrupts the predictability of professionalism, the manufactured techniques of presentation that are learnt within the industry. Meanwhile, media educators in China fear the *suzhi* of media professionals will be diminished.

Another perspective comes from a Beijing university graduate commenting on *Super Girl*: 'Most Chinese TV is formulaic. We can figure out after fifteen minutes what will happen, but on *Super Girl* we can't predict what they will say' (in Marquand 2005). Participating in such shows extends the rules of performance and, in the process, disrupts the repeated approximations of state-sanctioned role models that are intended to somehow 'scientifically' raise the intelligence and quality of the population. A different kind of social intelligence is required to perform 'against the grain', while watching popular reality shows involves a greater degree of emotional investment than conventional dramas and sit-coms (see Johnson 2005). This emotional intelligence factor includes tracking the emotional cues, looking for weaknesses and moments of tension, and evaluating the authenticity of performance. Evaluation by viewers thus incorporates more than only technical ability — a point often glossed over by critics keen to downplay the skill of performers. More importantly, it includes an appraisal of how the performance conforms or deviates, in the process, reinvigorating role models. The case of Li Yuchun's ambiguous sexuality worked in her favour in the eyes of many viewers, shifting the focus from male-dominated benchmarks of what constitutes aesthetics and *suzhi* (quality), to a liberated model more in tune with lived reality. In the process, the show also created a new surge in fan culture in China. The transliterated term *fensi* (literally meaning vermicelli) was coined to replace the standard word *mi*, which had the connotation of a lost and confused follower. The fans of winner Li Yuchun subsequently self-identified as *yumi* (corn) — inverting the word *mi* (second-tone pronunciation) to the gastronomic third tone *mi*. Other finalists had their own fan groupings, which would hold up supportive placards in the audience. Zhou Bichang's fans were *bimi* (followers of the pen), while others had similar savoury names: Zhang Liangying's admirers were *liangfen* (grain vermicelli), and He Jie's supporters were identified as *hefan* (snack boxes)(Duan and Deng 2006; Zhong and Wang 2006).

The appropriation of edible identities by fans of *Super Girl* led to the largest visible display of non-governmental organisation activity in modern

China. With three of the contestants originating from Chengdu, loyal fans formed the 'Snack Food Federation of Chengdu' (Zhong and Wang 2006: 32). Other smaller 'federations' were founded to support contestants of various geo-cultural linguistic origins — for instance, lychee, milk powder, honey, chicken wings, and cashew nuts. In a nation where products of television were hitherto regarded as 'spiritual food', fans' self-identification with tasty food rather than passive masses (*guanzhong*) is evidence of both agency and audience segmentation.

Concluding Remarks: High Politics and Everyday Culture

In 1980 the political scientist Bialer (1980) described two cultures operating in the post-Stalinist Soviet Union. Bialer spoke of different domains of political participation: high politics and low politics. The domain of high politics included the principal issues of society and the decisions of political leadership. These were couched in abstract official language. On the other hand, low politics was articulated in the day-to-day life of ordinary people. The cultural sphere in China from the 1950s until the mid-1990s was likewise organised from above. Television producers worked for the government and turned over the iconography of designated role models and official heroes. The relationship between producers and audience was one of distance, with the latter addressed as the viewing masses (*guanzhong*). Since 2000, new television has created a shift in such oppositions by bringing people into a more intimate relationship with each other as audience members, while undermining the stability of high culture and high politics. Reality TV and *Idol* shows have, in turn, opened the door for a more colloquial turn, an expanded desire for knowledge of what it is like to be inside an event, and a different kind of experience best described as 'emotional knowledge' (Corner 2004: 291). Inevitably, fragmentation of the television audience, combined with secularisation of taste, has led to new understandings of economic bottom lines. It is to this important question that we now turn.

9

The Artifice of Reality in East Asia

Reality is merely an illusion, albeit a very persistent one.
— Albert Einstein

Personally, I like the name reality TV because that is the whole thing about reality: it is performed, and it is edited.
— Beth Spencer, *Life Matters*, ABC Radio, March 2002

Reality television formats are omnipresent in global television schedules. Turn on a television channel in prime time and chances are you will be regaled by seemingly ordinary folk cast as players in games of chance and skill that include the engine of audience adjudication. The repertoire of reality television includes the fly-on-the-wall docu-soap variety that presents airport attendants, hotel staff, police, and emergency services interacting with the public; makeover programs; talent contests; court programs; various kinds of dating shows; cooking contests; reality-based sitcoms; and information challenge formats. In East Asia, however, it is the elimination model, broadly defined as the 'reality game show', which has provided a stimulus to local production, albeit with fine-tuning of the core elements to generate identification and appease cultural values.

This chapter examines the influence of reality television formats in East Asia and looks at how they function as alternative models of program investment and production. The relationship between artifice and reality is protean as production down-sizes, shifting from a limited repertoire of well-established genres utilising professionals to a diversity of forms that makes use of the labour of non-professionals and hidden cameras. Training and encouraging non-actors to 'act naturally' while surrounded by the machinations of production teams (directors, editors, make-up persons, and camera operators) adds to the incongruity of what constitutes contemporary reality TV.

The impetus for the 'new reality' movement — and, indeed, many of the actual manifestations of reality TV — has come from Europe and North America where reality television has evolved along with critical attention from scholars, pundits and politicians. With this in mind, we briefly look at some global critique before moving on to discuss the success and failures of reality TV in East Asia. In short, critics from different fields vary in their embrace of the genre. Critical screen studies accounts locate the focus on the evolution of the reality genre and its antecedents in documentary; media sociology tends to observe power differentials and the spectre of TV surveillance; while cultural studies celebrates active audiences, fan networks, co-creation, and mediated celebrity.

The concept of reality television is defined more loosely in East Asia where political correctness has presided over representations, denying outrageous reality of the kind associated with shows like *The Osbournes* and *Big Brother*. To understand the logic of new reality in East Asia, it is necessary to move beyond preoccupations with artificiality while remaining attendant to a standard critique of reality television — that it is in fact 'a misnomer' (Andrejevic 2004; Brenton and Cohen 2003). This critique, while central to media studies' interrogation of form, obscures the more important issue of how reality formats cross cultural boundaries. The key concern, therefore, is how reality television functions as a vehicle for flows of ideas and associated techniques of production.

According to Corner the emergence of reality television is framed by the relationship 'between *industrial* and *cultural* factors in innovation' (2004: 291; italics in original). The key point here is the correlation between bottom lines and what Frances Bonner (2003) calls 'ordinary television'. In Chapter 4 we suggested that the 'industrial' innovations provided by formats are flexibility tailored to the rapidly shortening product life-cycle of television programming. Demand for content — a consequence of digital technology allowing multiple channels to be broadcast over a previously crowded spectrum — has brokered new business models: music channels proliferate on cable because record companies are happy to give lavish pop videos to channels such as MTV for free, while low-cost TV shopping channels, likewise, find welcoming niches. Reality television, meanwhile, does away with much of the sunk cost of actors, scriptwriters, and elaborate sets.

Cultural factors in innovation, according to Corner (2004) include a 'colloquial turn', a shift towards private experience, the ascent of the ordinary (see Bonner 2003), and a desire for 'emotional knowledge', such as wanting to be in an event (Corner 2004: 291). In addition, as we argue in Chapter 12, the relationship between producer and audience has substantially modified, allowing the latter a more active role — not only in deciding which channel to watch, but in how the content is shaped.

While reality television is a product of European and North American television systems, it has a different provenance in East Asian society. Reality television provides a fresh alternative to documentary, an expository form that state-owned broadcasters actively exploited for the explicit purpose of state-building. 'New' reality allows the documentary mode of production to move across and refresh itself in the field of entertainment genres. In drawing attention to the transferability and tradability of reality across cultural boundaries, we recognise the subtle innovations that occur in making television in East Asia.

To further emphasise this point, reality television in East Asia provides an alternative to soap operas or television dramas, which in most Chinese communities serve as prime-time entertainment on major television channels. Dissatisfaction from viewers about repetitive themes in many so-called 'entertainment dramas' has provided reality television with opportunities to extend, diversify and enliven such themes. With television stations in East Asia subscribing to low-cost production models due to early uptake of cable multi-channelling, we note a tendency to favour alternative entertainment formats, particularly documentary and quiz shows. Producing reality TV formats is a pretext for the stations to diversify their program types while still maintaining relatively cheap cost structures and fulfilling obligations to produce shows that interpellate 'ordinary people'.

Reality — But Compared to What?

Whether reality TV programs provide authenticity is a moot point. Certainly, these programs in all their various manifestations offer a different perspective on reality than conventional news and documentary formats, which adopt an ideological position of some sort. The documentary is an artifice of authenticity in its positioning of the viewer vis-à-vis footage and spoken material chosen by the filmmaker. The news, on the other hand, reduces multiple events ranging from terrorism to human interest into a half-hour format. Neither has any absolute claim to representing reality; it is just that we have come to accept the factual reports that journalists provide as true eyewitness reflections of real events. Reality TV — or unscripted drama — is even further removed from reality. Many reality television shows (apart from the amateur video footage formats) are widely acknowledged as artifice, even deception. They aspire to capture the naturalness of non-professionals interacting in environments structured and manipulated by professional directors and production teams. For Andrejevic, 'Reality TV, to the extent that it demonstrates the artificial nature of mediated reality, highlights the reality of artifice in the mass media' (2004: 16).

According to Charlie Parsons, the devisor of the global format *Survivor*, the 'reality game show' is a hybrid term that brings together elements of docu-soap, game show, drama, and talk show (Brenton and Cohen 2003: 57). Echoing Andrejevic's (2004) point about reality TV being a 'misnomer', Brenton and Cohen point to the oxymoronic sense of 'reality television', as well as the often moronic nature of many reality formats. They assert that, 'It is about reality insomuch as it features neither actors nor scripts. Otherwise 'the term does not hold up to scrutiny' (Brenton and Cohen 2003: 8). In a similar critical vein, Boyle (2003), author of *Authenticity: Brands, Fakes, Spin and the Lust for Real Life*, writes of 'fake real', where products are made to look real, and 'virtual real', where experiences that are real are delivered by media technologies. In passing judgement on the British version of *Big Brother*, he writes:

> There's no doubt the emotions they feel are absolutely real — and that the TV show feeds a public which is demanding something more direct and emotional. But somehow the situation is so ludicrous and contrived, and the strings are being pulled by TV executives, that the end result is more fake real than virtual real. (Boyle 2003: 60–61)

Recent English-language literature on reality television is extensive and shows no sign of diminishing. Andrejevic's (2004) impressive study canvasses reality television's precedents in MTV's *The Real World*: its relationship with interactive media, surveillance, and voyeurism. Many others have weighed into the debate about the value of reality: reality TV is denigrated as dumbing down, or cast as 'tabloid television' (see Kilborn 2003: 25–28, 89–90). Nick Couldry (2003) has examined the symbolic aspects of reality TV from the relationship of ritual acts and social values. Many writers within media and cultural studies have reacted to the broadsides of television critics, and have celebrated popular reception and the democratising potential of reality television. The active audience and audience/fan engagement with the dynamics of celebrity and artifice is taken up in several studies (Tincknell and Raghuran 2004; Foster 2004; Mathijs and Jones 2004).

Writers working in screen studies address reality television as a sub-genre of popular factual television (Roscoe 2001; Dovey 2000), as a post-documentary phenomenon (Corner 2004), and as confessional, first-person narratives of everyday life (Dovey 2000; 2002). These descriptions confer upon reality television a greater sense of respectability — a point made by Corner, who points out that reality television forces us to reassess the very idea of the 'truth' that a camera can record — as much as 'our broader sense of why television continues to be important' (2004: 298). Accordingly, reality television is offered up as a revival of the documentary form, and a nail in the coffin of the traditional expository documentary form in which the subjectivity of the film-maker is intended to be masked. Brenton and Cohen subscribe to the view that the documentary in the United Kingdom only survived on television due to its support by government through public service broadcasting, notably, Channel 4 and the BBC (Brenton and Cohen 2003). There is a degree of disenchantment evident in this judgement of public support. During the 1990s, documentary was forced to confront its lack of appeal to (mainly) younger audience demographics who increasingly surf channels looking for engaging content. According to Peter Bazelgette, chairman of Dutch-owned production house, Endemol UK:

> One of the interesting things is that television has to be cleverer. That's why the format has risen in popularity. A format is a higher concept than a documentary, with a bit more a narrative to it. One way of hooking people is to make programmes which have more of a narrative and an outcome to them. (Cited in Griffiths 2003: 36)

Whether or not new reality formats have any substantive claim to being 'factual' forms remains a moot point. There are certainly real outcomes: prizes, celebrity status, and endless merchandising. Nevertheless, it cannot be disputed that reality television — or popular factual television, depending on one's degree of critical distance — is at least *claiming* to be a representation of real life. Participants compete for prizes, in contrast to narrative fictional forms in which actors are paid to act. Indeed, the subjects of reality shows could be someone we know — and this is a point of fine distinction. As Jane Roscoe notes, 'We know the characters in soap operas are fictional, but we expect the emotions and experiences to ring true' (2001: 13). In reality formats, the participants are working within the rules of the game rather than following scripts, so there is a tendency to overlook the fact that they are often heavily edited and manipulated. While we suspend disbelief in the act of viewing fictional narrative, the quasi-documentary mode of the reality game show, its 'non-actor' participants, and its prioritisation of the subjective voice encourage a different form of identification between participants and viewers.

One of the outcomes of this identification is that viewers are caught up, consciously or unconsciously, in searching for and adjudicating on authenticity in reality television shows such as *Big Brother, Survivor,* and *Idol.*

While this form of television is largely unscripted, it is heavily edited so that much of the dross is minimised. Moreover, what is often overlooked is that overweight, unattractive people are seldom selected for reality TV. In addition, reality television spawns a myriad of dedicated websites, offering fan commentary, analysis, merchandise, and viewer-cam. The viewer-cam adds an element of voyeurism to the internet site and, in turn, opens up the reality format to real-time online debates about characters, motives, and future directions.

Reality in East Asia

As Kilborn (2003) and Corner (2004) note, the origins of reality television in Europe evolved from action-incident programming along with surveillance, towards docu-soaps with some degree of narrative development, to a final stage where game elements add levels of audience interactivity. In East Asia, the evolutionary cycle is somewhat diverse, depending on location. The East Asian reality TV model owes a significant debt to the public educative role of television. The Chinese reality 'show' or *zhenren xiu* (literally, real-person show) originates from socialist realism documentary. Pedagogy was the rationale for documentary making in China and coincided with an official view that the media were the mouthpiece of the Chinese Communist Party and truth-telling was the highest profession. The domination of factual programming during the 1980s, and subsequent viewer over-exposure to socialist documentary at a time when the country was opening up to new ideas, led to widespread cynicism from those who commissioned such 'truth telling' in the name of progress. Early reality formats featured courtroom shows portraying petty criminals being duly admonished by the system and serious criminals getting their come-uppance. In a society where corruption of officials and black market activity are rife, police and justice shows struck a responsive chord well into the 1990s.

Documentary was intended to educate the broad masses, but it waned as a popular form as strong competition emerged in the late 1990s from light entertainment formats introduced from Taiwan, Hong Kong, and Japan. Disillusionment with the bland fare of politics also had the effect of driving the expansion of cable television, providing a more diverse and spicy buffet of audio-visual choices. Viewers migrated in mass numbers to quiz shows and variety shows, while television dramas remained as popular as ever. It was only a matter of time before reality television merged with propaganda. The marriage of entertainment TV and politics alerted Chinese leaders that unscripted drama was perhaps the best way to make a connection with the masses.

As we saw in the previous chapter, producers at the national broadcaster China Central Television (CCTV) had become cognisant of the international trend in reality programming that allowed ordinary people to become prime-time icons. Producers seized on the opportunity to promote reality formats, echoing those that have been massive hits in world markets over the previous few years.

Nevertheless, a shift in consciousness among producers towards the unscripted and the banal does not suggest that traditional documentary forms are endangered. Reality television has, in fact, reinvigorated the demand for factual television in other locations. During an address in March 2005, the General Manager of Television Broadcast Limited (TVB) in Hong Kong noted that stations had previously hesitated to feature documentaries on history, nature, and culture in prime time. After a few trials, they discovered that ratings were not particularly low in comparison with other genres. With increasing channels a consequence of digitisation, segmentation of audiences becomes more prominent. The key to reinvigorating traditional documentaries is adding greater appeal, and this repackaging is due to the challenge provided by the reality television formats, as well as new techniques of production and audience interaction that reality TV offers.

Looking at the phenomenon of reality television and reality game shows in East Asia, we can confidently state that the momentum has come from Europe via dedicated television format traders. If we disregard the pre-existence of socialist realist propaganda, the reality television format is a product of European television (Moran 1998). It has become a global format and, in the process, has gradually been indigenised. Whereas quiz shows seized the moment in Asia by capitalising on audience desires to see ordinary people competing for real money on television, the reality game show had a slower and more problematic uptake. Reality shows that have attempted to reversion *Survivor* and *Big Brother* formats have met with viewer resistance, despite huge amounts of capital being outlaid on production and cross-platform promotion strategies.

Reality Shows in Hong Kong, Japan, and China

In some respects, it can be argued that reality TV has found its natural home in East Asia. Reality television is regularly presented as excitement-packed adventures in exotic locations — for instance, when normally city-bound people discover a wilderness without any apparent connection to modern lifestyles. In an ideal form, reality offers a fly-on-the-wall scenario: subjects are unrehearsed, dialogue is unscripted, and spontaneity is the order of the day. As we have already mentioned, reality TV claims to be more real than (scripted) narrative forms: it seeks to capture real people, not actors, interacting in various natural settings in serial forms, quite often with these people taking on challenges and overcoming tasks. These can be physical, emotional or psychological, often pushing participants to experience a range of emotions — extreme joyfulness, the thrill of success or even the humiliation of dishonour in front of millions of people.

Reality programs are also relatively inexpensive to produce, particularly when compared with the costs of long-form television dramas. Reality programs with high-production values, such as US *Survivor*, cost about US$500 000 to US$600 000 per week (Seaton 2004); in many parts of Asia, modification of the format to more accessible or simpler adventures significantly reduces the cost. As we discuss in Chapter 10, reality is amenable to commodification. Due to the relatively cost-effective production budgets in East Asia, producers rarely license foreign formats. And, rather than directly adapting formats (or other programs) from overseas, they modify and tweak the format in ways that correspond to local contexts. For instance, reality formats that target family members interacting together are well received, more so than shows that feature individuals endeavouring to outwit and deceive fellow players.

Survivor in East Asia

As we discussed earlier, *Survivor* is generally regarded as the mother of all reality game shows. In the original *Survivor* concept, sixteen people are left at a far-away, often exotic, location and assigned to one of two tribes; members of these tribes compete together and against the other tribe in a series of challenges to win either rewards or immunity from elimination. Eventually the two tribes merge for the end-game, with the last 'survivor' being awarded the million-dollar prize. In 2002, the first survival reality show in East Asia was conceived in China. *Into Shangrila (zouru xianggelila)* was produced by the Beijing-based Weihan Cultural Production Company (Beijing Weihan), together with Sichuan Television and twenty other local TV stations. Within a short time, a program called *Perfect Holiday (wanmei jiaqi)* emerged, working off the *Big Brother* concept. *Perfect Holiday* was produced by Hunan Economic Channel. *Indiana Jones (duobao qibing)* was subsequently produced by Zhejiang Television and *Valley Survival Camp (xiagu shengcun ying)* by Guizhou Television. Most of these shows were promoted as exercises in documentary anthropology rather than just escapist game shows (Ran 2002). Distancing the Chinese survival-in-the-wilderness concept from CBS's *Survivor* in the wilderness was necessary due to widespread consumer awareness in China of global television. It was said the US version's correlation with market individualism, crass commercialism, and the survival-of-the-fittest concept expressed values that were at odds with the both the Chinese Communist Party's ethic of 'spiritual civilisation' and Chinese Confucian values.

Likewise, the *Temptation Island* format, in which prospective couples are flown to an exotic tropical paradise and separated from their partners, then tempted to temporarily forego monogamy by cavorting with other playful participants, was deemed too risky for Hong Kong viewers. The cautious approach to risqué reality is attributable to the local regulatory regime. Both government and viewing publics subscribe to stringent moral standards in television programs and media representation in general. Several notable cases of public outrage against perceived media licentiousness have made headlines. In 2002, the public censure of a photo of a naked female artist on the front cover of the Hong Kong magazine *Eastweek* resulted in government intervention and, finally, in the owner's voluntary closure of the magazine. In television, the rules are equally stringent. In mainland China, periodic crackdowns on unhealthy content have taken place since television began broadcasting in 1958. In such environments of moral conservatism, broadcasters cannot afford to risk directly importing controversial formats which, despite their titillation effects, would inevitably precipitate public outcry. In short, a significant degree of fine-tuning is required to re-version these formats.

Faced with such impediments to creativity, how do local producers construct reality television formats? An illustrative example is *The Wild (redai yulin miyue kuangben)*. *The Wild* was a local production, a generic variation of the global format *Temptation Island* (produced by Twentieth Century-Fox). Shown on Hong Kong's TVB in February 2002, *The Wild* adapted many of the core ingredients of *Temptation Island*. In this romantic adventure lasting ten days, newly engaged males were asked to confront problems and surmount physical obstacles in the tropical wilderness of north Queensland, Australia, while their female partners engaged with the material temptations of southern Queensland's affluent lifestyle centre, the Gold Coast. *The Wild* is a hybrid format, incorporating elements of *Temptation Island* as well as the globally recognised *Survivor* format. Both programs feature city-dwelling participants who are transported to remote wilderness locations to compete with and against each other. In *The Wild*, the competition consists of extreme challenges such as jumping from waterfalls and cliffs, parachuting, running across deserts, sand tobogganing, canoeing in open seas, a 45-metre bungee jump in a jungle location, and the tasting of strange food. The ultimate prize was HK$300 000 (US$40 000). Losers were duly punished in novel and exciting ways, such as being forced to dash across a shallow pool infested with crocodiles.

Drawing on the core ingredients of *Temptation Island* and *Survivor*, the producers reduced the incompatibility of this new kind of format with local cultural values. *The Wild* diluted the obvious sexual connotations that branded *Temptation Island* as an exciting diversion in the US. In short, the overt sexual temptations that render the former titillating are objectionable in Hong Kong society. Interestingly, Hong Kong has one of the world's highest rates of usage of internet pornography. The de-eroticisation of the program makes it generative, allowing it to be refashioned into even more spin-offs. In November 2002, TVB also launched a student version of *The Wild* — incidentally, also shot in Queensland — entitled *The Mission (daxue qunying yueye kuangben)*. In this modified version, college student 'survivors' were asked to work as both teams and individuals, demonstrating perseverance, fortitude, and stamina in outdoor activities such as rock-climbing, hiking and other forms of 'healthy competition'.

The nature of survival reality makes such games a marketing access point, or even 'advertainment' (Deery 2003). The scarcity of resources in the wildlife settings, combined with the disciplinary actions and restrictive rules of the games, foreground the importance of commodities and 'delayed rewards'. As we discuss in more detail in the following chapter, the placement of sponsor products naturalises consumerism. In *The Wild*, sponsors Coca-Cola and Siemens were able to exploit the environment and its isolation. Competitors were rewarded with Coca-Cola, hardly the most appropriate rehydrating beverage of choice, while couples communicated and exchanged pictures of the day's activities via MMS with their Siemens mobile technology.

Reality — whether constructed domestic artifice *(Big Brother)* or simulated natural environment formats *(1900 House* and *Frontier House)* — becomes a means to remind us of the luxuries of contemporary life missing in the constructed reality of the house or the remote location. The scarcity of resources in the wild, together with disciplinary regimes and restrictions, foreground the importance of commodities. For example, in the documentary-style format *Frontier House* (PBS) three families 'experience' life on the American frontier in 1883. Similarly, in *1900 House* (PBS) a family is transported back to Victorian England. Rather than conjuring some fantasy outside our daily life, the adventure reality show, best typified by *Survivor*, casts the competitive reality of social Darwinism in front of the participants who are exposed to and disciplined by an environment that is, ironically, a metaphor for neo-liberal capitalism. The irony of stripping away the accoutrements of consumer modernity is brought home in the shape of rewards for success in the various challenges. In one instance, the prize for the winner in the US *Survivor* was a 'civilised' cooked breakfast served on a table on the beach with silver cutlery, toast racks, and orange juice (Brenton and Cohen 2003). By struggling and forming alliances — and by scoring higher in the competitions — participants gain material rewards and commodities.

Moreover, rather than conjuring some fantasy narrative outside everyday reality, the reality game show portrays the competitive nature of society as something that is physical and tangible. 'Players' are exposed to, and 'taught' to confront, a competitive environment parallel and analogous to the materialist environment in their, and the audience's, *real life*. For instance, the dilemmas that confront participants can be paralleled with struggles in real life as one ascends the social ladder or the office hierarchy. We saw the same kind of process at work in the information challenge show *The Weakest Link* (see Chapter 7). In the survival formats, the necessity of forming into tribes, working cooperatively to overcome challenges, and finally thinking as an individual by eliminating contenders, replicates real life under conditions of contemporary capitalism. Only by struggling throughout — and literally scoring higher marks in competitive games — are participants deserving of material rewards and commodities. Materialistic desire matches and reproduces audience expectations of real life in contemporary consumer society.

Berger and Luckmann (1967) argue that reality is constructed by participation in everyday life through an inter-subjective process. Audience members, situated in a living-room environment, make sense of the world from messages received; by evaluating and interacting with these meanings, they then construct a reality. The film *The Truman Show* (directed by Peter Weir), in which the protagonist (Jim Carrey) constructs his pocket reality from producer-instigated events and cues, might well be seen as an indictment of reality television — or the medium of television itself, for that matter. In the constructionist view, legitimation and reification of reality are stabilised through viewing — and by viewing as if participating in reality TV. While there is a certain suspension of belief and second-guessing in negotiating the motives of players, the decisions made by players confirm narratives of everyday life, such as dog-eat-dog; don't give a sucker an even break; cooperation is important; men are stronger than women, but women are more empathetic; men are from Mars and women from Venus; and so on. While dramas and sitcoms may be fictional and commonly regarded as entertainment, reality shows introduce facets of real-life interaction that impinge upon audience experience and imagination. In reality game show formats, the wilderness in which the contestants compete is remote from the audience, but the spirit of 'survival of the fittest' is not. These shows collectively convey a capitalist, materialistic view of society. The end result — at least the result presumably desired by advertisers and sponsors in Asia — is that audiences will feel more connected to consumerism, value the commodities advertised, and ultimately desire more.

In Hong Kong, reality television programs have not achieved the measure of ratings success found elsewhere. Indeed, the most conspicuous reality formats are youth game shows rather than overtly individualistic winner-takes-all shows, such as *Survivor* and overtly hedonistic formats such as *Temptation Island*. In the case of the former, it needs to be noted that the idea of casting two tribes of people on an island with limited resources has not translated well across cultures. The show was not a success in the United Kingdom, it did not take off in Hong Kong, and it failed to excite in Japan. It is not a question so much of whether individualism or materialism is the defining issue here. One of the most popular and successful shows of the past few years in Hong Kong has been *Who Wants to Be a Millionaire?* (see Chapter 6). It appears that the lack of cooperation inherent in the *Survivor* game and identification with the much-publicised US versions doomed it to still-birth.

Reality TV has blended with weight-loss advertisement campaigns in Hong Kong. In addition to supposedly 'real' celebrity endorsements of slimming in TV commercials, beauty salons have also sponsored makeover reality television programs. Such formats are premised on the assumption that audiences already accept that the actors in commercials are authentic cases. For example, Sau San Tong, a leading slimming salon in Hong Kong, produced a 'documentary' featuring two females and one male travelling overseas with famous TV artists (April–May 2005). In the television program, they invited nutritional experts and professionals to comment on the three participants' daily habits and slimming regimes. The program ends with shopping episodes, which indirectly acknowledged the necessity of slimming. Only by undergoing the body-shaping regimes offered by these salons are the women able to buy and wear glamorous clothing and face the public.

Japan

In Japan, the uptake of reality television took a somewhat different trajectory. *Survivor* was the first global reality format to surface in Japan, and it entered via the United States where it had already achieved huge success. Japanese *Survivor* commenced in April 2002 (Tokyo Broadcasting System [TBS], 6:30 pm every Wednesday), accompanied by considerable media promotion. About 2500 people applied to be one of sixteen challengers. It was reported in the press that most participants were not simply attracted to the big money payoff, but were seeking to discover a true self through involvement in highly stressful physical and mental challenges with other contestants (Iwabuchi 2004).

However, the Japanese *Survivor* struggled to survive. It rated on average 6–8 percent, far below the benchmark rating in the prime-time slot. Iwabuchi's (2004) study of Japanese reality TV draws attention to the incompatibility of the Western format with Japanese value systems, a fact acknowledged by the producer who stated that the program failed in the market because the depiction of contestants' emotions in *Survivor* was too fine-grained to be clearly understood. The emphasis on the search for a true self did not develop into unexpected interpersonal relationships, such as love affairs among contestants (*Asahi* newspaper, 27 June 2002, cited in Iwabuchi 2004). The original premise of the *Survivor* game show — the utilisation of engines such as the prisoner's dilemma, immunity, and voting-off — failed to achieve traction. Iwabuchi's study found that interpersonal alliances tended to be translated into inward-looking exposures of unattractive aspects of contestants' egoistic personalities — and this had more to do with the fear of actually being excluded from the group. In short, the meaning of survival of the fittest worked differently in Japan: it was collectivist logic rather than individualistic tactics that negatively determined losers and winners. As we see below, the same logic apply to mainland China.

Chinese Reality: Socialist Realism Meets *Big Brother*

The concept of popular factual television programming is one that is likely to evoke strong feelings in the minds of many propagandists. The national form throughout the revolutionary period (1949–78) was socialist realism which was inscribed into all popular art forms. The propaganda documentary was the staple of Chinese broadcasting throughout the development of Chinese television, and the prevalence of this form of factual television meant that its reception was bound to suffer when confronted with the emergence of entertainment genres, coupled with a desire on the part of producers and advertisers to capture audiences. Socialist documentary was left with no alternative but to redefine its relationship with the viewer or be banished to rarely viewed timeslots and channels.

The first examples of reality television in China were revealed in south China, arguably a more tolerant environment for experimentation with new ideas than the more political north. *The Great Survival Challenge (shengcun da tiaozhan)*, produced by Guangdong Television in 2000, set a precedent by incorporating elements of foreign reality shows at a time when the reality genre was still being redefined in global markets. In fact, both *Survivor* and *Big Brother* only appeared in the United States in 2000 (Murray 2004). The manner in which this show took root says something important about the hybridity of formats and supports Corner's proposition that contemporary reality television has evolved from the hidden camera, via the docu–soap, to the reality game show (Corner 2004). The idea was first conceived as a segment of a summer holiday program targeted at young adults with a camera tracking an outdoor survival challenge in Guangdong province. When this gained popularity, the concept was expanded to a more ambitious survival challenge, following the route of the Chinese Long March (in the 1940s) along the border regions and up into north China. The young participants found themselves tracing the footsteps of Communist Party icons, such as Mao Zedong and Zhou Enlai.

Not unsurprisingly, given the proximity of Guangdong viewers — probably the least politically attuned population in China — to Hong Kong television, this stoic re-enactment of the Long March failed to capture imaginations. The following season saw the *Great Survival Challenge* duly presented as an all-female survival affair in a *Temptation Island*-style location. Images of young women revealing their fantasies of success and scrambling up coconut trees soon inspired another wave of reality television a little further north.

Into Shangrila (zouru Xianggelila) was an ambitious attempt to introduce reality TV into the Chinese market. If one were to accept the producer's account of the logistics, it was the biggest event since the communist Long March itself. Produced by documentary filmmaker Chen Qiang whose previous output had included a 1990 documentary ode to the Yellow River and the people living alongside its banks, *Into Shangrila* saw two teams of young Chinese encountering the ultimate survival test: the Himalayan foothills in Sichuan province. Members of the Sun and Moon Teams were drawn from eighteen different provinces and thirty cities. From the many (230 000 applicants) only a few were chosen to compete for the honour of belonging to the winning team and revealing their fears and aspirations to the nation. The young pioneers in this media event were left in the wilderness for thirty days with food and matches for ten days and expected to work together to overcome the hazards of altitude, cold, physical duress, and emotional conflict.

Into Shangrila's producer was obliged to defend the program against charges of cloning, despite its packaging as a Chinese survival-against-all-odds documentary. According to Chen, he had drawn minimal inspiration from the foreign model. In justifying the adoption of many elements of the Western format, critics pointed out that, whereas *Survivor* was evidently a game show, the Chinese version was 'an exercise in anthropology and sociology' (CCTV 2002). Furthermore, the Chinese version distanced itself from the capitalist grandeur of the Western original by emphasising that *Into Shangrila* was not produced by a transnational media company (Columbia Broadcasting), but by a small yet enterprising Chinese company, his own Beijing Weihan Cultural Broadcasting Company. Other differences were advanced to placate the censors. The dog-eat-dog antics of the foreigners were contrasted to the comradely cooperation exhibited by the Chinese when facing harsh conditions, a trait that evidently had its provenance in revolutionary struggle.

Indeed, *Into Shangrila* did go much further into the traditional documentary mode, allowing extra-dimensions, such as portraits of the contestants' lives in their home locations prior to competing, and post-competition interviews. In this way, it pre-empted much of what is common in contemporary reality and docu-soaps — the milking of such formats for added value. And, whereas the foreign *Survivor* promised the winner the mother of all prizes, the participants in *Into Shangrila* were rewarded with the glory of being seen on television. This was not artifice. In the words of the producer:

> The program's sense of reality is authentic. On the surface the contents and format of the program were controlled by us to the extent that we had chosen the rules of the game and the environment, even the conditions and the volunteers. However the sense of reality of the whole package was authentic. (Chen Qiang, interview by Keane, 7 June 2002)

Echoing the influence of the international model, *Into Shangrila* had coverage on more than a hundred websites, in more than 160 newspapers and on four mobile phone networks, as well as participation from twenty-nine television stations nationwide. In explaining his approach to formatting reality television Chinese style, Chen admitted that he had only become aware of the international version as he was completing his format, and that extensive media cross promotion was his own methodology, one that he had developed to promote his former documentary productions (Chen, interview 2002). In describing the convergence of documentary film making and the virtual sphere of mass marketing, Chen commented that *Into Shangrila* combined two spaces — the real and the unreal — and mixed up mediated events with real life:

> Through the platforms of Internet, satellite communication systems, and the telephone there were links between these two spaces and with our audiences. This made our program both a game and an interactive social revelry. (Chen, interview, 2002)

In terms of how the format was rolled out for Chinese viewers, we note striking similarities. In the beginning, the program had simple game rules and a simple scenario: how could people survive on the uninhabited plateau for thirty days with only ten matches and ten days' supply of food? Chen goes on:

> In making the program we soon become aware that the people who were confronting these conditions were in fact not supernatural beings: their personal development and levels of maturity were different: they came from different occupations, had distinctive education backgrounds, personalities, family, and lifestyles. So, we then added many aspects of their personal background into the program. (Chen, interview, 2002)

The Great Survival Challenge and *Into Shangrila* were pioneers of reality game shows in China. However, neither took the market by storm. In hoping to catch the crest of the new television format wave that was impacting upon bottom lines in surrounding television industries, these programs were probably guilty of over-estimating audience willingness to engage with hybrid program forms. After all, Chinese broadcasting had been built on a pedagogic model in which paternal leaders spoke directly to the masses. A similar predicament faced the Hunan Economic Channel when it introduced its version of *Big Brother* on 21 July 2001. Soporifically entitled *Perfect Holiday (wanmei jiaqi)*, this version of the housemate elimination format isolated thirteen contestants — whose ages ranged from nineteen to forty-three — in a specially designed luxury house replete with swimming pool, games room and modern appliances. Sixty cameras monitored the proceedings, which were broadcast twice weekly. One person was eliminated each week with the last person standing acquiring a prize worth RMB500 000 (US$60 000). While the production of *Perfect Holiday* was a great step forward for innovation, it achieved only moderate ratings and did not recoup investment costs.

Concluding Remarks: The Future of Reality TV in East Asia

Although reality television is a relatively recent addition to the buffet of viewing choices awaiting television viewers, it has gained a foothold in popular consciousness and is not likely to go away, as some of its critics might wish. As the examples have shown, reality's focus on ordinary people, often doing extraordinary things, challenges the presumption that television is produced and dispensed by experts who know what's good for audiences. Financial concerns have driven the proliferation of reality formats globally, and this low-cost, flexible model applies even more in East Asia. Furthermore, reality TV embraces a wide and ever-expanding variety of forms and allows for innovative ways to attract sponsors and advertisers. These financial strategies are the subject of the next chapter.

10

Ad Magazines, Care of the Self, and New Windows of Opportunity

The bottom line of the television industry — the financing of its programs — is under siege from the threat of diminishing audiences, or at least, substantial reductions in audience numbers per channel. This chapter addresses some of the strategies that producers and networks adopt to offset the tide of audience fragmentation and advertiser apathy. These include advertorials, magazine and lifestyle shows, tie-ins, product placement, and various forms of merchandising. The role played by formats as a kind of circuit-breaker in the trend towards low-cost programming illustrates the profound institutional shifts confronting the medium of broadcast television.

The first section looks at some of the strategies that have emerged in the wake of multi-channel delivery and competition from digital platforms. Following this, the discussion turns to examples of these strategies in Hong Kong, mainland China, and Taiwan. The final section advances a 'cultural compatibility index' to explain why some formats succeed and others fail in cross-cultural incarnations. In short, while social values are generally regarded as the prime index of localisation, the alignment of government and economy helps explain why television channels in East Asia are predisposed to produce programs that incorporate merchandising and product integration.

What we discern in much East Asian programming are symbolic representations of society, the economy, and the state. This convergence allows us to expand the concept of governmentality introduced in Chapter 8. By invoking care of the self and entrepreneurial conduct as dual conditions for living in modern liberal societies, ad programs and reality shows reveal rules that bind social relations. Many of these rules are culturally based; others are politically inscribed, while others are in the process of formation. In particular, we suggest that the notion of 'entrepreneurial governmentality'

(Yurchak 2002) can explain relationships between symbolic representations of risk, capital, personal interaction, reward, and penalty as people attempt to improve their personal status or that of their family. In the final section, we describe how formats broker more multifarious forms of content that rub up against social and ideological conventions.

The Economics of Production

As the economics of production encounter the realities of advertiser unwillingness, the amount spent per hour of television is diminishing. According to Looms, there is 'a downward pressure on production and distribution budgets, apart from flagship fiction in primetime television, blockbuster films and high-flying console games' (2005: 4). An increase in production of low-cost lifestyle, magazine, and travel programs is symptomatic of this transition. Theme lifestyle channels target niche and premium demographics, those who may be inclined, due to lifestyle and income, to purchase products and services featured in these programs. Many of these commodities are readily integrated into program formats. Such a trend is an indication of the demise of the traditional spot advertising model. The shift to a post-broadcasting multi-channel environment — along with the appearance of technologies, such as the digital video recorder, that allow viewers to skip advertising — dilutes the effectiveness of spot advertising targeted at mass audiences. At the same time, advertisers have become aware of the problem of commercial clutter and are actively embracing new ways of getting their messages across effectively. Some of these new strategies are, in fact, a return to the past: a repurposing of techniques first used in the radio broadcasting business where advertisers' goods are integrated into the script by willing hosts.

Television game shows have frequently functioned as vehicles for soft advertising. However, many newer television formats, including reality television, provide more effective vehicles for product placement and integration by allowing ancillary merchandising strategies through branded commodities, e-commerce, and revenue-sharing agreements with telecommunications companies. Promotional websites, celebrity magazines, and spin-off programming maintain viewer interest in the show, thereby extending the brand value for as long as the program (or format) exists. While TV and celebrity magazines are not new to commercial programming, online technology has enabled a virtual and continuous community of interest that can be tapped into by advertisers and marketers. Further, reality show spin-offs and branded internet quiz shows provide opportunities to broaden the economic base of programs.

East Asia: A World of Products

Television in East Asia is less mature than the dominant US media market, a fact reflected in the variety of programming on offer. Lack of revenue constrains development of quality branded programming, such as HBO or Discovery Channel. Despite a global aggregate trend to greater diversity due to audience fragmentation, cable systems in Taiwan still offer a limited program buffet on multiple channels. By 2004, Taiwan had 68 cable operators and 128 satellite channels (Liu and Chen 2004). Most of these deliver low-cost genres, such as news, talk shows, game shows, and lifestyle programs. In the People's Republic of China (PRC) television drama alone absorbed 80 percent of advertising in 2004 and dominated schedules (Keane 2005).

Conservatism within television networks and a focus on economic bottom lines reflect an ethic of low risk taking. The cost of television production is high compared with other mass media, such as print and radio. On average, a television drama in Hong Kong in 2003 cost about HK$200 000 (US$25 000) per episode. This figure reflects direct costs and does not include indirect costs, such as crew and post-production. Extra costs — of between HK$1 million and 2 million (US$128,000 and 256,000) — are sometimes required for special effects such as explosives and the renting of police cars in dramas involving crime scenes (production assistant of TVB, interview by Fung, 9 June 2003). Because of the high costs associated with the production of blockbusters, stations devote an annual budget to production of a few 'quality' works — that is, programs that attract conventional forms of advertising revenue. High-production costs have always existed in TV drama production, although recent trends indicate greater financial commitment on the part of networks to high-profile *Idol* reality shows.

The use of expensive television drama for channel headlining and branding means that foreign programming fills other timeslots. Alternatively, stations utilise a range of low-cost programming strategies. One cost-effective route is where local stations license foreign programs and translate them into the local idiom. Japanese cooking shows such as *Versus V-6 (V-6 zhushi yingdi)* and reality game shows *Future Diary (weilai riji)* have been rendered in Cantonese. Elsewhere, Mandarin programs produced in Taiwan, such as CTS's *Young Boy Zhang Sanfeng (shaonian Zhang Sanfeng)*, have been re-purposed into Cantonese for Hong Kong consumption. Hong Kong programming is also 'translated' for Mainland and Taiwanese audiences.

Minimal Formatting Strategies

This minimal formatting strategy — what Lee (1991) has termed the 'parrot model' — does not require production crews and production studios. Translation of pre-formed content is an expedient and direct means of 'filling' program schedules. However, minimal formatting often requires an ombudsman, or a cultural mediator, who can bridge the foreign and the local. When this cultural intermediary is absent, audiences may perceive the program as detached from the local culture.

Minimal formatting strategies are clearly less costly than buying global brand formats, and are cheaper and less time-consuming than new program development. The utility of the minimal formatting route also exploits linguistic variation within the region. Unlike English and Spanish-speaking worlds, where television finds numerous global markets, television programs in East Asia are produced in several local dialects, mostly for local consumption with only a few titles achieving sales in other countries. Audiences in East Asia are well conditioned to dubbing and sub-titling, strategies employed to advantage by Hong Kong's film industry (Lo 2005). Japan's NHK Television and Taiwan's CTS (since 1996) have sold TV dramas to Hong Kong, and some distributors — for example, Asia Video Publishing — have acquired Korean dramas and Japanese cartoons, and distributed these to Chinese-speaking communities, such as Hong Kong, Malaysia, and Singapore. The fact that television is primarily a domestic medium feeding sub-regional markets (in comparison with the national and international aspirations of cinema) explains why programs derive their return on investment from local sales and advertising revenue.

One of the most effective strategies to make foreign programs more popular is the substitution of foreign elements, such as the inclusion of video footage from other countries. The practice illustrates flexibility and often adds a competitive and attractive edge to local programming. While episode insertion is adopted by many stations that are recipients of foreign content, especially documentary forms, the practice is widespread in Hong Kong, Taiwan and mainland China. This prototype of formatting utilises a local host — a cultural ombudsman who introduces the foreign into the local context. Judicious translation — as well as use of voice-overs — filters out non-local elements that don't make sense. In short, this minimal censorship ensures that the content accords with local taste sensibilities. The genres where these practices occur are usually entertainment programs, documentary forms, or programs that endorse consumption. In contrast with narrative genres, such as drama, where continuity is essential, these genres follow a loose, magazine-type structure so that unsuitable episodes can be selectively omitted.

The practice of inserting episodes of foreign programs into a locally hosted and produced program — or employing well-known local hosts to introduce and moderate foreign material — does not imply cultural integration or minimisation of cultural contrasts within Asia. Rather, it creates a cultural mosaic that reflects variation in local values and discourses, further illustrating the cultural and geographical differences existing in East Asia (Evans 1993). The program is (re)presented from a perspective that attracts the curiosity of the local audience. In China, the travel information challenge format *Chia Tai Variety Show (zhengda zongyi)* utilised the practice of buying episode segments and fusing these into such a global–local mosaic. These were interspersed with content actually filmed by the team.

Similarly in Taiwan, episode insertion is a means to incorporate new material. Liu and Chen (2004) call this 're-production'. *Hello Kitty Wonderland (Hello Kitty leyuan)* is a show that exploited the popularity of the Japanese Hello Kitty fashion icon among Taiwanese youth culture. In the Taiwanese format, the lyrics of the Japanese songs were dubbed into Chinese and the voice-over of a local host was added. Likewise, the Taiwanese travel program, *Travel Around the World (huanyou shijie)*, used video footage acquired from around the world. Japanese companies have taken advantage of the demand for such content by selling segments from successful shows such as *Wakuwaku Animal Land* and *Show-by Show-by* (Iwabuchi 2004). Indeed, episode insertion formatting is not limited to voice-over documentaries. They include family variety shows, such as *Funniest Home Videos*, as well as programs introducing gourmet consumption, tourist spots, and associated commodities. One gastronomic example was a Japanese eating contest introduced by local presenters in Hong Kong. The presenters localised this by performing a Hong Kong version of the contest prior to the broadcast of the imported content. An example of this was TVB's *The Strongest Tendon*, in which Japanese-originated games were spliced into local contests.

Ad Magazines

Many television channels in East Asia currently favour a format that we describe as 'ad magazines'. These promote commodities within program time, but differ from dedicated cable shopping and lifestyle channels. In this embedded advertising magazine format, the strategy is to covertly use the program to promote advertisers' products and the ideology of self-improvement. The products offered in these shows service specific consumer niches, emphasising transformation and care of the self through options for gourmet food, travel or simply consumption of everyday commodities. Importantly, the products and services featured in these programs are not distant from the viewing audience (as in imported episodes), but are readily acquired in nearby shopping malls.

The presentation style approximates the layout of popular magazines, with different elements catering for different classes and tastes. Products and services vary from labour-saving devices to commodities targeted at upwardly mobile and aspirational segments. Local hosts — pre-selected with acknowledged expertise or embodying a particular class disposition — introduce the subject-matter. In general, the emergence of the ad magazine format is a derivative of episode insertion and reflects the fundamental cultural tolerance for consumerism in East Asia's large urban centres.

In Hong Kong, the programs *Quality of Life (youzhi shenghuo pai)* (July–September 2002) and *Quality of Life 2* (May–July 2003) on TVB best illustrate the commodity nature of the format. Featuring an assortment of commodities — toys, cars, dining places, sports goods and high-tech goods — *Life* directly promoted certain combinations of goods as lifestyle choices. Commodities conspicuously displayed brand names, while sales outlets and prices were provided for the products. These programs were also integrated into other specialist channels. The TVB Xinghe satellite television channel broadcast a program titled *Good Eating and Good Living* (every weekend in 2003) that featured travelogues and lifestyle enhancement. TVB Xinghe is a Mandarin-language channel targeted at mainland China and diasporic Chinese viewers, such as those in Indonesia, Malaysia. Its staples are classic costume dramas, light-hearted sitcoms, action thrillers and cosmopolitan modern dramas.

In mainland China, the China Satellite Travel Channel (formerly the Hainan China Travel Channel) incorporates a range of lifestyle and reality programming to supplement its core business of travel journalism. The concept of lifestyle television is also widespread, with the extension of multi-channel networks. China Central Television (CCTV) now broadcasts fifteen channels with many shows providing opportunities for sponsor involvement, although this is necessarily covert due to its status as a public broadcaster. The national broadcaster, moreover, provides a dedicated Economic Channel (Channel Two), which features a mix of programming that aims to reflect China's 'socialist market economy', such as formats celebrating entrepreneurship interspersed with quiz shows, including the top rating copy of *Who Wants to be a Millionaire?* — *The Dictionary of Happiness (kaixin cidian)* (see Chapter 6).

The sponsorship mechanism is also widespread throughout China's increasingly bottom-line conscious provincial stations. Zhejiang's TV's Beauty Channel (Lianghuang Channel) incorporated agreements with a number of modelling and cosmetic companies, including the Beijing Xinsilu (New Silk Road) Model Company, with models from the company acting as hosts for programs. In north China, the Tianjin TV group has a channel called Tianshi Home Supplies Channel *(Tianshi jiaju pindao)*, dedicated to home/apartment remodelling, renovation and decoration. Many television shows and formats incorporate sponsors' names and products. For example, a Japanese-based company, Xizhilang (in Chinese), that produces jelly products, was the named sponsor of Hunan Satellite TV's popular dating show, *Romantic Meeting (meigui zhiyue)* (Keane 2004). Likewise, Lycra sponsors Shanghai Dragon TV's popular *Idol*-style format *My Way*. Cross-border sponsorship, where Chinese products are displayed in Hong Kong or where Japanese products sponsor Hong Kong programs, is also common in more conventional forms of programming; quite often, the name of the sponsor is prominently displayed. Matsunichi was a regular sponsor of the Hong Kong prime-time television dramas *Fatewisters* (June 2003) and *West 3* (in early 2003).

The lifestyle and makeover boom in much of the East Asian region is driven by attention to self-transformation, an ethic linked to economic reform and consumerism. Nor is this confined to capitalist enclaves such as Hong Kong. Since the economic reforms of the 1980s, mainland Chinese cities have moved inexorably towards a love affair with consumerism, reflected in the conspicuous display of international brand names on streetscapes, subways and high-rise buildings. Revitalisation of self-image, formerly associated with political power and connections, is directly expressed through food, living space and luxury products (Davis 2000; Fan 2000). During the 1990s, a fast-moving economy, increased personal mobility and gradual formalisation of property rights saw the growth of a middle class, as well as a *nouveau riche* social segment — people conspicuous in their consumption and dedicated to presenting an image of being totally modern (Robinson and Goodman 1996). In other words, as people climb 'a consumption ladder', they aspire to products that are markers of social transformation (Fan 2000). In contrast with the Maoist doctrine which stressed values of frugality and thrift, and the practicality of goods, the new affluent classes are concerned with expressing their wealth and status. New television formats reflect such social 'upgrading', as well as promoting consumer ethics and the ideology of self-transformation.

In Hong Kong, the expression of identity framed by cultural taste is more evident. The media are the principal conveyors of information for those aspiring to upgrade their body image or their social status (Fung 2003). Hong Kong, of course, is a cosmopolitan centre where global ideas and fashions have long found fertile soil. With consumption an essential component of collective identity in the former colony (McCracken 1990), it is not surprising that those media with a propinquity to consumer values and rituals of self-transformation are popular. Moreover, as cultural traffic between mainland China and Hong Kong has increased in intensity, Chinese shampoos, health goods and other appliances feature as major sponsors of Hong Kong television programs.

While public interest concerns regulate product placement within television and entertainment programming in many international television systems, the practice in East Asia is hardly controversial — at least not sparking debates in society and among public bodies. In the United States, for instance, the Federal Communications Commission (FCC) has set strict rules to regulate covert product placement on television (Galician 2004). Product placement is allowed for brands that are listed as sponsors. The practice of product placement has become so widespread, however, that one critic notes 'the idea that advertising is somehow far removed from the real world is a reassuring bromide, but unfortunately the world we live in is coming to resemble the world of product placement' (Olsen 2004: 66). In *Global Hollywood 2*, Miller et al. (2005) examine disturbing impacts of product placement and the increasing incidence of cigarette products within film and television. Payment of direct revenues to stations from companies wishing to gain covert endorsement is monitored by consumer groups. However, ad magazine programming, along with creative modes of product placement, is widespread in East Asia. It provokes no such controversy and no consumer backlash. This perhaps reflects a more fluid modality of capitalism that prevails in places such as Hong Kong, and indeed in many urban spaces on the Mainland. In this modality, the seller is more prioritised than the consumer; subsequently, the idea that the latter ought to be protected from excessive advertising has not found support from regulators intent on ramping up economic activity.

In Hong Kong, moreover, there have even been moves to loosen restrictions on advertising in the light of decreasing advertising sales on television. In mid-2003, contradictory to conventional practices and international legal frameworks, the Hong Kong Broadcasting Authority moved to allow product placement and product sub-titling as an alternative mechanism for soliciting advertising revenue. In China, regulations set out by the State Administration for Industry and Commerce (SAIC) prohibit subtitles beneath programs. At the same time, regulations do not address the issue of product placement (Chan and Co. 2002), and selling products within programming is quite often regarded as a legitimate means to raise revenues that are not available through sales of program rights. In China, covert advertising is a preferred means to attract advertisers. And, despite regulations against advertising sub-titles, the practice is widespread.

Integrating Products and Self-transformation

The reality of contemporary life is mirrored in consumption and reflected in media images, particularly for residents of East Asia's large cities. Fascination with consumption opens the door to reality show merchandising. As we saw in the previous chapter, international 'brand formats' like *Survivor* and *Big Brother*, in which participants are placed in environments devoid of creature comforts, provide a platform where products can be introduced as 'rewards'. In the United States, the *Survivor* format was founded on brokering a unique financial arrangement between the production company and the network. Mark Burnett, the producer of *Survivor*, established a relationship with CBS that entailed him pre-selling sponsorship — including ad time, product placement, and a website link (Magder 2004: 140). As discussed in Chapter 9, many reality television shows are complicit with the merchandising of products and the promotion of consumption. Winner-takes-all reality game shows celebrate the survival of the fittest, fastest and sharpest-witted. Variants on the *Survivor* format, often promoted as an exciting experience that places contestants in a wilderness without direct connection to the world of consumption, serve the interests of the market.

On an hour–by-hour basis, reality programs are inexpensive to produce, particularly when compared to the inflated costs of television dramas with paid actors, expensive sets and production schedules. Low-cost copies of international formats can be made using more accessible locations or simpler adventures. Reality formats have fewer industrial overheads than drama, while providing newer revenue streams. The content of the reality show, and even the impromptu, unscripted utterances of the participants generate additional down-stream value: these include newspaper reports, magazines, sound-bites, websites, promotional documentaries, spin-offs, and video and quiz games, as well as improvisational comedy programs. The high cost efficiency and return on investment through ancillary merchandising and the self-generating publicity has spurred many producers in Asia to attempt indigenous reality shows.

Reality programs in East Asia rarely 'clone' international formats. The local product is often a 're-version' of the original — or, indeed, of a version of a re-version — depending on how many format iterations have preceded. Even when the program is licensed from an international distributor, latitude exists for localisation. *The Weakest Link (zhizhe wei wang)* in China did away with the bitchy host engine so central to the concept. In other instances, modifications suit the social context. *Into Shangrila* opted to emphasise cooperation over competition. Producers are more inclined to experiment with formats that correspond to cultural values. Nevertheless, locally produced formats do need to take account of the success of international versions, such as CBS's *Survivor*. As we have seen, adventure-based game shows in Hong Kong and China borrow from international models, particularly in marketing and merchandising strategies. The nature of reality adventure television allows multiple levels of commercial synergy. As Olsen writes, this is the 'practice among media conglomerates of using one medium to promote products in another, using each to sell the other' (2004: 66). He breaks marketing synergy into a number of 'multifaceted marketing opportunities': merchandising, intertextuality, placement, theming and simulacra (Olsen 2004: 69). Merchandising and placement have already been documented in our discussion so far. Intertextuality refers to the linking of media narratives such as the appearance of characters or celebrities across different mediums. Theming is the exploitation of visual logos, puns, or other iterations to extract as much value as possible. An example of theming was the *Big Brother* logo adopted in Australia, where a pair of billboard eyes helped create a sense of intrigue and debate about the show. In the context of TV formats, simulacra are artificial places, such as theme parks that are spun off from high-profile shows. In Australia, *Big Brother* transformed into a virtual theme park within a real theme park, serendipitously located at Dreamworld on the Gold Coast (Moran 2004).

From Layman to Celebrity

From the viewpoint of the media, reality television works to satisfy the industry's appetite for spin-offs by transcending recognisable individuals into brands or celebrities and selling them to advertisers or other media (Deery 2003). This strategy of celebrity is consistent with the logic of branding in most large urban centres in East Asia. Such phenomena are more overt in 'soft' reality formats — those where contestants are not forced to survive in 'natural settings'. Instead, they compete in quasi-competitive domestic settings.

The most notable examples are personal makeover shows and weight-loss challenges. In TVB's *SlimFlight* (Hong Kong), six women relocated to a lifestyle centre where they received training from physical advisers and nutritional professionals. Viewers were able to monitor their profiles, news, physical condition (for example, BMI, a weight-to-waist ratio) and slimming progress on the internet and on television. The winner was the person who lost the most weight. She was duly rewarded with gifts amounting to HK$100 000 (US$12 000). Within a short period of time, the daily routines of participants became public concerns and these formerly inexperienced women learnt to speak confidently in front of the camera as if they were celebrities.

The emergence of these lifestyle celebrities — who care enough to care for themselves by submitting to the widest exposure possible — focuses on the ethic of self-transformation. Their public disclosure of dissatisfaction with body shape and self-image draws advertising revenue for the stations, but it also reinforces the impression that the station is in tune with social discourses of personal hygiene, weight management and beauty. In other words, the cultural mores of 'looking good in the city' align with the economic interests of different parties. These agents of care and self-renovation are the companies that produce slimming products, cosmetics and nutritional supplements, as well as advertising agencies and the media that are vehicles for their dispersion. The local television station echoes a cultural and commercial theme, formerly a staple of women's magazines, within a reality show. A number of similar docu-soaps about slimming took off in Hong Kong in 2003. There were shows sponsored by Royal Bodyperfect, Beauty Concept, and Sau San Tong (literally, "a place for slimming"): they selected both celebrities and ordinary women to undergo the slimming training processes and to tell their experiences and progress of weight reduction on prime-time television. Such shows have format cousins in reality shows such as *I Want a Famous Face* (MTV) and *The Biggest Loser* (NBC). Moreover, the fetishisation of care of the self in these shows not only benefits the ratings and ad revenue of the broadcaster, but also boosts the beauty business in Hong Kong.

Compatibility Index

In Chapter 3 we proposed two models of cultural exchange and economic development: the first described the gradual process of how texts are read, translated, modified and reinvigorated when crossing cultural boundaries; the second accounted for media industry growth strategies starting from a low base. We have also noted throughout that the relationship between cultural values and political norms is critical in determining success or failure. We refer to this relationship as a 'compatibility index'.

The television format production model is based on adaptation, and this process entails compatibility with local values. A producer from the company, Endemol, has summed up international format transactions in this way: 'We take a format that works in one country, strip everything cultural off of it, export it to a new country, and then, over time, add cultural aspects of that country to it' (cited in Magder 2004: 147). The success of many new formats in East Asia has to do with such stripping and adding — more specifically, adding in culturally specific attributes of modernity, success and personal transformation.

Adaptation by definition means changing certain elements while observing others that anchor meaning. While these added elements are usually portrayed as embedded cultural values, they also embody political and economic relationships. Despite Hong Kong's return to the China in 1997, the content of many programs still reflects the former British colony's self-identification with *laissez-faire* capitalism and an ideological distancing from state socialism. In contrast to the Chinese mainland, where information challenge shows such as *The Weakest Link* signify a shift away from egalitarianism and frugality, myths of economic progress and entrepreneurship are pivotal in Hong Kong. Ma (1999) has written about the entrepreneurial Hong Konger represented in the 1970s television series *The Good, the Bad, and the Ugly* and 1990s programs *Great Times (Dashidai)*, *Under the Lion Rock*, and *Hong Kong Legend* (TVB) that celebrate the ethos of liberalism within Hong Kong's development as a world business centre. Ma's argument is that economic success is an ingredient of Hong Kong cultural identity. Other countries in the region embrace the centrality of the economy in differing ways: mainland China is rapidly transforming into an economic powerhouse; Taiwan and Korea are so-called dragon economies; and Japan is the world's second-largest economy. In addition, the cultural traditions of these countries attach importance to accumulated knowledge and family asset management.

Variations on the relative weighting attributed to state management and individual freedom occur in the region (from resolutely statist mainland China to *laissez-faire* Hong Kong to the 'state capitalism' of Japan), but it is evident from public endorsement of information challenge and renovation formats that these shows are ideologically useful in promoting the message that social responsibility is shared between state and individual subject, with the latter responsible for proper conduct in accordance with social rules. New television formats are in these ways agents of a model of governmentality that nurtures a neo-liberal ethic of self-management. According to Michel Foucault's later writings, government is broadly defined as 'the conduct of conduct', a 'form of activity aiming to shape, guide or affect the conduct of some person or persons' (cited in Gordon 1991: 5). The operations of government can thus be construed as a contact point where techniques of domination — or power — and 'techniques of the self' interact (Burchell 1996: 20).

In contradistinction to technologies of power, techniques of the self refer to the myriad ways individuals regulate their own conduct (Miller 1993). The function of government here is not so much to discipline, but rather to put in place strategies and policies that lead individuals to self-government. Of course, how these strategies are implemented depends upon the kind of political system that organises social relations. As we have seen in examples from Hong Kong, the contact point between governmental care and care of the self is reflected in a number of ways, not the least being the idea that people (and families) are ultimately responsible for managing success.

The longevity of imported programs and formats in the East Asian mediascape is therefore heavily dependent on compatibility. Why do some of the cultural elements within international formats appeal to mass audiences? Further, when unfamiliar elements are circulated, how do audiences react? Does familiarity with global television breed acceptance? Does it broaden local horizons of expectations, and in doing so, infuse new elements in the local culture? Or is this inimical to the local culture?

To be more specific, there are two dimensions to compatibility: cultural and political. 'Cultural compatibility' refers to the coherence of the values, norms and lifestyle of the local context with the values promoted by the programs. 'Political compatibility' describes the ruling elite's tolerance of the ideological content of the program. High compatibility across both dimensions facilitates local adoption. A failure to achieve cultural compatibility may result in low ratings and acceptance, whereas neglecting to make the content sensitive to political realities often leads to some form of interference from the state.

Despite global integration of countries within the region, the political landscape of East Asia is complex and diverse. China is the epitome of a politicised media environment where imported popular culture requires political approval. The Chinese government is more vigilant towards potential ideological effects of foreign media than their economic impact. The State Administration of Radio Film and Television (SARFT), which operates in tandem with the Chinese Propaganda Bureau (now referred to, somewhat ironically, as the Chinese Publicity Bureau), examines applications to produce programs, vets local scripts, and scrutinises imported program formats. Television formats that incorporate propagandist elements and that maintain compatibility with the ideology of the state are welcomed. Production is guaranteed when struggles for personal or group success concur with Marxist

— or at least, contemporary governmental — interpretations of progress. The domestic reality shows *Into Shangrila* and *The Great Survival Challenge* (see Chapter 9) strategically incorporated elements of historiography and illustrate what Tao, as early as 1995, called the compromise of official mainstream and popular culture. He writes:

> One of the main trends in the 1990s is the compromise and interpenetration of official culture and commercial popular culture. In comparison with the period 1949–1979, the current official culture has significantly absorbed the values, tastes, and styles of commercial popular culture. In doing so it embraces many new characteristics. Moreover, commercial culture in the 1990s can only develop under the policies of the government and the dominant ideology. (Tao 1995: 175)

Cultural compatibility is a more important determinant of success than politics in some locations. Hong Kong, in particular, is a good example of how this plays out; the entrepreneurial island is acknowledged as a centre of global capitalism, and yet it is ideologically over-determined by its sovereign, the People's Republic of China. Hong Kong represents a hybrid type where program formats of mixed compatibility and origin coexist. Ownership of television is entirely private in contrast with the Mainland's policy of state ownership. More importantly, the most popular station, Television Broadcast Limited (TVB), has been incorporated since 1983. Its shares are freely traded on the stock market and this commercial imperative impels TVB to readjust its focus accordingly, lessening critical political content during Hong Kong's return to the Mainland in 1997, and largely tilting its mission toward maximising economic profitability (Fung 2003). With investors' economic interests a priority, it is no surprise that the Hong Kong mediascape favours formats that have an economic logic embedded — for instance, heavily ad-laden reality shows that follow what many critics consider vulgar commercial formulae.

Yet another variation on the theme of cultural and political compatibility was *Everyone Wins*, produced by Singapore-born Robert Chua and first broadcast on Shanghai's Oriental Television in 2003. On the surface, this is an information challenge show like *Who Wants to Be a Millionaire?* (UK) and CCTV's *Dictionary of Happiness* (see Chapter 6), *Everyone Wins* is not so much reliant on voting as on accidental good fortune, a well-tempered theme in Chinese societies. In this oriental variation of *Millionaire*, later sold in Korea, the last digits of the contestants' constantly changing scores generate a stream of 'lucky numbers'. These enable viewers to play and win prizes by matching numbers of their own on anything from national identity cards and lottery tickets to sponsors' numbered tickets.

The producer logic here is that gambling by numbers appeals to Chinese societies. With information challenge shows endorsed by the Chinese government, and with lotto competitions integrated within the former leader Deng Xiaoping's 1980s 'get rich is glorious' manifesto, the hunch was that the proclivity of Chinese viewers to trust in fate would add an extra dimension to the standard information challenge format. Despite the hype associated with *Everybody Wins* in China, the show failed to take the local Singaporean market by storm, prompting Chua to launch a letter-writing campaign against what he saw as a lack of coverage in the local Chinese-language press. Chua complained against bias towards his company and the lack of a 'can do' attitude in Singapore (see Chua 2003).

Concluding Remarks: Towards a Society of Consumption

Both reality shows and the ad magazine formats result in the forging of an imagined transformation that engenders comparison with an idealised self or body image. Transformation is supposedly attained through consuming the products on offer, hearing expert advice, and listening to the philosophies of the successful contestants. However, these culturally inflected formats are not born of the local context. For the most part, they are imported from overseas and modified to accommodate local structures of feeling.

Overseas programs might need to be localised to accommodate local tastes, especially where there are fundamental cultural differences, but if the ethic of consumerism is deeply embedded in the television format and this coincides with the local desires for consumption, the need for explicit localisation is not deeply felt. Or, if they have to be modified, they are changed — not so much to be non-foreign — but to be more unambiguously commercial and to appeal to the locale which is already manifestly capitalist.

Do new formats reinforce social rules? Or do they challenge the status quo? The former position suggests that programs such as ad magazines, lifestyle shows and some reality game shows are complicit in reinforcing the commodification of experience by reducing lived reality to a form of televised video game or a cut-throat contest. And, more than simply fetishising consumer culture by offering the spoils of a sponsor's prizes — as in old-style game shows — they demonstrate that there is an ever-changing regime of rules in contemporary society. For instance, much of the pleasure of viewing reality formats is the uncertainty provided by increasing complexity. There are rules, but these are conditional and change as contests get ever more challenging and as the bar is raised higher: Johnson writes that '"playing" a reality show requires you to both adapt to an ever-changing rulebook, and scheme your way through a minefield of personal relationships' (2005: 96). Risk takers, those who form strategic alliances, and those who are able to present themselves as likeable are often rewarded. Reality shows extract a model of entrepreneurship from the scripts of narrative drama, while ad magazines promise social rewards through personal transformation. The certainty in these rituals of success is that there is, indeed, reward for initiative; the uncertainty is how to conduct oneself in achieving this prize. In societies in which the rule of law provides some safeguards against the vagaries of imperfect markets, we expect certainty. But viewers know differently: it is not always 'good' people who earn the reward.

New formats, however, can and do challenge social and political status quos, often in an incremental way. To use a cliché of business, they provide a window of opportunity to broker new kinds of relationships that extend the compatibility index: relations between self and others, between self and family, between self and peer groups, and between self and authority. What Yurchak (2002) has called entrepreneurial governmentality is knowledge of entrepreneurship, of what it means to speak about entrepreneurship, and how this is embedded within social relations. In transitional states such as China, entrepreneurship had existed previously, but was managed by political bureaucrats and cadres. Under the current regime, the responsibility for wealth creation and social status moves into the private sphere. How do people conduct themselves as citizens, moving between responsibility to the family and themselves, and to the state?

As we have seen, Hong Kong provides a template for a mode of governance that draws citizens into forms of acceptable entrepreneurship. New television formats provide tutorials for those who wish to understand the vagaries of the market economy; at the same time, they provide entertainment for viewers, seeing others on the screen negotiating relationships while imagining that it could be them. Formats have, in this way, provided 'windows of opportunity' for the representation of what was formerly unspeakable. Slimming contests in which contestants publicly display shame about body size were never part of Chinese society in the past. They have become normalised. Game shows in which individuals outwit others to win prizes were once considered bourgeois heresy by Chinese cultural commissars. Now they are accepted and promoted as part of the socialist market economy. Ad magazines that promote subliminal and often intrusive messages were regarded until recently as crass commercialisation of a public resource, the electro-magnetic spectrum. Now it seems they are here to stay.

PART III

New Television

11

Adaptation, Imitation, and Innovation

If franchising is a strategy for producing programs that can generate local as well as international sales, what should we then make of copying, a practice that is endemic — and, some would say, even essential to doing business in East Asia? As argued in the five-stage export growth model germane to developing or peripheral markets (Chapter 3), the format/franchise model is based on the idea of trading copyrights and exchanging knowledge. The notion of trade is paramount in this stage of development. The previous stage in the model is cloning or copying and, while not precluding trade, it limits this possibility because what is produced is recognised as a copy, both by audiences and by would-be purchasers of the program.

The propensity to imitate raises a number of important questions. Is this behaviour exploitative or expedient, excessive or necessary? Alternatively, is the idea of copyright, defined as the legal right to make copies, a means of assuring market growth, or a Western notion with little relevance to East Asian television? Two issues illustrate this conundrum and therefore remain to be considered in this penultimate chapter: these are innovation and its parallel, the impulse to imitate.

These themes have been ever-present within the case studies. But, in order to bring together economic and cultural aspects of the global format momentum, we need to recognise legalities that impact upon formatting. Some benchmark examples from the Western hemisphere illustrate how a different focus on copyright has come about with the advent of hybrid formats and genres. In particular, the relationship between innovation and imitation has moved into sharper relief with the popularisation of reality TV; similarly, formats have provided the engines to move reality TV into a greater number of living rooms. The momentum moves in two directions.

While reality TV's provenance is fly-on-the-wall hidden camera formats, its emergence as a prime-time commodity is largely due to the elimination engine. Some of the most ground-breaking elimination engines in the past decade have ensued from the *Survive!* prototype initiated by UK producer Charlie Parsons. The story of *Survivor/Survive!* is a valuable frame of reference to investigate the complexities of legal protection. The original concept was conceived in 1987 and came from a Channel 4 show called Network 7 — a kind of desert island skit where five members of the public were despatched to a remote location (Brenton and Cohen 2003: 45). Putting real people in unreal situations devoid of modern comforts was the seed for *Survivor*, as we now know it. According to Parsons, it was only in the United States a decade later, when pitching the show to network executives that the 'killer engine' appeared — elimination. The idea of a wilderness survival show took on a strong sense of drama when the idea of voting off the castaways 'one by one' suddenly emerged. When this breakthrough eventuated, it triggered an abundance of elimination-style program formats (*The Mole, The Weakest Link, Idol,* etc). Certainly, what at first seemed like another superficial media trend has shown surprising resilience. The well shows no sign of drying up.

By the time Parsons's show made it to the small screen, via an earlier incarnation as *Expedition Robinson* (Sweden), another elimination-driven format had surfaced — coincidentally, in a company employing a former colleague of Parsons. The *Big Brother* reality format in which a dozen or more people are confined together in a communal house was incubated in the studios of Endemol, a Dutch company founded by Joop van den Ende and John de Mol.

The key issue at stake in the ensuing litigation was the legal doctrine of 'substantial similarity'. Parsons's claim to the Amsterdam District Court was that the *Big Brother* format violated the copyright of his company, Castaway Television Production Ltd. He claimed that *Big Brother* was a copy of *Survive!* which he had earlier offered to the Dutch company Endemol. Unsurprisingly, the lawyers for Endemol refuted this claim, but Parsons argued that twelve fundamental ingredients from his format *Survive!* had turned up in the globally successful format for *Big Brother*. These were as follows:

1. A small group of very different people are separated from the outside world and are thus severely restricted in their freedom of movement.
2. The group is being followed by TV cameras and there are one or more presenters.
3. The group is being filmed 24 hours a day.
4. The program is set up as a daily record in which the reporting period is always one day.

5. The group has to fulfil tasks set by the producers and earn bonuses.
6. The group must be self-supporting.
7. The group themselves must vote who to remove or who to nominate for removal; the participants must constantly choose between their own interests and their loyalty towards the group.
8. The group is selected by psychologists and the producer.
9. The group is not allowed to have contact with the outside world unless allowed by the producers.
10. The group may only take a limited number of personal items with them.
11. The members of the group are asked to maintain a personal video diary to record their impression of the experiment.
12. The last remaining participant wins the big prize, the rest get nothing.
   (Cited in Malbon 2003: 36–37)

The first stage in the legal process in 2000 involved the case being heard in front of the members of the court on their own. This is known as the *Castaway Television Production Ltd v Endemol Entertainment International* judgement. Here, the judge ruled the *Big Brother* format did not infringe on Parsons's format, although the judgement agreed there was substantial similarity between the shows in relations to points 9 and 11. In these initial judgements, expert witnesses were not called as the requirement was that 'similarity of expression', if it existed, was 'based on the response of the ordinary reasonable person' (Malbon 2003: 35). Points of dissimilarity were deemed to exceed similarity, so there was no copyright infringement. Parsons appealed the judgement and, in 2002, the Amsterdam Court of Appeal heard the matter. This time, however, witnesses could be called. In an important reversal of an earlier verdict (the *Opportunity Knocks* case: see Moran 1998), the court ruled that, although the *separate* elements of the format were non-copyrightable, the *combination of several elements* could be protected under a copyright.

However, in this particular case, there was no infringement because it was deemed that the general impression of the two formats, *Survive!* and *Big Brother*, differed too much. In other words, the court recognised that the two had elements in common but also had elements that were different, suggesting that they were examples of the same genre or species while also exhibiting significant variations.

This was not the end of the legal trail so far as Parsons was concerned. His company now trained its gun-sights on another format which it felt had infringed on the original format. CBS had licensed another desert island reality format, *I'm a Celebrity ... Get Me Out of Here!*, from the format owner Granada.

CBS took legal action against rival network ABC on the grounds that the latter adaptation had infringed the format of *Survivor*, which it had developed from Parsons' original concept. Parsons was on record as confidently predicting that CBS would win the action. The network sought an injunction to prevent *Celebrity* going to air.

The matter was heard in the US District Court in New York at the beginning of 2003 with CBS claiming that *Celebrity* was a direct copy of *Survivor*. ABC countered by arguing that both were instances of a generic theme. The judge accepted this view and said that program-making was 'a continual evolutionary process with both shows borrowing heavily from earlier formats' (Malbon 2003). *Celebrity* borrowed no more heavily from *Survivor* than previous US shows with similar concepts, such as *The Honeymooners* and *I Love Lucy* or *Bewitched* and *I Dream of Jeannie*. CBS was refused an injunction and, although the network claimed to be considering what subsequent action it might take, nothing further eventuated. In the face of both the Dutch decisions about *Big Brother* and the US one on *Celebrity*, the format owners of *Survive!* abandoned plans to take any action against Granada in the United Kingdom. However, over and above the individual judgements regarding the claims of *Survivor* against both *Big Brother* and *Celebrity*, there is the fact that a higher court in the shape of the Amsterdam Court of Appeal held that particular TV formats were protected by copyright.

The IP Equation

In the past decade, intellectual property has become a contentious issue as digital technology makes it easier to replicate and circulate creative content. Where then do television formats fit into all of this? After all, most of the copyright claims and counter-claims in East Asia currently concern piracy and redistribution of digitised content via DVD and internet platforms. The appropriation of formats is less litigious, purely for the reason that it is difficult to prove and even more bothersome to prosecute, as the above example from Amsterdam has illustrated.

In Chapter 4 we noted the pie and crust format recipe: that is, the crust remains the same but the filling changes. This provides a way of thinking about the protection of ideas and the impact that formats will have on the circulation of content in the global media economy. Before we go on to discuss the ethics of copying, however, we should remind ourselves of why copying occurs at such significant levels in Asia. In countries with Confucian traditions, copying signifies respect and recognition. In fact, our research confirms that, when questioned about origins, producers will tend to use the terms 'emulating' or 'localising' — more euphemistic ways of describing copying. In traditional Chinese society, emulating is a compliment, while these days the concept of localising 'with Chinese characteristics' is an expedient way to claim ownership of ideas that have originated elsewhere. A more modern explanation of copying stems from communism. Under this system, all property belonged to the state. The idea that creative ideas and expressions could be used for personal wealth was akin to heresy during the high tide of Maoism in the 1950s and 1960s.

This heritage, however, does not justify the practice of imitation in media industries, and Japan, in particular, has led the way in policing copyright protection. Incidentally, Japan was known for many years as a copying nation rather than as an innovator. In this regard, we can see the role that copying plays in the five-stage model (factory/cloning/formatting/niche and flying geese/media clusters). Japan has moved up the value chain over the past few decades; it produces original content and then formats this for export, drawing on synergies within the 'new East Asian cultural co-prosperity zone'. As we discuss later in relation to Japanese television formats, there have been numerous instances of the copyright originator threatening offending imitators.

The desire to protect formats is clearly related to maintaining a business model. The high cost of first-up production relates back to a core principle in the creative industries: that the costs associated with producing a hit are usually high. Or, to use the lexicon of business, producers incur marginal costs in production because of the use of supplies and equipment in bringing products to market. Audiences of reality television and countless makeover programs are only too aware of the many flops and pale imitations. Those television shows that are successful generally offer some innovation — what we have called an 'engine'. According to one format producer, a key cause of program failure is the slew of look-alike programming that often accompanies the success of one program: 'If you like the occasional chocolate, try spending a week in a chocolate factory. The novelty and the experience are subsumed under the availability of so much of it, particularly when they are clones' (Adair and Moran 2004: 29).

Formats certainly need some form of protection against those who would use them without authorisation and without paying licence fees to the devisor or the owner. Unsanctioned copies of formats exist not only across Asia, but also across all other parts of the world. However, the copying of a program in a small, domestic, regional market is one thing; the violation of confidential agreements in major markets is quite another. In the age of multi-channel television where the value of licence and syndication rights is diminished, there is an identified need to derive as much financial mileage out of ownership as possible. This move to safeguard and control content-related ideas formalises ownership under the protection of property laws, such as those relating to trademarks, brand names and registered designs, as well as those of copyright law (Lane 1992; van Manen 1994; Moran 1998; Freeman 2002). Indeed, the format era may come to be characterised as one of a heightened awareness of, and emphasis on, program rights.

Nevertheless, this emphasis on rights helps secure the general conditions for the process of selling the same content over and over again across a series of different media. Within the broader phenomenon of piracy and intellectual property violation in the East Asian region, we note the proclivity to copy — or, to use a more pejorative term, to clone — television formats (Thomas and Kumar 2004). Copying creates value without extensive research and development and risks associated with new program development. For many producers operating in an environment where fragmenting audience and multi-channelling conspire against the longevity of program ideas, copying is expedient and, some would argue, entirely necessary.

In recent years many writers have defended developing and newly developed countries against charges of copyright infringement, the core argument being that copyright is a Western concept used by copyright-rich nations to force developing countries to adopt practices that are less directly applicable to non-Western traditions. A fundamental point of opposition to the implementation of copyright from many developing countries is that the costs of acquiring the product in its original form are too high to bear. The rich media industries of the United States, therefore, have a competitive advantage: not only do they have international distribution systems, but they have money and lawyers.

From the perspective of powerful copyright industry organisations like the Motion Pictures Association (MPA), an ongoing 'war' is being waged against individuals who infringe copyright in any form — from downloading content to actually copying the *expression* of ideas. From the opposing perspective, however, the international copyright system under the World Trade Organization/Trade-related Aspects of Intellectual Property Rights (WTO/TRIPS) regime requires all countries to embrace a particular worldview: that 'works' are private property, or at least the private property of their owners or the person or company that purchases the rights. Thus they are commodities and items of international trade and commerce. The protocols of free trade agreements are subsequently underpinned by a modern form of property.

Legal Instruments and Institutions

The tools that allow some safeguarding of formats are to be found in two different arenas. The first is that of commerce and the second that of the law. As we have already suggested, to ask the question 'What is a format?' is to ask the wrong *kind* of question. It implies that a format has some core or essence. Instead, as our discussion has suggested, the label 'format' is a loose term that covers a range of items that may be included in a format licensing agreement. There are only a handful of ways that help in the protection of formats, and these mechanisms have been found wanting in East Asia. In most international television industries, the more elaborate and well documented a format is, the harder it becomes to copy. In order to prove origin, devisors (and their collaborators) will develop their format ideas as fully as possible and record them in writing with photographs and/or drawings in a permanent form. This is done to ensure that evidence of authorship of the original work and all revisions with the relevant dates are available in the event of infringement. In addition, some of the larger format owners and distributors have either set up branches and established joint venture agreements with companies in another territory. In some instances, this even includes setting up joint ventures with companies known to be pirating. In that way, they ensure a stream of revenues from an adaptation and also pre-empt the likelihood of more rip-off versions as the known 'pirate' now assumes responsibility for protecting the copyright.

The industry safeguard resides with the Format Registration and Protection Association (FRAPA). This trade body was formed in 2000, a sign of how extensive the international TV format trade was becoming, as much as an indicator of the increase in disputes and conflicts. As its name implies, the association seeks to introduce better manners in the industry by codifying various areas of practice. FRAPA is a self-regulatory body that promotes the concept of the format as a unique intellectual property to producers, broadcasters and to the legal community. In principle, at least, it aims to provide a fast, cheap and effective dispute-resolution procedure for format owners, producers, and broadcasters in cases of alleged format infringement, and to provide a pre-clearance mechanism for broadcasters when they are pitched with conflicting formats. It is interesting that one of the more recent members of FRAPA is Robert Chua, the Singaporean media proprietor and producer of the 'Asian' gambling game *Everyone Wins* (see Chapter 10).

Adopting a broad historical perspective, we can suggest that coincident with the international television industry's elaboration of the elements of the format has been the attempt to secure legal protection for the creator and owner of a format. Business development and legal development have gone hand in hand. However, the position of such a figure under the law in relation to TV formats is not clear cut. Accordingly, when writers of TV formats, producers or broadcasters seek to protect their investment, they have to rely on cobbling together a jigsaw of pieces drawn from different areas of intellectual property law. In particular, format protection has been sought through four legal instruments: copyright, breach of confidence, passing-off and an assortment of law to do with trademarks, patents and so on (Mummery 1966; Lane and Bridge 1990).

Copyright is the most important of the four legal mechanisms for protecting TV program formats. As is widely known, copyright does not protect ideas as such, but rather the expression of ideas. In fact, this distinction is far from useful, suggesting as it does that ideas are somehow anterior or platonically beyond some kind of form. The formulation of the notion of 'idea' here pays no attention to duration or length of time. An idea may be the result of a moment or a lifetime of thinking and reflection, yet the term does not help us to distinguish between the two. Similarly, the term may refer to a single, basic notion or to a complex set of interrelated concepts, but again, there is no way of making the distinction. Finally, too, the idea/expression distinction presupposes a one-way street between a first-level activity of thinking which, when complete, gives way to a second-level activity of giving form to that thought.

However, the distinction has long been accepted and it has had a determining effect in legal thinking about TV program formats. As defined in various copyright acts in different jurisdictions, the law prohibits the reproduction of original literary, dramatic, musical, or artistic works. However, while the copyright protection afforded to a book or an article is clear, a TV format and its characteristic features are usually less tangible. Copyright protection may be available in relation to certain elements of a television program — for example, the theme song, scripts, schedules, and so on — but copyright in the format itself is less certain. In addition, the international distribution of TV program formats complicates matters by setting in train laws of other jurisdictions. Particular difficulties come into play where an unauthorised adaptation is put to air in another territory.

Many successful format-based TV programs generate brand consciousness and the titles of programs are often registered as trademarks, including *Big Brother* and *The Weakest Link*. In addition, *Who Wants to Be a Millionaire?* is registered both as a trademark and as a logo. Provided they are sufficiently distinctive, slogans and catch phrases can also be registered to help with claims for trademark infringement in the event of unauthorised use.

The Asian Copyists

In critiquing the rate of change in television systems, we need to be attentive to imitation and opportunistic cashing in on others' creativity. As we have stressed throughout, the recent surge in adaptation — exemplified by the format, the remake, the sequel and the spin-off — is a consequence of a demand for proven content. However, the search for security increases the likelihood that ideas will be replicated and that copyrights will be transgressed. These are not new issues within global media industries, particularly within East Asia. Policing copyrights has become a contentious issue with claims and counter-claims of cloning.

Industrial practices in Asia are notably different from the Western hemisphere where companies are more inclined to seek redress from courts. Television industries have adopted strategies that we can usefully describe under a range of practices: 'cultural borrowing', imitating, cloning, and emulating, depending on one's distance from the plaintiff. In most cases instances of blatant imitation have attracted the indignation of copyright owners who have either complained to higher political authorities or made light of the infringement to the point of advertising the fact.

An example of the latter strategy illustrates a characteristically Asian (or perhaps even Japanese) way of dealing with such problems. The offenders were Taiwanese television producers who were making a practice of imitating successful shows. But, rather than threatening to sue for infringement, Japanese television used the Taiwanese copyists as content for variety shows (Iwabuchi 2004: 33). Shows such as ANB's *Flaming Challengers* and Fuji TV's *Mecha x 2 Iketeru!* have made light of the Taiwanese copies of Japanese shows with comedians parodying the copyists. The blurring of boundaries of copy and original now provides ample material for entertainment formats.

The issue of copying versus originating, once again, in relation to Japanese formats, gathered fresh momentum during the 1990s in Korea. Copying practices were quite common in Korea which, until the end of 2004, restricted Japanese popular culture. Korean producers had regarded Japanese programs as an index of new trends in television production. Lee (2004) notes that, as Korea moved closer to opening its gates to Japanese culture, the common practice of copying from Japan began to be viewed as detrimental. Obviously, it would be harder to copy surreptitiously when Japanese pop culture was widely accessible. But there were other reasons: it led to legal conflicts, economic penalties and international condemnation; it created a kind of cultural dependency on Japan; it paralysed the ethical consciousness of local broadcasters; it weakened local creativity; and it reduced the competitive power of Korean programming in the global market (Lee 2004).

For example, the Korean SBS show *Special Task! Dad's Challenge* was a close copy of Japanese TBS show *Happy Family Plan*. Incredibly, the tasks in the Korean show included challenges that were virtually identical with those appearing several weeks earlier in the Japanese show (Iwabuchi 2004). TBS officially complained to SBS and the show finally ended in June 1999 after only two years on air. A different phenomenon occurred following the same program's licensing to Beijing TV in the People's Republic of China. As with successful formats elsewhere in China, it was not long before other stations were intent on cloning and cashing in on the success of the original. Stations in Sichuan and Zhejiang provinces even used the same title. TBS subsequently issued a complaint to the Chinese media regulator, the State Administration of Radio, Film, and Television, and to the Ministry of Culture, seeking to control this 'infringement'. However, the most they could hope for was trademark protection of their logo and their name (producer of *Happy Family Plan*, interview by Keane, 2004).

Likewise, the successes of the international format industry watchdog FRAPA have been few and far between in Asia. One instance of litigation occurred, however, when the information challenge *Lucky 52* was bought by Shenzhen Cable Television in southern China in 1997. The local broadcaster defaulted on payment, leading to legal action by ECM, with costs of US$200 000 finally being cleared in 2001 (Stein 2002: 20). In another example of a pre-emptive strike, FRAPA notified the Chinese travel quiz show *Chai Tai Variety Show (zhengda zongyi)* of claims by ECM against the CCTV production company. *Chai Tai* was a long-running show on CCTV, but by the end of the 1990s its audiences were waning. In 2002, the producers revised the format, but the resulting makeover bore a substantial similarity to the English elimination game show *Dog-Eat-Dog*, enough to make it a target. *Dog-Eat-Dog* was a game show using an elimination engine pitting contestants against each other. Of course, this was more than coincidental. When contacted by FRAPA intermediaries alerting them to the alleged infringement of copyright, the producers subsequently reverted to a hybrid that allowed them to maintain a degree of 'substantial dissimilarity'.

The first Chinese reality game show, *Into Shangrila,* was also similar in many areas to the international brand desert island *Survivor* (CBS). How substantial these elements were, however, was never put to the test, although the concept for the reality show was obviously borrowed, as were the marketing strategies. According to producer Chen Qiang, the show was a totally new concept in China, whereas such shows were familiar to Western audiences:

You asked if this (programming) was influenced by the international formats. Without a doubt, it was. However I had not seen *Survivor* when we were starting to plan our programming in October the year before last. But I had heard that there was such programming in Britain and Europe. (Chen, interview by Keane, 15 October 2003)

Similarities were more than just serendipitous. Filmed in the foothills of the Himalayas in Sichuan province, two teams — the Sun and Moon teams — tested their survival skills in a series of challenges, against the elements and against themselves. The promotional material closely echoed its international cousins. The opening credits even saw the word 'China' burning across the ground, a branding strategy reminiscent of the opening credits of the Western versions.

Into Shangrila attempted to generate publicity through its novelty, using similar promotional strategies to those utilised for *Survivor*. At least the program was sufficiently differentiated to make litigation futile. The producer also pointed to differences in the hosts. In the US version there was a visible host; in the Chinese version there was a documentary-style voice-over. The US version was shot in open spaces as well as on a *Survivor* set, while the Chinese version had no *Shangri-La* 'set'. The emphatic difference, according to the producer, consisted of *before* and *after* visits by producers to each of the eighteen contestants' home towns, wrapping the event in the respectable cloak of social documentary.

If we accept the claim of serendipitous innovation, we can discount the substantive similarity between the two projects. A year later, another program caught international attention. *Perfect Holiday (wanmei jiaqi)* featured a group of twelve people living together in a large house for a period of twelve weeks, with one person being evicted each week and the winner taking all. In this case, the prize was a house worth approximately RMB500 000 (US$60 000). This time, Endemol, the owners of the *Big Brother* franchise and themselves no strangers to lawsuits, invited a legal person to try to dissuade the television station, Hunan Economic Channel, from using the *Big Brother* format (personal correspondence of lawyer with Keane).

The Weakest Link (see Chapter 7) was another international brandname format that had imitators. ECM had franchised *The Weakest Link* in Taiwan where it failed to impress as *The Wise Survive (zhizhe shengcun)*. In Hong Kong, the format rights for *The Weakest Link (Yibi OUT xiao)* were purchased by TVB in 2001 to counter the sudden success of *Who Wants to Be a Millionaire?* on rival network ATV. *The Weakest Link* was re-versioned as *The Wise Rule (zhizhe wei wang)* in China. The distributors of *The Weakest Link* format had offered the rights to Shanghai Oriental Television which declined the opportunity, citing the fact that it was not culturally appropriate for Chinese viewers. In a further indication that the station believed there was something that could be extracted from the international format, however, a spokesperson for Shanghai Oriental's entertainment channel said that producers of all these kinds of quiz shows were eating from the same bowl, and so it was difficult to see who was violating another person's copyrights. He said that it was important for each show to have some unique point that differentiated it from rivals (Wang 2002). Meanwhile, Nanjing Television, a smaller station, took up the franchise. In justifying the deal, the producer at Nanjing TV, Yin Yang, said, 'These kinds of shows are already reaching to highest prize levels. This is an international trend' (Wang 2002). In the interim, Shanghai Television considered its options and went ahead and made an unlicensed version called *The Examination Room of Riches (caifu da kaocha)* with a prize of RMB220 000 (US$25 000).

Two further examples demonstrate how copyright is coming into sharper focus. The television serial *Pink Ladies (hongfen nülang)* had great success in the Shanghai market in 2003. The concept was adapted from a cartoon series *Hot Ladies (se nülang)* by Taiwanese artist Zhu Deyong. Zhu himself acknowledged the provenance, although he claimed no royalties, happy to draw attention to his own medium. The success of *Pink Ladies* inspired another Beijing-flavoured 'pink drama'. The serial *Falling in Love (haoxiang haoxiang tan lianai)* had to fend off somewhat different claims of plagiarism. The lawyer for the plaintiff, Qixinran Audiovisual Company (Qixinran), argued that the owner of the successful script was a person called Li Qiang, whose version was optioned to the company where he was working as an editor. At the time, the Assistant Manager of Qixinran had offered the project to the Beijing Television Arts Centre — a high-profile production house. Four months before the option lapsed, she set up her own company, the Tongle Media and Zhongshi Company, and produced the series (*Beijing Morning News,* 5 November 2003). The lawyers for Qixinran asked for RMB500 000 (US$60 000) in damages and a stop to the series. The attempt to secure damages was, however, unsuccessful.

Concluding Remarks: Where to for Certainty?

One of the late billionaire Paul Getty Jr.'s more memorable declarations was that intellectual property would be the oil of the twenty-first century. The exploitation of intellectual property now accounts for about 10 percent of the US economy and nearly 5 percent of the UK's (Stevenson-Yang and DeWoskin 2005). For countries such as China, rights derived from intellectual property are low. In an article published in the *Far Eastern Economic Review*, Stevenson-Yang and DeWoskin (2005) suggest that if the United States really feared the threat China posed in terms of intellectual property rights infringements, it should actively encourage counterfeiting instead of trying to eliminate it. The argument is hypothetical but still pertinent to our argument. Widespread copying in China has the capacity to stifle innovation and kill off the development of original content that can be traded across networks. Why would you bother to spend time and money developing a new idea if you can't guarantee that it won't be plundered a day after its release? One statistic in particular makes interesting reading and draws attention to the scale of the problem: of the fake artefacts confiscated by US customs, three-quarters come from mainland China and Hong Kong (Stevenson-Yang and DeWoskin 2005: 11).

The TV format industry in Asia, like its counterparts elsewhere, needs to appear as though it is ordered and bound by legal rules rather than being characterised by chaos and anarchy. Clearly, both realities are true — even if for the most part those involved behave as though only the former is the case. In the past few years, the flow of formats has increased, as has the awareness of intellectual property. Rather than greater clarity as to what constitutes imitation, it is probable that the trend will progress towards smarter imitation — or to use the appropriate euphemism, emulation.

12

New Television

When people talk about the golden age of television in the early seventies — invoking shows like *The Mary Tyler Moore Show* and *All in the Family* — they tend to forget to mention how awful most television programming was during that decade.

– Johnson (2005)

Documentaries — wildlife documentaries and the like — are incredibly female. However, if you want to get males in it is very easy, because they want two things in documentaries: the destruction of the planet with weather disasters or people being eaten by sharks.

– David Franken, program director of the Seven Network,
Australia, cited in Adair and Moran (2004)

So what's new about *new* television? Is it platforms or content, spectrum or distribution? Should we be circumspect about a demise of television in the post-broadcasting era? Certainly, electronic consumer technologies like the internet and video gaming are reshaping the role of television. But to what extent are such changes impacting upon the evolution of content? Do digital technologies substitute or supplement existing media? How does the ease of replication associated with digitisation determine the menu of choices available to consumers?

In the preceding eleven chapters, we have suggested that adaptation has become the prime currency of contemporary television markets, particularly when ideas are transferred across cultural borders. In all of our discussions, the need to create compelling content has remained central, even if the adaptations in question have frequently taken advantage of limited international copyright protection. The key issue, however, is the relationship between novelty, industry volatility, and consumer attention in this current age of adaptation. In this final chapter, we draw together a number of threads that have a direct bearing on the future of television.

The Role of Technology

Multi-channel platforms are providing new opportunities for aspiring producers, hopeful of making their ideas accessible to different audiences. Cross-platform delivery strategies and marketing have become imperative to the survival of commercial broadcasters. Broadband internet and digital television have been rolled out in East Asia. Internet Protocol Television (IPTV), which allows access to video on a computer, and internet via the television monitor, is available in Taiwan, Korea, Japan, and in large urban centres in China. These and other impending technologies are transforming the way people access and consume content. But, despite cross-platform profusion and pay-TV niching, many programs — including drama, sport, news, and game shows — appear to carry on much as they have for fifty years. Where changes are apparent, it is in the amounts of revenue spent per hour of program production (along with new strategies for generating finance), the shift to niche programming on pay platforms, the transition from blockbuster creation to concept programming on both free-to-air and cable, and the use of formatting to ensure continuity of ideas.

In the age of adaptation, more and more media are turning to 'test-tube concepts', reality formats and synthetically produced pop idols. The key advantages that these offer are greater opportunities to cascade rights and monetise branded content (Aris and Bughin 2005). In contemporary media industries, it makes economic sense to re-purpose content across platforms, increasing opportunities to accrue intellectual property rents. Video streamed from fast broadband connections reinvigorates programming schedules while providing opportunities for audiences to respond to content. Accessing through high-speed broadband allows almost simultaneous qualitative feedback, in comparison to slower quantitative industry-ratings technologies. These developments are indicative of a shift in how we understand television. The 'old' network strategy of keeping audiences in their seats and building program or channel loyalty was based upon a proposition that viewing was a passive activity, 'valued in part because it is bereft of thought and the need for considered choice' (Owen 1999: 103). An even more fundamental challenge is evident, with industry analysts predicting that digital media are likely to be substitutes rather than supplements to existing media. As convergence increases across platforms, mature media — including television — will struggle to maintain loyal audiences (Aris and Bughin 2005: 8).

The Market and the Institution

The industry practice of formatting is both symptom and driver of change in television in East Asia and elsewhere. The international practice of format-driven program-making (with its attendant practices in the realm of imitation, copying, cloning, 'simultaneous accidental innovation', and so on) is a major development in program production. Over the course of broadcast television's history of more than half a century, there has only been one previous seismic movement in the area of production — the shift in program-making from a Fordist model of production to a post-Fordist system of content derivation. In the past broadcasters had insisted on controlling the circumstances of production, requiring that programs be made in-house at television stations. These organisations employed many people whose task was to ensure that stations had sufficient resources for purposes of broadcast. To understand the transition that is now occurring, we need to reflect on the evolution of programming.

The US television system has been the benchmark which many international systems aspire to emulate, at least in models of production and licensing. The US model largely followed the commercial model already adopted for radio broadcasting (Preston 2001: 200). One characterisation of the US international model of broadcasting is Television I, II, and III. Rogers, Epstein and Reeves (2002) contend that the golden days of TV I were from the 1950s through to the mid-1970s, and were about satisfying the core values of mainstream American culture. TV I — at least in the United States — was 'a period when television broadcasters profited by delivering a largely undifferentiated mass audience, in lots of a thousand, to advertisers' (2002: 46). A period then ensued from the 1980s in which quality TV offerings such as *ER* and *Hill St. Blues* targeted high-value advertising niches — those 'sophisticated viewers with money to burn' (2002: 44). Rogers at al (2002) refer to this as TV II. These programs broke narrative conventions, introducing greater complexity into plot and characterisation. However, despite their appeal to high-value demographics, these programs were fundamentally mainstream in that they sought to attract mass audiences on free-to-air channels in order to generate advertising sales. In addition to free-to-air, they served cable demands for dramatic content during a period of widespread uptake of pay TV in the United States.

TV III illustrates a particular pay TV strategy: the trend to premium-brand channels like HBO and Showtime. Subscriber loyalty towards non-mainstream and sometimes 'alternative' content supports these channels. Boutique dramas like *The Sopranos* and *Sex and the City* feature in this stage, more directly reflecting the age of narrowcasting.

Not all television systems have followed the United States, however, so applying the TV I, II, and III model across the global media is problematic. For instance, many European television systems have a legacy in public service broadcasting institutional frameworks; others, such as the Australian system, emerged from a dual track public-private model. Moreover, as discussed in Chapter 2, television systems in East Asia have their own logics of production, typified by a history of direct state regulation in China, Taiwan and Korea, and more *laissez-faire* oligopolies in Hong Kong and Japan. Another factor that challenges this TV I, II, and III model is the emergence at different times — and with differing degrees of social uptake — of time-shifting media technologies such as the analogue VCR, the digital PVR (personal video recorder) and other uses for the TV monitor such as DVD, games, and karaoke. These changes have led to new technological platforms and new revenue sources for audio-visual industries.

In contrast to the TV I, II, and III typology, we propose a different phase of development in TV's mid-life crisis. The prototype is a 'publishing model', in which production is sub-contracted out to the independent sector. Beginning with the US network television during the 1950s, the in-house (studio) system was reorganised to allow the farming-out of production to independent producers whose task it was to provide the required programming. The independent production moment occurred much later in Europe, but its eventual advent was perhaps more noteworthy. The establishment of Channel 4 in the United Kingdom in the early 1980s was the catalyst for change. In Western Europe, the privatisation of public channels and the licensing of new commercial channels during the 1990s promoted the role of independent producers. It is not altogether coincidental that independent television format production emerged from this region. In East Asia, independent production occurred much later, however, due to the nature of the market and a propensity to maintain control of content. In Hong Kong, much domestic programming was produced within TVB and ATV. It has really only been in the past few years that the outsourcing model has come into practice, and one of the catalysts for change was the licensing by ATV of the TV format *Who Wants to Be a Millionaire?*. In mainland China, independent production companies are a recent occurrence and have moved quickly into making television formats.

Reframing Industrial Creativity

This institutional shift towards independent production is matched by another structural change that formatting has brought in its wake. The international production industry has been reorganised in such a way as to centralise much of the devising and development work associated with programming. Of course, program ideas and innovations have always been capable of moving beyond their original circumstances. Programs have been imitated, remade, translated, and so on since the beginning of broadcasting. The production process still includes three segments: development and pre-production of the 'property'; production and actual shooting of the television program; and post-production (Christopherson 2005: 31). However, what is new in the present era is the systematic attention now given to the development and pre-production phase to increase the adaptability of programs in other industries and territories. Indeed, the very idea of production has been redefined in such a way as to suggest a more elongated series of steps that now not only takes in the actual making of a program, but can also involve further trialling, including broadcast itself.

Yet another part of the shift associated with the institutional advent of the format trade is the centralisation of creativity associated with the devising and development phase of the operation. In Chapter 5, we suggested that this work is a form of industrial research and development equivalent in its own way to the work undertaken in concentrated settings by scientists, engineers, and others. Production company offices and auxiliary settings, most especially the production floor of a television station, become the scientific laboratory or workshop in which systematic aesthetic labour is taking place. Large television companies have been quick to recognise this analogy so that particular labels, such as 'the greenhouse', have been set aside as a way of designating them. These are format think-tanks especially organized to incubate TV reality concepts. However, creativity is by no means confined to these settings, and there is an obvious opportunity to make cultural contributions to formats throughout the full cycle of their gestation and development.

By way of comparison with cinema and subscription-based media — such as the internet — television figures relatively low on creativity and high on imitation. Television relies on incremental adjustments to tried-and-trusted formulas. According to Magder, 'The day to day business of TV runs on habit not on hits, making shows that are marginally better than other offerings at the same time' (2004: 143). However, the global turnover of television ideas is inevitably eroding the conservatism of programmers. Smaller-budget programs have emerged that are not solely dependent on ratings, finding alternative revenue sources. At the same time, many of these shows have become more complex, echoing the video gaming culture that is competing for youth demographics.

If we look at the evolution of TV formats during the past two decades, we can draw a parallel with *Survivor*. The early formats were mostly game shows that offered a few lucky people a chance to be on television and win prizes — programs such as *Wheel of Fortune* and *The Price is Right*. The arrival of the Celador format of *Who Wants to Be a Millionaire?* changed the landscape. By introducing audience participation directly into the quiz show, it killed off weaker species — that is, they were voted off by viewers. Likewise, information shows about making better gardens, renovating homes, or ideas for vacations became popular because they gave viewers something to take away — tips about how to solve a problem or advice about an inexpensive holiday. The next wave was information challenge shows, including challenge makeovers, where a renovation occurs under restrictions of time and budget. While these kinds of shows distanced the traditional audience of documentary and information genres, they attracted the twenty-five- to thirty-nine-year-old audience. Unscripted drama (reality shows), in turn, regenerated information challenge shows, introducing the engine of 'built-in conflict', and forcing the more conservative makeover genres off mainstream free-to-air and on to public channels or specialist lifestyle pay TV. In the process, the program idea became more complex and creative by allowing in more elements: 'You hybridise by taking something that's familiar, say, in an information show like renovation, then you add a challenge, and then you get a bunch of people together to create conflict. That way you move beyond information, beyond information challenge, into a new form' (Franken, cited in Adair and Moran 2004: 25).

Audiences, New Creative Labour, and the Bottom-line

In the present environment of multi-channelling and convergence, producers have responded to the challenge of capturing and maintaining the attention of audiences who have no loyalty to broadcast television. Television — particularly free-to-air broadcasting — has lost audience share to media technologies that exploit advantages inherent in interactive, mobile, and niche-oriented content. Many of these new technologies utilise business models that have no fixed assumptions about audiences.

The success of mass media during their short history has been founded on celebrities as well as programs. Networks maintained an expensive list of talent: newsreaders, current affairs anchors, and quiz and variety show hosts. Owning and continuously branding these celebrities adds to content and production costs, which are estimated at 65 percent of the total expenditure of free-to-air broadcasters in northern Europe (Aris and Bughin 2005: 120). In a shift away from talent-driven to other forms of content, the role of the blockbuster hit (and channel celebrities) is diminishing. The format business, in turn, shifts the relationship between labour, creativity, and talent. The end-user now contributes directly to 'the talent'. As television competes with new, interactive, 'lean forward' technologies, such as video gaming, the internet, and SMS, people are less willing to relax and be entertained: they want to *influence* television and they want *to appear* on television. In this age of (interactive) access and shortened product lifecycles the distinction between producer and audience has muddied. New television formats are instrumental in giving a motley crew of non-professionals a greater role in determining what is ultimately presented for popular viewing consumption.

Many formats place ordinary, unpaid people in front of the cameras where their behaviour is recorded — an inversion that represents a major cost-saving benefit in an age of continuously rising above-the-line talent costs (Christopherson 2005: 32). Reality programs rarely employ professional actors. According to media analysts, Aris and Bughin, (2005), 'in all media sectors there has been a shift to retort-made content'. Developing this kind of content requires 'a deep understanding of potential consumers and their triggers' (2005: 22). Similarly, format programs based on scripts mostly dispense with the local screenwriter in favour of a translator. Equally, too, other labour is also redefined. In reality programs the role of editors is greatly enhanced in scope and importance.

Notwithstanding continuing debates about a perceived reduction in the quality of programming on offer, new program formats have been instrumental in changing the way that television networks imagine their audience. Reality formats, such as *Big Brother* (Netherlands/Endemol) and *Survivor* (Castaway Productions), challenge the core assumption of professionals that creative ideas are confined to writers, ideas people and producers.

The question of how innovative the adaptation of formats might be in any particular television broadcasting industry inevitably leads into critical cul-de-sacs. After all, what might seem like imitation and derivation to one investigator might seem like creative enterprise or hybridity to another. In concluding our analysis, we therefore need to acknowledge critiques of popular television, namely, the stream of critical perception that asserts programming is much the same on most of the channels most of the time.

Television formats, in particular, are frequently the subject of these kinds of allegations. However, similar charges of repetitions were made against Hollywood feature films, especially in the classical studio. In the contemporary era, many critics apply a 'fast-food' metaphor to argue that culture has become franchise-like in its production — that is, it doesn't require creativity as much as packaging and marketing. Indeed, Japanese celebrity *Iron Chefs* are presented in a gladiatorial format, syndicated across cable networks. Is this a creative reinvigoration of a tired old genre (the cooking show) or globalised triviality?

Our position here is more neutral. Throughout this book, we have maintained that new television formats have brokered new opportunities in television production, reshaping conventions of how the industry operates. We contend that television formats represent an important stage in a progression to a new mode of television production, one in which producers and consumers meet as co-creators of hybrid formats and genres.

To understand the importance of this progression, we need to return once again to the bottom line. Outlaying large amounts of money for development of drama, sit-coms, and television movies has become increasingly risky in a media environment in which the passivity of living room relaxation is complemented by the active engagement of users. The digital TV environment promises to add to this uncertainty principle. With bandwidth savings, content disseminated on one platform can be enhanced on others. More than simply viewing, audiences vote for favourite performers, buy products online, and use the video screen as a computer monitor, games console, or karaoke screen. In Chapter 10 we saw how advertising is used to fill channel space or is embedded in reality and improvement shows. These changes are global in scope and, in turn, change how we understand the medium of television. Likewise, content is responding within this landscape. Television producers and network executives see light entertainment formats as insurance against uncertainty: they offer broadcasters more commercially efficient strategies of maximising audiences. Genres such as quiz, talk, and lifestyle, which were once tributary programming flows, now capture prime-time viewers.

Merchandising and Distribution

The other important element of the franchise movement as it applies to global television production is the relationship of the primary work to ancillary elements. The global television program is not difficult to make or emulate — or even improve. However, the value of formats will often reside in ancillaries, more so than pre-formed content like drama and sit-coms. These include CDs, concert revenue, T-shirts, board games, trivia games, and revenue from SMS. The key to maintaining profitably is maintaining control of name, logos, set designs, and catch phrases — 'the distinctive (and yet homogenous) look and feel of the product' (Malbon 2003: 26). While global media corporations, such as Disney and News Corporation, have been keen to build synergy in their movie business through tie-ins and product placement, they have yet to adopt the television format and its ancillaries as core global strategies, possibly because their business models to date have primarily revolved around selling merchandise through association with pre-formed content — the Harry Potter model, for instance.

Distribution has also taken on new shades of meaning. Once, the term referred to the organised dispersal of programs licensed for broadcasting. Formatting changes this cycle; now the process is both reinforced and extended, as in the complex gears of a mountain bike, whereby each broadcast of a format adaptation in another territory or another time becomes part of a snowballing package that is the continuing object of distribution. Hence the distribution history of a format is likely to be a more complicated and ongoing process than that of a finished program available for broadcast. Every broadcast of the latter does nothing to change or alter its physical or aesthetic dimensions. With a format, on the other hand, adaptation and rebroadcast add markedly to its industrial and cultural richness, as well as to its complexity. In the distribution of formats internationally there are categories of value. The most valued market — the 'super A' market — is the United States, where payment for each episode are highest (as they are for pre-formed programming). 'A' level territories include Germany, Spain and France; 'B' level territories include Portugal, Australia and Scandinavian countries; and 'C' territories are Russia, Poland, and many countries in Asia, such as Indonesia, Singapore, and Hong Kong. Mainland China remains a 'D' territory, simply because of the low return and high probability of cloning.

Imitation, Adaptation, and Globalisation

As mentioned earlier, innovation in television production is incremental rather than risk-taking. This has always been the case, in comparison to cinema which recoups its costs through various distribution windows. According to Bonabeau (2004), imitation is the natural mechanism of both inspiration and aspiration. Imitation provides benefits to television industries in that it reduces risk. But imitation also leads to negative consequences when businesses follow the leader. Consider the decision of the French conglomerate, Vivendi, to acquire the entertainment business of Seagram. This copycat merger was initiated, despite AOL's ill-fated acquisition of Time Warner. Bonabeau (2004) cites three reasons why humans imitate. The first is safety (following a well-worn path); the second is conformity (fads and fashions); and third, there is a belief that the other guy may know better (abdicating responsibility for decisions). In television production in East Asia, we have seen ample evidence of safety, conformity and emulation.

Throughout this study, we have argued that television is undergoing unprecedented change in production, financing, marketing, and reception. Globalisation and adaptation are defining elements of the new television landscape. Inevitably, globalisation creates tensions as societies encounter ideas that are sometimes irreconcilable with cultural values and political ideologies. During the past five decades, the threat of inappropriate foreign media values to local cultures has led to censorship, quotas and, more recently, electronic firewalls. Most regulatory attention is directed at foreign cultural goods — movies, TV programs, books, and magazines. Globalisation, however, proceeds on another level as inappropriate elements of these foreign programs are stripped away and substituted with local flavour and values. The foreign program provides the DNA, the recipe, and the technology for invigorating local television industries that are struggling with committing funds to program development.

Concluding Remarks: The East Asian Cultural Imagination

As local content production in East Asia has grown in confidence, and as inter-Asian networks of production and distribution have increased, formerly successful Western media products have met with increased consumer resistance. One response to the new competition has been to pursue localisation strategies. The international program is invested with local flavour and modified so as to allow it to speak directly to local cultures. As examples of national versions of *Who Wants to Be a Millionaire?* attest, international programs can be localised and out-rate imitators.

When formats are introduced across television systems through licensing arrangements, they bring about sharing of knowledge. Localisation and cultural translation occur with cross-border flows of television formats. But there is a multi-directionality to this process that, until recently, has remained under-researched. Our bottom-up model of cultural production is a corrective to the tendency to focus on the activities of transnational media. The midstage franchise (or formatting model) is a way of enabling the international and the local to come together. The television franchise has brought about a transfer of ideas, capital and technology — more so than the clone.

Finally, to return to our opening images in this book, a dynamic interplay persists between processes of homogenisation and heterogenisation. The incidence of global franchises in unfamiliar locations — for instance, KFC in Beijing or *Who Wants to Be a Millionaire?* in Hong Kong — leads many observers to conjecture about the social effects of such colonisation of the peripheries by Western companies and products. However, what we see and hear less of is the internationalisation of East Asian culture into Western mediascapes. The issue of whether or not the localisation of television formats is detrimental to host cultures (and host television industries) is, therefore, a complex one. Do formats transmit non-appropriate values across national cultures, or are these stripped down in the localisation process? While the latter is an argument used to manage the negotiation of local content regimes and nervous censors in many countries, format traffic is about more than just representations and imposition of inappropriate cultural values. Local format-makers insert local values and these in turn are assimilated into regional cultural production. Quiz shows become information challenges; documentary merges with reality TV; and cooking shows become cook-offs. In the process, the ready-made production template, the format, becomes a low-cost means of translating ideas across national boundaries. This is the East Asian cultural imagination at work.

At the same time, the format model is unlikely to lead to the demise of locally originated content — although, as we have seen, it has been taken up by more and more producers in East Asia. Coincident with an increase in infotainment genres, television formats have become mainstays of the economics of modern television and in the process of their evolution during the past decade they have led to a regeneration of ideas about delivering creative content.

References

Abel, Sue (2005). '"Forward-looking" news? Singapore's News 5 and the marginalization of the dissenting voices', in John Nguyet Erni and Siew Keng Chua (eds.), *Asian Media Studies*. Malden, MA: Blackwell.

Adair, David, and Albert Moran (2004). *At the TV Format Coalface: Mark Overett and David Franken in Conversation*. Working Papers in Communication, No. 2: Griffith University.

Anagnost, Ann (2004). 'The corporeal politics of quality *(suzhi)*', *Public Culture* 16 (2): 189–208.

Andrejevic, Mark (2004). *Reality TV: The Work of Being Watched*. Lanham: Rowman and Littlefield.

Anthios, Floya (1999). 'Theorising identity, difference and social divisions', in Martin O'Brien, Sue Penna and Colin Hay (eds.), *Theorising Modernity: Reflexivity, Environment and Identity in Giddens' Social Theory*. London: Longman.

Appadurai, Arjun (1990). 'Disjuncture and difference in the global cultural economy', *Public Culture* 2 (2): 1–24.

Appadurai, Arjun (2001). 'Grassroots globalization and the research imagination', in Arjun Appadurai (ed.), *Globalization*. Durham and New York: Duke University Press.

Aris, Annet and Jacques Bughin (2005). *Managing Media Content: Harnessing Creative Value*. Chichester: John Wiley and Sons.

Bakker, Gerben (2003). 'The decline and fall of the European film industry: Sunk costs, market size and market structure 1890–1927', Working Paper no. 70/03, Department of Economic History, London School of Economics.

Barboza, David (2005). 'Seven Habits of Highly Effective Cadres', *New York Times*, 19 February, accessed online at: http://www.octanner.com/php/files/7Habits2.pdf/ [on 5 October 2005].

Bates, Benjamin J. (1998). 'The economics of transborder video', in Anura Goonasekera and Paul S. N. Lee (eds.), *TV Without Borders: Asia Speaks Out*. Singapore: AMIC.

Bennett, Tony (1998) *Culture: A Reformer's Science*. Sydney: Allen & Unwin.

Berger, Peter L. and Thomas Luckmann (1967). *The Social Construction of Reality: A Treatise in the Sociology of Knowledge*. London: Penguin.

Berry, Chris and Mary Farquhar (2006). *China on Screen: Cinema and Nation*. New York: Columbia University Press.

Bhaba, Homi. K. (1985). 'Signs taken for wonders: Questions of ambivalence and authority under a tree outside Delhi, May 1817', in Francis Barker et al (eds.), *Europe and Its Others*, Vol. 1. University of Essex, 89–106.

Bialer, Seweryn (1980). *Stalin's Successors: Leadership, Stability and Change in the Soviet Union*. New York: Cambridge University Press.

Bodycombe, David (2002). 'Format Creation', accessed online at: http://www.tvformats.com/formatsexplained.htm/ [on 17 April 2006].

Bonabeau, Eric (2004). 'The perils of the imitation age', *Harvard Business Review*, June: 45–54.

Bonner, Frances (2003). *Ordinary Television*. London: Sage.

Bourdieu, Pierre (1984). *Distinction: A Social Critique of the Judgement of Taste*. Cambridge, MA: Harvard University Press.

Boyd-Barrett, Oliver and Daya Thussu (1995). *Contra-flows in Global News*. London: John Libbey Press.

Boyle, David (2003). *Authenticity: Brands, Fakes, Spin and the Lust for Real Life*. London: Flamingo.

Brenton, Sam and Reuben Cohen (2003). *Shooting People: Adventures in Reality TV*. London and New York: Verso.

Brown, L. (1977). *The New York Times Encyclopaedia of Television*. New York: New York Times Press.

Brunsdon, Charlotte (2004). 'Television Studies', in Horace Newcomb (ed.), *The Encyclopaedia of Television*, second edition. New York: Fitzroy Dearborn.

Burchell, Graeme (1996). 'Liberal government and techniques of the self', in Andrew Barry, Trevor Osborne and Nikolas Rose (eds.), *Foucault and Political Reason*. London: UCL Press.

Butler, Judith (1990). *Gender Trouble, Feminism and the Subversion of Identity*. New York: Routledge.

Caldwell, John Thornton (1995). *Televisuality: Style, Crisis and Authority in American Television*. New Brunswick, NJ: Rutgers University Press.

Canclini, Néstor Garcia (1992). 'Cultural reconversion', in G. Yúdice, J. Franco and J. Flores (eds.), *On Edge: The Crisis of Contemporary Latin American Culture*. Minneapolis: University of Minnesota Press.

Carey, John (2005). *What Good are the Arts?* London: Faber and Faber.

CCTV (2002). 'Reality TV: Television programme format characteristics and the localization trend' *(zhenren xiu: dianshi jiemu de xingtai tezheng he bentuhua qushi)*, internal documents: Beijing.

Chadha, K. and A. Kavoori (2000). 'Media imperialism revisited: Some findings from the Asian case', *Media, Culture & Society* 22: 415–432.

Chan, Joseph Man (1994). 'Media Internationalization in China: Processes and Tensions', *Journal of Communication* (US) 44 (3): 70–88.

Chan & Co Hong Kong (2002). 'The Advertising Race in China: Legal and Practical Issues', October, accessed online at: http://www.ahk.org.hk/Archive/02_10_legal.pdf/[on 18 April 2006].

China Cue Online (2000). 'How children's television shows are borrowing from overseas' *(ertong dianshi jiemu ruhe jiechuan chuhai)*, accessed online at: http://www.chinacue.com.cn/cue/topic/zmj.htm/ [on 12 April 2004].

Chow, Rey (1995). *Writing Diaspora* ('Xie zai jia quo yiwai'). Hong Kong: Oxford University Press.

Christopherson, Susan (2005). 'Divide and conquer: Regional competition in a concentrated media industry', in Greg Elmer and Mike Gasher (eds.), *Contracting Out Hollywood: Runaway Productions and Foreign Location Shooting*. Lanham: Rowman & Littlefield.

Chua, Robert (2003). Robert Chua website, accessed online at: http://www.robertchua.com/PROFESSIONAL/lobby/root.asp?menuid=25.2/[on 17 April 2006].

Ci, Jiwei (1994). *Dialectic of the Chinese Revolution: From Utopianism to Hedonism*. California: Stanford University Press.

CNNIC (2005). 16th Statistical Survey on the Internet Development in China, July, China Internet Network Information Center, accessed online at: http://www.cnnic.net.cn/en/index/0O/ [on 17 April 2006].

Coleman, Stephen (2003). *A Tale of Two Houses: the House of Commons, the Big Brother House and the People at Home*. London: The Hansard Society.

Collins, Richard (1998). *From Satellite to Single Market: New Communication Technology and European Public Service Television*. London: Routledge.

Compaine, Benjamin (2000). 'Distinguishing between Concentration and Competition', in B. M. Compaine and D. Gomery (eds.), *Who Owns the Media? Competition and Concentration in the Mass Media Industry,* third edition. Mahwah, NJ: Lawrence Erlbaum Associates.

Cooper-Chen, Anne (1994). *Games in the Global Village: A 50-nation Study of Entertainment Television*. Bowling Green, Ohio: Bowling Green State University Popular Press.

Corner, John (2004). 'Afterword: Framing the new', in Su Holmes and Deborah Jermyn (eds.), *Understanding Reality Television*. London: Routledge.

Couldry, Nick (2003). *Media Rituals: A Critical Approach*. London: Routledge.

Cowan, Tyler (2002). *Creative Destruction: How Globalization is Changing the World's Culture*. Princeton: Princeton University.

Cunningham, Stuart, and John Sinclair (eds.) (1999). *Floating Lives: The Media and Asian Diasporas*. St. Lucia: University of Queensland Press.

Curran, James and Myung-Jin Park (2000). *De-Westernizing Media Studies*. London: Routledge.

Curtin, Michael (2003). 'Media Capital: Towards the Study of Spatial Flows', *International Journal of Cultural Studies* 6 (2) 202–228.

Curtin, Michael (2005). 'Murdoch's dilemma, or "What's the price of TV in China?"' *Media, Culture & Society* 27 (2) 155–175.

Curtin, Michael (2007). *Playing to the World's Biggest Audience*. Santa Cruz: University of California Press.

Dayan, Daniel (1997). 'Public Events Television', in Horace Newcomb (ed.), *Encyclopaedia of Television*. New York: Fitzroy Dearborn.

Derry, June (2003). 'Reality TV as advertainment', paper presented at the International Conference on Television in Transition, Massachusetts Institute of Technology, 2–4 May.

Dicken, Peter (1998). *Global Shift: Reshaping the Global Economic Map in the 21st Century*, fourth edition. London: Sage.

Dirlik, Arif (2001). 'Markets, culture, power: The making of a "second Cultural Revolution" in China', *Asian Studies Review* 25 (1) 1–35.

Dovey, John (2000). *Freakshows: First Person Media and Factual TV*. London: Pluto Press.

Downing, John, and Yong Cao (2004). 'Global Media Corporations and the People's Republic of China', *Media Development* 4: 18–26.

Duan, Dong, and Bin Deng (2006). 'An exploration of *Super Girl* *(pandian chaoji nüsheng)*, in Zhang Xiaoming, Hu Huilin and Zhang Jiangang (eds.), *The Blue Book of China's Culture*. Beijing: Social Sciences Academic Press.

Dyer, Geoff, and Richard McGregor (2005). 'China's answer to Larry King', *Financial Times*, 31 January.

EITF (2004). 'Edinburgh International Television Festival Launches Programme 2004', 13 July, accessed online at: http://www.mgeitf.co.uk/news/detail.asp?id =4014/ [on 20 September 2006].

Elmer, Greg and Mike Gasher (2005). *Contracting Out Hollywood: Runaway Productions and Foreign Location Shooting*. Lanham: Rowman and Littlefield.

Evans, Grant (1993). *Asia's Cultural Mosaic: An Anthropological Introduction*. New York: Prentice Hall.

Erni, John Nguyet and Siew Kang Chua (2005). *Asian Media Studies: Politics of Subjectivities*. Oxford: Blackwell.

Fan, Chengze Simon (2000). 'Economic development and the changing patterns of consumption in urban China', in Chua Beng-Huat (ed.), *Consumption in Asia: Lifestyles and Identities*. London: Routledge.

Fevrier, Philippe and Laurent Linnemer (2002). 'Strengths of The Weakest Link', *Economics Working Paper*, accessed online at: http://ideas.repec.org/p/wpa/wuwpex/0210002.html/ [on 17 April 2006].

Fiddy, D. (1997). 'Format Sales, International', in Horace Newcomb (ed.), *Museum of Broadcasting Communication Encyclopaedia of Television*. Chicago and London: Fitzroy Dearborn.

Fladmoe-Lindquist, Karin (2000). 'International Franchising: A Network Approach to FDI', in Yair Aharoni and Lilach Nachum (eds.), *Globalization of Services: Some Implications for Theory and Practice*. London: Routledge.

Florida, Richard (2005). *The Flight of the Creative Class: The New Global Competition for Talent*. New York: HarperBusiness.

Foster, Derek (2004). '"Jump in the pool": The competitive culture of *Survivor* fan networks', in Su Holmes and Deborah Jermyn (eds.), *Understanding Reality TV*. London: Routledge.

Foucault, Michel (1977). *Discipline and Punish*. New York: Vintage Books.

Freeman, M. (2002). 'Forging a Model for profitability', *Electronic Media* 21: 13–15.

Freedman, Des (2003). '*Who Wants to Be a Millionaire?* The politics of television exports', *Information, Communication and Society* 6 (1) 24–41.

Frow, John (1997). *Time and Commodity Culture: Essays in Cultural Theory and Postmodernity*. Oxford: Clarendon.

Fung, Anthony (2003). 'Media Economics of the Hong Kong press in political transition: Towards a new viable political economy', in Gary D. Rawnsley and Ming-Yeh T. Rawnsley (eds.). *Political Communications in Greater China: The Construction and Reflection of Identity*. London: RoutledgeCurzon.

Fung, Anthony (2004). 'Coping, Cloning, and Copying: Hong Kong in the Global Television Format Business', in Albert Moran and Michael Keane (eds.), *Television Across Asia: Television Industries, Programme Formats and Globalization*. London: RoutledgeCurzon.

Fung, Anthony (2005). 'Hong Kong as the Asian and Chinese Distributor of Pokemon', *International Journal of Comic Art* 7(1): 432–448.

Fung, Anthony and T. Y. Lau (1993). 'The emergence of cable TV and TV ratings' (Part II) *Hong Kong Economic Journal*, 18 September, 11.

Galician, Mary-Lou (ed.) (2004). *Handbook of Product Placement in the Mass Media: New Strategies in Marketing Theory, Practice, Trends and Ethics*. Binghamton, NY: Best Business Books.

Giddens, Anthony (1998). *The Third Way: The Renewal of Social Democracy*. London: Polity.

Giddens, Anthony (1990). *The Consequences of Modernity*. Cambridge: The Polity Press.

Gillespie, Mary (1995). *Television, Ethnicity and Cultural Change*. London and New York: Routledge.

Goldsmith, Ben and Tom O'Regan (2005). *The Film Studio: Film Production in the Global Economy*. Lanham: Rowman & Littlefield.

Goonasekera, Anura and Paul S. N.Lee (eds.) (1998). *Television Without Borders: Asia Speaks Out*. Singapore: Asian Media Information & Communication Centre.

Goonasekera, Anura and D. Holaday (eds.) (1998). *Asian Communication Handbook*. Singapore: Asian Media Information and Communication Centre & School of Communication Studies, Nanyang Technological University.

Gordon, Colin (1991). 'Government rationality: an introduction', in Graham Burchell, Colin Gordon and Paul Miller (eds.), *The Foucault Effect: Studies in Governmentality*. London: Harvester Wheatsheaf.

Grammaticas, Damian (2001). 'Hong Kong warns on Economy', BBC News Online, 21 August, accessed online at: http://news.bbc.co.uk/2/low/business/1502252.html/[on 30 March 2006].

Grantham, Bill (2003). 'International law and TV formats: Perspectives and synthesis', in Michael Keane, Albert Moran and Mark Ryan (eds.), *Audiovisual Works, TV Formats and Multiple Markets*. Brisbane: Griffith University.

Griffith, Alan (2003). *Digital Television Strategies: Business Challenges and Opportunities*. Basingstoke: Palgrave Macmillan.

Gutmann, Ethan (2004). *Losing the New China: A Story of American Commerce, Desire and Betrayal*. San Francisco: Encounter Books.

Hall, Stuart (1997). 'The local and the global: Globalisation and ethnicity', in Anthony D. King (ed), *Culture: Globalisation and the World System*. Minneapolis: University of Minnesota Press.

Hartley, John (2006). '"Reality" and the plebiscite', in Kristine Riegert (ed.), *Politicotainment: Television's Take on the Real*. New York: Peter Lang Publishers.

Hawkins, Gaye and Jane Roscoe (2001). 'New Television Formats': theme issue of *Media International Australia*. Brisbane: Griffith University.

Heller, Dana (2003). '"Russian" sitcom adaptation: The Pushkin effect', *Journal of Popular Film and Television* 31 (2) 60–86.

Herman, Edward and Robert McChesney (1997). *The Global Media: The New Missionaries of Global Capitalism*. London: Cassell.

Heinderyckx, F. (1993). 'Television News Programmes in Western Europe', *European Journal of Communication* 8 (4) 425–450.

Hindess, Barry (1996). *Discourses of Power: From Hobbes to Foucault*. Oxford: Blackwell.

Holmes, Su (2004). 'The only place where "Success" comes before "Work" is in the Dictionary … ?', Conceptualising Fame in Reality TV, *M/C Journal*, 7 (5), accessed online at: http://journal.media-culture.org.au/0411/07-holmes.php/ [on 17 April 2006].

Hoerschelmann, Olaf (2004). 'Quiz and game shows', in Horace Newcomb (ed), *The Encyclopaedia of Television,* second edition. New York: Fitzroy Dearborn.

Hoskins, Colin and Stuart McFayden (1991). 'The U.S. competitive advantage in the global television market: Is it sustainable in the new broadcasting environment?', *Canadian Journal of Communication* 16 (2) 207–224.

Hoskins, Colin, Stuart McFayden, and Adam Finn (1999). 'International joint ventures in the production of Australian feature films and television programs', *Canadian Journal of Communication* 24 (1), accessed online at: http://www.cjc-online.ca/viewarticle.php?id=508&layout=html/ [on 17 April 2006].

Hoskins, Colin and Rolf Mirus (1988). 'Reasons for the U.S. dominance of the international trade in television programmes', *Media, Culture and Society*, 10: 499–515.

Hu Angang (2003). 'The new catch up strategy', in Bhajan Grewal, Lan Xue, Peter Sheehan and Fiona Sun (eds.), *China's Future in the Knowledge Economy: Engaging the New World*. Melbourne and Beijing: Victoria University Press and Tsinghua University Press.

Iwabuchi, Koichi (2002). *Recentering Globalization: Popular Culture and Japanese Transnationalism*. Durham: Duke University Press.

Iwabuchi, Koichi (2004). 'Feeling glocal: Japan in the global television format business', in Albert Moran and Michael Keane (eds.), *Television Across Asia: Television Industries, Programme Formats and Globalization*. London: RoutledgeCurzon.

Jakes, Susan (2005). 'Li Yuchun: Loved for being herself', *Time Asia*, 10 October, 166 (15).

Jameson, Fredric (2000). 'Globalisation and political strategy', *New Left Review* 4, July–August, accessed online at: http://www.newleftreview.net/NLR23803.shtml/[on 17 April 2006].

Jeon, Gyuchan and Tae-Jin Yoon (2005). 'Two different stories of the Korean Wave and new television flows in East Asia', paper presented at the International Communications Association Conference, 'Questioning the Dialogue', New York, 24–29 May.

Johnson, Steven (2005). *Everything Bad Is Good for You: How Today's Popular Culture Is Actually Making Us Smarter*. New York: Riverhead Books.

Johnson, J. C. and K. Jones (1978). *Modern Radio Station Practices*. Belmont CA.: Wadsworth.

Jones, Judith, 'Coronation Street', in Horace Newcomb (ed). *The Encyclopaedia of Television*, Second Edition, New York: Fitzroy Dearborn, pp. 601–603.

Jung, S. (1991). *Past and Present of Korean Broadcasting (Hankook Bangsongeui Eojewaoneul)*. Seoul: Nanam.

Kapner, S. (2003). 'US TV shows losing potency around the world', *The New York Times*, January 2.

Kato, Hidetoshi (1998). 'Japan', in Anthony Smith (ed.), *Television: An International History*. Oxford: Oxford University Press.

Kawatake, K. and Y. Hara (1994). 'Nihon o chūshin to suru terebi bangumi no ryūtsū jōkyō' (The international flow of TV programmes from and into Japan), *Hōsō Kenkyū to Chōsa*, November.

Keane, Michael (1998). 'Television and moral development in China', *Asian Studies Review* 22 (4): 475–504.

Keane, Michael (2002). 'Send in the clones: Television formats and content creation in the People's Republic of China', in Stephanie Hemelryk Donald, Michael Keane, and Hong Yin (eds.), *Media in China: Consumption, Content and Crisis*. Surrey: Curzon.

Keane, Michael (2004). 'A revolution in television and a great leap forward for production', in Albert Moran and Michael Keane (eds.), *Television Across Asia: Television Industries, Programme Formats and Globalization*. London: RoutledgeCurzon.

Keane, Michael (2006). 'Once were peripheral: creating media capacity in East Asia', *Media, Culture & Society* 28 (6).

Keane, Michael (2005). 'Television drama in China: Remaking the market', *Media International Australia* 115: 82–93.

Keane, Michael (2001). 'Television drama in China: Engineering souls for the market', in Richard King and Tim Craig (eds.), *Global Goes Local: Popular Culture in Asia*. Vancouver: University of British Colombia Press.

Keshishoglou, John E. (2005). 'Television content in transition: Today's entertainment landscape is moving by leaps and bounds leaving consumers bewildered', *Media Asia* 31 (4) 218–223.

Khalil, Joe (2004). 'Blending in: Arab Television and the Search for Programming Ideas', *Transnational Broadcasting Studies* 13, Fall.

Kilborn, Richard (2003). *Staging the Real Factual TV Programming in the Age of Big Brother*. Manchester: Manchester University Press.

King, Richard and Timothy J. Craig (2001). 'Asia and global popular culture: The view from He Yong's garbage dump', in Timothy J. Craig and Richard King (eds.), *Global Goes Local*. Vancouver: University of British Columbia Press, 3–14.

Kipnis, Andrew (2006). '*Suzhi*, a keywords approach', *The China Quarterly*, 186: 295–313.

Kleiner, Art (2001). 'The Next Wave of Format', *Deeper News*, Global Business Network, June.

KNTO (Korean National Tourism Organization) (2003). *Research Report on the Korean Wave and Tourism*. Korean National Tourist Corporation, Seoul.

Kraidy, Marwan, M. (2005). *Hybridity or the Cultural Logic of Globalization*. Philadelphia: Temple University Press.

Krupto, Robert (2005). 'American Idol's William Hung found dead of heroin overdose', *Broken Newz*, HomorFeed.com, accessed online at: http:// www.brokennewz.com/displaystory.asp_Q_storyid_E_1027hungdeath [on 22 September 2006].

La Pastina, Antonio C. (2004). 'Telenovela', in Horace Newcomb (ed), *The Encyclopaedia of Television*, second edition. New York: Fitzroy Dearborn.

Lane, Shelley (1992). 'Format rights in television shows: Law and the Legislative Process', *Statute Law Review*, 24–49.

Lane, Shelley and Richard McDee Bridge (1990). 'The protection of formats under English law: Part 1, *Entertainment Law Review*, 96–102; Part 2: 131–142.

Lau, Chun Tao (2003). 'All senior secretaries of the Hong Kong government step down as the public wishes?', *Ming Pao Weekly*, 19 July, 20–21.

Lee, Dong-Hoo (2004). 'A local mode of programme adaptation: Korea in the global television format business', in Albert Moran and Michael Keane (eds.), *Television Across Asia: Television Industries, Programme Formats and Globalization*. London: RoutledgeCurzon.

Lee, Dong-Hoo (2005). 'Transnational imagination: Co-produced drama and national identity', paper presented at the International Communications Association Conference, 'Questioning the Dialogue', New York, 24–29 May.

Lee, Tain-Dow and Yingfen Huang (2002). '"We are Chinese": Music and identity in cultural China', in Stephanie H. Donald, Michael Keane and Yin Hong (eds.), *Media in China: Consumption, Content & Crisis*. Surrey: Curzon.

Lee, Paul S. N. (1991). 'The absorption and indigenisation of foreign media cultures: a study on a cultural meeting point of the East and West', *Asian Journal of Communications*, 1 (2): 52–72.

Li, Conghua (1998). *China: The Consumer Revolution*. Singapore: John Wiley and Sons.

Li, Zhan (2002). 'Intelligent shows will soon cause disaster' (zhili jiemu kuai chengzai le). *China Youth Daily*, 19 May.

Lie, Rico and Jan Servaes (2000). 'Globalization, consumption and identity: Towards researching nodal points', in Georgette Wang, Jan Servaes and Anura Goonasekera (eds.), *The New Communications Landscape: Demystifying Media Globalization*. London and New York: Routledge.

Lim, Tania (2004). 'Let the Contests Begin: Singapore Slings into Action', in Albert Moran and Michael Keane (eds.), *Television Across Asia: Television Industries, Programme Formats and Globalization*. London: RoutledgeCurzon.

Liu, Kang (2004). *Globalisation and Cultural Trends in China*. Honolulu: University of Hawaii Press.

Liu, Xiaobo (2005). Comments available online at: http://www.zonaeuropa.com/20050829.1.htm/.

Liu, Yu-Li and Chen, Yi-Hsiang (2004). 'Cloning, adaptation, import and originality: Taiwan in the global television format business', in Albert Moran and Michael Keane (eds.), *Television Across Asia: Television Industries, Programme Formats and Globalization*. London: RoutledgeCurzon.

Liu, Yu-li (1994). 'The growth of cable television in China', *Telecommunications Policy*, 18 (3) 216–28.

Lo, Kwai-Cheung (2005). *Chinese Face/Off*. Hong Kong: Hong Kong University Press.

Looms, Peter Olaf (2005). 'Convergence of telecommunications, media and Internet: case studies in Denmark, Japan, Singapore and Taiwan', paper at the Asian Media and Communication Centre Conference, Beijing 18–22 July.

Lotman, Yuri M. (1990). *The Universe of the Mind: A Semiotic Theory of Culture*, translated by Ann Shukman. Bloomington and Indianapolis: Indiana University Press.

Ma, Eric Kit-Wai (1999). *Culture, Politics and Television in Hong Kong*. London: Routledge.

Ma, Eric Kit-Wai (2005). 'Re-advertising Hong Kong: Nostalgia industry and popular history', in John Nguyet Erni and Siew Kang Chua (eds), *Asian Media Studies*. Oxford: Blackwell.

MacKenzie, Tyler (2004). 'The Best Hope for Democracy in the Arab World: A Crooning TV *Idol*?,' *Transnational Broadcasting Studies* 13, Fall.

Magder, Ted (2004). 'The End of TV 101: Reality Programs, Formats, and the New Business of Television', in Susan Murray and Laurie Ouellette (eds.), *Reality TV: Remaking Television Culture*. New York: New York University Press.

Malbon, Justin (2003). 'Taking formats seriously', in Michael Keane, Albert Moran and Mark Ryan (eds.), *Audiovisual Works, TV Formats and Multiple Markets*. Brisbane: Griffith University.

Marquand, Robert (2005). 'In China it's Mongolian cow yoghurt *Super Girl*', *Christian Science Monitor*, accessed online at: http://www.csmonitor.com/2005/0829/p01s04-woap.html/ [on 17 April 2006].

Marshall, P. David (1997). *Celebrity and Power*. Minneapolis: University of Minnesota Press.

Mathijs, Ernest and Janet Jones (2004). *Big Brother International: Formats, Critics and Publics*. London: Wallflower Press.

McLuhan, Marshall (1962). *The Gutenberg Galaxy: The Making of Typographic Man*. London: Routledge and Kegan Paul.

Meisner, Maurice (1982). *Marxism, Maoism and Utopianism*. Madison: The University of Wisconsin Press.

Miller, Toby, Nitin Govil, John McMurria, and Richard Maxwell (2001). *Global Hollywood*. London: British Film Institute.

Miller, Toby, Nitin Govil, John McMurria, Richard Maxwell, and Ting Wang (2005). *Global Hollywood 2*. London: British Film Institute.

Miller, Toby (1993). *The Well-tempered Self: Citizenship, Culture, and the Postmodern Subject*. Baltimore: Johns Hopkins University Press.

Mok, Lai Kong (2003). 'Culture of Employee in Silicon Valley Sun bleeds Creative Spirit', *Ming Pao Daily*, 17 June, B5.

Montgomery, Lucy and Michael Keane (2006). 'Learning to love the market: Copyright, creative and China', in Pradip Thomas and Jan Servaes (eds.), *Communications, Intellectual Property and the Public Domain in the Asia-Pacific Region: Contestations and Consensus*. New Delhi: Sage.

Moran, Albert and Michael Keane (eds.) (2004). *Television Across Asia: Television Industries, Programme Formats and Globalization*. London: RoutledgeCurzon.

Moran, Albert (1998). *Copycat TV: Globalisation, Program Formats and Cultural Identity*. Luton: University of Luton Press.

Mummery, John (1966). 'The protection of ideas, Part 1', *The New Law Journal*, 27 October, 1455–1456.

Newcomb, Horace (ed.) (2004). *The Encyclopedia of Television*, second edition. New York: Fitzroy Dearborn.

Nordenstreng, K. and T. Varis (1974). *Television Traffic — A One-way Street? A Survey and Analysis of the International Flow of Television Programme Material*. Paris: UNESCO.

Olsen, Scott Robert (2004). 'The extensions of synergy: product placement through theming and simulcra', in Mary-Lou Galician (ed.), *Handbook of Product Placement in the Mass Media: New Strategies in Marketing Theory, Practice, Trends and Ethics.* Binghamton NY: Best Business Books.

Olson, Scott Robert (1999). *Hollywood Planet: Global Media and the Competitive Advantage of Narrative Transparency.* Mahwah, NJ: Lawrence Erlbaum.

O'Regan, Tom (1999). 'Cultural Exchange', in Toby Miller and Robert Stam (eds.), *A Companion to Film Theory.* Oxford: Blackwell.

O' Sullivan, Tim et al (1983). *Key Concepts in Communication.* London: Metheun.

Ohmae, Kenichi (2005). *The Next Global Stage: Challenges and Opportunities in our Borderless World.* New Jersey: Wharton School Publishing.

Otake, Akiko and Shuhei Hosakawa (2005). 'Karaoke in East Asia: modernization, Japanization or Asianization', in Ackar Abbas and John Nguyet Erni (eds.), *Internationalizing Cultural Studies: An Anthology.* London: Blackwell.

Owen, Bruce M. (1999). *The Internet Challenge to Television.* Cambridge, MA.: Harvard University Press.

Ozawa, T., S. Castello and R. J. Phillips (2001). 'The Internet Revolution, the "McLuhan Stage" of Catch-up, and Institutional Reforms in Asia', *Journal of Economic Issues* 2: 289–98.

Page, David and William Crawley (2001). *Satellites Over South Asia: Broadcasting, Culture and the Public Interest.* New Delhi, Sage.

Paul, D. A. (1997). 'Rethinking technology transfers: incentives, institutions and knowledge-based industrial development', in Charles Feinstein and Christopher Howe (eds.), *Chinese Technology Transfer in the 1990s: Current Experience, Historical Problems, and International Perspectives.* Cheltenham: Edgar Elgar Press.

Pearson, Robert A. and William Uricchio (eds.) (1999). *The Many Lives of the Batman.* London and New York: Routledge.

Preston, Paschal (2001). *Reshaping Communications.* London: Sage.

Ramo, Joshua Cooper (2004). *The Beijing Consensus.* London: The Foreign Policy Centre.

Ran, Ruxue (2002). 'A Study on Reality Television's Form and Characteristics and Its Localization in China' *(zhenren xiu dianshi jiemu de xingtai tezheng ji zai Zhongguo de bentuhua wenti yanjiu)*, masters thesis. Journalism and Communication Department, Beijing: Tsinghua University China.

Rifkin, Jeremy (2000). *The Age of Access: How the Shift from Ownership to Access is Transforming Work.* London: Penguin.

Robertson, Roland (1992). *Globalization: Social Theory and Global Culture.* London: Sage.

Robertson, Roland (1994). 'Globalisation or glocalisation', *Journal of International Communication* 1 (1): 3–6.

Rodrigue, Michael (2000). Paper presented at Special Event at 2000 Montreux Rose D'Or Festival, 9 May, accessed online at: http://www.tvformats.com/devising/d03.htm/ [on 12 June 2001].

Rogers, Mark C., Michael Epstein, and Jimmie L. Reeves (2002). 'The Sopranos as HBO brand equity: The art of commerce in the age of digital reproduction', in David Lavery (ed.), *This Thing of Ours: Investigating the Sopranos*. Columbia: Wallflowers Press.

Rojek, Chris (2001). *Celebrity*, London: Reaktion Books.

Roscoe, Jane (2001). 'Real entertainment: New factual hybrid television', *Media International Australia* 100: 9–20.

Roscoe, Jane and Gaye Hawkins (2001). 'New Television Formats', *Media International Australia* 100: 5–7.

Rose, Nikolas (1999). *Powers of Freedom: Reframing Political Thought*. Cambridge: Cambridge University Press.

Ryan, Bill (1992). *Making Capital from Culture: The Corporate Form of Capitalist Cultural Production*. Berlin: Walter de Gruyter.

Santos, Josefina (2004). 'Reformatting the Format', in Albert Moran and Michael Keane (eds.), *Television Across Asia: Television Industries, Programme Formats and Globalization*, 157–168. London: RoutledgeCurzon.

Seaton, Beth (2004). 'Reality programming', The Museum of Broadcast Communications website, accessed online at: http://www.museum.tv/archives/etv/R/htmlR/realityprogr/realityprogr.htm/ [on 17 April 2006].

Schiller, Dan (1999). *Digital Capitalism: Networking the Global Market System*. Cambridge, MA.: Massachusetts Institute of Technology Press.

Schiller, Herbert (1989). *Culture, Inc: The Corporate Takeover of Public Expression*. New York: Oxford University Press.

Schiller, Herbert (1991). 'Not yet the post-imperialist era', *Critical Studies in Mass Communication* 8: 13–28.

Scott, Allan (2004). 'The other Hollywood: the organizational and geographical bases of television-program production', *Media, Culture, and Society* 26 (2): 183–205.

Shami, Seteney (2001). 'Prehistories of globalization: Circassian identity in motion', in Arjun Appadurai (ed.), *Globalization*, 230–250. Durham and London: Duke University Press.

Sinclair, John, Elizabeth Jacka, and Stuart Cunningham (eds.) (1996). 'Peripheral Vision', in *New Patterns in Global Television: Peripheral Vision*. New York: Oxford University Press.

Sinclair, John (1999). *Latin American Television: A Global View*. Oxford and New York: Oxford University Press.

Skinner, W. G. (1964). 'Marketing and social structure in rural China: part 1', *Journal of Asian Studies* 24 (1) 3–43.

Smith, Anthony (1998). 'Introduction' in Anthony Smith (ed.), *Television: An International History*, second edition. New York: Oxford University Press.

Spence, Joseph (1990). *The Search for Modern China*. New York: W.W. Norton Press.

Stein, J. (2002). 'Dollar values', *Television Asia*, October: 20–22.

Stevenson-Yang, Anne and Ken DeWoskin (2005). 'China destroys the IP paradigm', *Far Eastern Economic Review* 168 (3) 9–18.

Storper, Michael (1989). 'The transition to flexible specialization in the U.S. film industry', *Cambridge Journal of Economics* 13: 273–305.

Straubhaar, Joseph (1991). 'Beyond Media Imperialism: Asymmetrical interdependence of television programming in the Dominican Republic', *Journal of Communication* 41 (5) 53–69.

Sun Wu (1996). *The Essentials of War.* Beijing: New World Press.

Surowiecki, James (2004). *The Wisdom of Crowds: Why the Many Are Smarter then the Few.* New York: Random House, Doubleday.

Tao, Dongfeng (1995). 'Guanfang wenhua yu shimin wenhua de tuoxie yu hushen' (The compromise and interpenetration of official and civil culture), *China Social Sciences Quarterly* 12, 173–186.

The Wit (2003). 'A very serious article about formats', first published in the SIS Briefings, The European Broadcasting Union, Number 44, accessed online at: http://www.thewit.com/news_article/inner_content.asp?id=177/ [on 20 September 2006].

Thomas, Amos Owen (2005). *Imaginations and Borderless Television: Media, Culture and Politics Across Asia.* New Delhi: Sage.

Thomas, Amos Owen and Kevel J. Kumar (2004). 'Copied from without and cloned from within: India in the global television format business', in Albert Moran and Michael Keane (eds.), *Television Across Asia: Television Industries, Programme Formats and Globalization,* London: RoutledgeCurzon.

Thompson, Kristin (1999). *Storytelling in the New Hollywood: Understanding Classical Narrative Technique.* Cambridge, MA: Harvard University Press.

Thompson, Kristin (2003). *Storytelling in Film and Television.* New Haven, MA: Harvard University Press.

Thrift, Nigel (1996). *Spatial Formations.* London: Sage.

Thrift, Nigel (2005). *Knowing Capitalism.* London: Sage.

Tinctnell, Estella and Parvati Raghuram (2004). 'Big Brother: Reconfiguring the "active" audience of cultural studies?', in Su Holmes and Deborah Jermyn (eds.), *Understanding Reality TV.* London: Routledge.

Tracey, Michael (1988). 'Popular culture and the economics of global television', *Intermedia* 16 (2): 9–25.

Tu, Chuangbo (1997). 'Woguo guangbo dianshiwang de fazhan jiqi falu zhengce' (The development and legal policies of China's broadcasting network), *Dianshi Yanjiu* (Television research) 6, 4–7.

Tunstall, Jeremy (1977). *The Media Are American.* New York: Columbia University Press.

TVB (2003). 'The Chinese winner' *(Zhonghua zhuang yuanhong),* accessed online at: http://app2.tvb.com/tvcity/special/culture/index.asp/ [on 17 April 2006].

Van Manen, J. (1994). *Televisie Formats: En-iden nar Nederlands Recht.* Amsterdam: Otto Cranwinckle Uitgever.

Waisbord, Sylvio (2004). 'McTV: Understanding the global popularity of TV formats', *Television and New Media* 5 (4): 359–383.

Wang, Bingwen (1999). 'A report on the TV program The Citadel of Happiness' (guanyu 'kuaile da benying' de qingkuang huibao), *Hunan Television Correspondence.*

Wang Xiaofang (2002). 'How to become a millionaire', *Chengde Evening News (Chengde wanbao)*, 15 July.

Wang, Jing (2005). 'Youth culture, music and cell phone branding in China', *Global Media and Communication* 1 (2) 185–201.

Wang, Shaoguang (1995). 'The politics of private time', in D. Davis et al. (eds.), *Urban Spaces in Contemporary China: the Potential for Autonomy and Community in Post-Mao China.* Cambridge, MA: Woodrow Wilson Press.

Williams, Raymond (1961). *The Long Revolution.* London: Chatto and Windus.

Williams, Raymond (1974). *Television, Technology and Cultural Form.* London: Fontana.

Williams, Raymond (1979). *Politics and Letters: Interview with New Left Review.* London: New Left Books.

Woodside, Alexander (1998). 'Territorial order and collective-identity tensions in Confucian Asia: China, Vietnam, Korea, *Daedalus*, Summer 1998, v. 127 n. 3.

Woodside, Alexander (2006). *Lost Modernities: China, Vietnam, Korea and the Hazards of World History.* Cambridge, Massachusetts: Harvard University Press.

Xiao, Hui (2006). 'Chaoji nvsheng de jige guanjianci' (Keywords of the 'Super Girl' Idol Show), *Tianya* (Frontiers), December, 27–34.

Xie, Jiang (ed.) (2001). *I Love Quiz Show.* Wuhan: Changjiang wenyi chubanshe.

Xu, G. G. (2004). 'Remaking East Asia, Outsourcing Hollywood', *Senses of Cinema*, November, accessed online at: http://www.sensesofcinema.com/contents/05/34/remaking_east_asia.html/ [on 17 April 2006].

Yang, Bin (2000). *Feeling the pulse of the contestant (bamai jiabin).* Beijing: Zhongguo guoji guangbo chubanshe.

Yeh, Yueh-Yu and Darrell Davis (2002). 'Japan Hongscreen: PAN-Asian cinemas and flexible accumulation', *Historical Journal of Film, Radio and Television*, March, available online at: http://www.findarticles.com/cf_0/m2854/1_22/84409366/print.jhtml/.

Yoon, Sun-kyung (2001). 'Swept up on a wave', *Far Eastern Economic Review*, 18 October.

Young, Doug (2004). 'Asian piracy costs movie makers $718 million in 2003–MPA', Forbes.com. 2 February, accessed online at: http://www.forbes.com/home_asia/newswire/2004/02/02/rtr1238879.html/ [on 31 March 2006].

Young, David (2000). 'Modelling media markets: how important is market structure', *The Journal of Media Economics* 13 (1) 27–44.

Yúdice, George (2003). *The Expediency of Culture.* Durham, NY: Duke University Press.

Yurchak, Alexei (2002). 'Entrepreneurial governmentality in post-socialist Russia', in Victoria Bonell and Thomas Gold (eds.), *The New Entrepreneurs of Europe and Asia*. Armonk, NY: M.E. Sharpe.

Yuan Chunpei (2002). *Liaoning Broadcasting Journal (Liaoning guangbo dianshi bao)* 3 (4).

Zhong, Yong and Qianting Wang (2006) 'Cannibalising the Chinese "Watching Mass": Documenting and analyzing the evolution of Chinese terms of address from "the watching mass" to "snack food"', *The Journal of International Communication*, 12 (1): 23–36.

Zhu, Ying, Michael Keane, and Ruoyun Bai (forthcoming). *TV Drama in China: Unfolding Narratives of Tradition, Political Transformation and Cosmopolitan Identity*. Hong Kong: Hong Kong University Press.

Index